The postmodern professional:
Contemporary learning practices, dilemmas and perspectives

the Tufnell Press,
London,
United Kingdom

www.tufnellpress.co.uk

email contact@tufnellpress.co.uk

British Library Cataloguing-in-Publication Data
A catalogue record for this book is
available from the British Library

paperback ISBN	*1872767443*
ISBN-13	*978-1-872767-44-4*
Kindle	*978-1872767-49-9*

Printed in England and U.S.A. by Lightning Source

The postmodern professional: Contemporary learning practices, dilemmas and perspectives

edited by
Karen Borgnakke, Marianne Dovemark and
Sofia Marques da Silva

The Ethnography and Education book series aims to publish a range of authored and edited collections including both substantive research projects and methodological texts and in particular we hope to include recent PhDs. Our priority is for ethnographies that prioritise the experiences and perspectives of those involved and that also reflect a sociological perspective with international significance. We are particularly interested in those ethnographies that explicate and challenge the effects of educational policies and practices and interrogate and develop theories about educational structures, policies and experiences. We value ethnographic methodology that involves long-term engagement with those studied in order to understand their cultures, that use multiple methods of generating data and that recognise the centrality of the researcher in the research process.

www.ethnographyandeducation.org

The editors welcome substantive proposals that seek to:

explicate and challenge the effects of educational policies and practices and interrogate and develop theories about educational structures, policies and experiences,

highlight the agency of educational actors,

provide accounts of how the everyday practices of those engaged in education are instrumental in social reproduction.

Details of recent titles in this series can be found at the end of this book

Contents

Contributors

Estibaliz Aberasturi-Apraiz has s Ph.D. in Pedagogy and works at the University of the Basque Country (UPV/EHU). Her research and teaching career is primarily focused on teacher education, pedagogical innovation and visual arts in educational contexts. She is a coordinator of a community of practice where teachers reflect critically on learning from experiences in visual arts. She is part of the research group Elkarrikertuz and REUNI+D[1].

Lawrence Angus is a Professorial Research Fellow in the Faculty of Education and Arts at Federation University Australia. He was previously Head of the School of Education at the University. His publications are mainly in the areas of educational policy and reform, continuity and change in education, equity and democratic schooling. His research is informed by a critical ethnographic perspective and critical notions of power and cultural identity.

Karen Borgnakke, dr.paed., Professor in Education, University of Copenhagen. She has undertaken research, taught and published in the fields of education and learning research. She has carried out fieldwork, developed case studies, participated in development projects and evaluation research, including projects on strategies for organisational and pedagogical innovation throughout education. She has more than twenty years experience with developing research methodology in education and learning research, including comprehensive experience with research education. Currently research project: Ethnographic studies in scholastic, profession-oriented and academic learning contexts.

Jose Miguel Correa has a Ph.D. in Pedagogy and works at the University of the Basque Country (UPV/EHU). He is a faculty member of the Department of Teaching and School Organisation (San Sebastian, Spain). In the last decade he has been teaching Information and Communications Technologies (ICT) to future Early Childhood Education teachers. He is the coordinator of the educational research group Elkarrikertuz. He is also a member of the network for research and educational innovation REUNI+D.

Amalia Creus is a Senior Lecturer at the Universitat Oberta de Catalunya where she coordinates the BA Degree on Communication. She is also an external faculty member of the Department of Education at University of Vic, Central University of Catalonia. As a member of the research Group KIMO (Knowledge and Information Management in Organisations), she is currently working in the research Project KIBIS, which has the objective to explore knowledge transfer and knowledge creation at the ATLAS Experiment, at CERN. Her main research interests are professional careers and professional identities, network society, education and communication, and organisational culture.

1 REUNI+D — University Network for Educational Research and Innovation. Social Changes and Challenges to Education the Digital Age, http://reunid.eu (MINECO. EDU2015-68718-REDT).

Laura Domingo Peñafiel is a Junior Lecturer and researcher at the Faculty of Education, Translation and Humanities, Department of Pedagogy, of the University of Vic, Central University of Catalonia. Her research areas are rural education, multi-grade teaching and inclusion. Her PhD thesis was titled *The pedagogical contributions of the Rural School: Inclusion in multi-grade classrooms. A Case Study*. She participates as a researcher in different national and international projects.

Marianne Dovemark is a Professor in Education at the Department of Education and Special Education, University of Gothenburg, Sweden. Her research interests are in educational ethnography, focusing on structural factors such as class, gender and ethnicity. She is devoted to issues of power and influence as these relate to school governance and market orientation.

Luispe Gutierrez has a Ph.D. in Pedagogy and works at the University of the Basque Country (UPV/EHU). In the last years he has been teaching to future Early Childhood Education teachers. His research interests include teacher education, educational innovation and physical education. He is part of the research group Elkarrikertuz and REUNI+D.

Fernando Hernández is a full Professor at the Unit of Cultural Pedagogies in the Fine Arts Faculty of the University of Barcelona. Director of the Master's program on *Visual Arts and Education: a constructionist perspective* and Doctoral program on *Arts and Education*. He is member of ESBRINA- Cotemporary Subjectivities, Visualities and Educational Environments (2014SGR 0632) http://esbrina.eu/en/home/, and REUNI+D. He directs and participates in several national and international projects.

Ann-Sofie Holm is an Associate Professor at Gothenburg University, Department of Education and Special Education. Her main research field is the sociology of education with the focus on gender constructions in school, but also on aspects of inclusion and marketisation of the Swedish education system.

Bob Jeffrey was appointed Honorary Research Fellow at Exeter University in 2012 following retirement from The Open University. He researched from 1992 the work of primary teachers with Professor Peter Woods and Professor Geoff Troman. They focused on the opportunity for creative teaching and the effects of the reforms of the 1990s in England on this form of pedagogy and teacher identities. In the 2000s they developed this focus to learners and their opportunities for creative learning including a nine nation European study from 2004-2006. He also worked closely with Professor Anna Craft developing research and promoting creative teaching and learning in the educational research community. They have published extensively including a great many methodology articles focused on an ethnographic approach including a focus on cross cultural approaches. Bob is co founder of the *Ethnography and Education* journal and edited it from 2008-2012 and co-organised an annual ethnography conference in Oxford for ten years as well co-editing a book series from 2007-2012 www.ethnographyandeducation.org.

Michalis Kakos is a Senior Lecturer in education at Leeds Beckett University, UK. Previously he was leading a Postgraduate course in Citizenship education at the University of Leicester. Michalis' research interests include: citizenship and intercultural education; institutionalisation in education; and inclusive and special education. Michalis has conducted research and he has taught in a variety of schools in Greece, USA and the UK.

Sofia Marques da Silva is anAssistant Professor at Faculty of Psychology and Educational Sciences, University of Porto, Portugal, and member of CIIE (Educational Research and Intervention Centre). She teaches Research Methodologies and Sociology of Education. She has been researching ethnographies on youth cultures, gender and education and lately has been involved in online and offline ethnographies with young people from border regions. She is a Co-convenor of the European Conference on Educational Research (ECER) and the vice-president of the Portuguese Society of Educational Sciences (SPCE). She is deputy editor of Ethnography and Education (Taylor and Francis).

Analía E. Leite Méndez has a Ph.D. and is a teacher of the Didactics and School Organisation Department of the University of Malaga. She was also taught an the University of the Northeast of Argentina for twenty years. She is member of research group *Teacher, Culture and Educational Institution* (Procie) focused on school and university learning, with which she has several publications, and with educational memories.

Asunción Martínez-Arbelaiz holds a Ph.D. in Linguistics from Cornell University, New York. She is currently the Spanish Language Coordinator for the University Studies Abroad Consortium, where she also teaches a variety of courses of Spanish for speakers of other languages. She is part of the research group Elkarrikertuz and REUNI+D, where she contributes ideas related to language and discourse to the challenge of how to prepare the teachers of the future.

Alejandra Montané López holds a PhD in Pedagogy and is a senior lecturer in the Faculty Education (Department of Didactics and Educational Organization at the University of Barcelona). She is a member of the accredited research group *Teacher Training and Innovation in Education* (FODIP). She is the author of numerous publications in books and journals, and a member of the editorial board and referee for several Spanish, Portuguese and Latin American specialised publications. She has participated in a number of national and international research and inter-university cooperation projects

José Ignacio Rivas Flores is the Professor of Didactics and School Organisation, Department of University of Malaga. He is Doctor in Educational Sciences. He coordinates the research group *Teacher, Culture and Educational Institution* (Procie). Also he is the coordinator and adviser of research projects in Argentina and Mexico. His research is focused on narrative biographical methodology around the school experience of diverse participants. He has publications in school management, the teacher professional development, research methods and educational policy.

Juana M. Sancho is the Full Professor of Educational Technologies at the University of Barcelona. Coordinator of the research group ESBRINA- Cotemporary Subjectivities, Visualities and Educational Environments (2014SGR 0632) esbrina.eu/en/home/, and REUNI+D. She has a long and steady experience in promoting research policy at institutional level, advising research programmes and projects, and assessing and managing research projects.

Alaster Scott Douglas, has a Ph.D. and is the Assistant Director of Education and Reader in Education and Professional Practice at the University of Roehampton, London. He is director of the research group Teaching and Learning in Schools and the author of *Student teachers in school practice* (Palgrave Macmillan). He is a fellow of the Higher Education Academy in the UK. His current research focuses on the roles of universities and schools in the preparation of teachers.

Pablo Cortés González is an Assistant Teacher in the Department of Didactic and School Organisation at the University of Malaga (Spain), and member of Procie research team. Also he is part of the BSA (British Sociological Association, UK) and the SEP (Spanish Society of Pedagogy). His research interests focus on resilience, ecologies of learning , critical pedagogy and narratives.

Geoff Troman is Emeritus Professor of Education at Froebel College, School of Education, Roehampton University, London. He was also Visiting Professor at the University of Boras, Sweden. He was Director of the Economic and Social Research Council funded project: Primary Teacher Identity, Commitment and Career in Performative Cultures (PTICC) 2005-2007. This project was linked to a cross Europe research project Profknow involving eight European partners exploring nurses and teachers' constructions of professional knowledge. He was also Co-Director (with Bob Jeffrey) of the 2005-2007 ESRC project Creativity and Performativity in Teaching and Learning (CAPITAL). And has recently been a methodological consultant for the EC funded CLASP project (directed by Bob Jeffrey) a comparative study of ten European countries. Previously he was a Research Fellow and Associate Lecturer in the Faculty of Education and Language Studies at the Open University. He taught science for twenty years in secondary modern, comprehensive and middle schools before moving into Higher Education in 1989. Throughout his time in schools he carried out research as a teacher researcher. His Ph.D research was an ethnography of primary school restructuring. Geoff is foundation Editor (with Bob Jeffrey, The Open University; Geoffrey Walford, University of Oxford; and Tuula Gordon, University of Helsinki) of the international *Journal Ethnography and Education* published by Routledge, Taylor and Francis Group.

Introduction

Karen Borgnakke, Marianne Dovemark and Sofia Marques da Silva

The contributions in this book discuss the processes of professionalisation related to professional teaching practice, teacher education and the organisation of professional education. The chapters identify different trends, dilemma and perspectives through empirical research and analysis at the political macro-level as well as the institutional and practical micro-level. Contributions cover the experiences of different European and non-European countries making it possible to understand historical perspectives, different educational systems and teacher training traditions, adding complexity to the discussion of political discourse and the demands of professionalisation in educational and teaching practice.

It is possible to consider that the period from 1990 to the present day has been characterised by a loss of autonomy. Professional collegiality has been replaced by school managerial team work, that aims, in many cases, to implement policies, practices and performances devised and controlled centrally by government. Previous 'professional' dispositions, such as mutual respect, authenticity, courage and compassion were threatened and recultured by the values of the market place.

The identification of ages of professionalism, like the pre professional, the age of autonomy, the collegial and the post professional age or postmodern, refer, at the same time, to common trends in Europe and to different phases in the process of modernisation and professionalisation in different states, regions and traditions, like the Afro-American curriculum or the central European 'didactic-tradition'. The editing process will integrate contributions to which an international audience can relate.

In general, the chapters give a particular overview on the idea of the post modern professional as a diverse/complex/hybrid, taking on board some of the characteristics of past ages and at the same time incorporating a more performative professional role, mandate and purpose. The book as a whole will account for ethnographic approaches to teachers' experiences and professional pathways. However, even if all chapters are ethnographically based, each of them make their own unique contribution by exploring and interpreting empirical data and/or discussing theoretical possibilities for visioning what it means to be a professional teacher in the post-modern era of professionalism.

The chapters

In chapter 1 Bob Jeffrey and Geoff Troman, *The governance turn, institutional embrace and the postmodern professional,* focus on how the role of the post-modern teacher in the UK has been fashioned over the last twenty years. The authors argue that each of the identified postmodern professional identities is a challenge to the self, in order to maintain and develop the former and to meet the challenges faced by external demands and the progression of the learners. Chapter 2 *The performative culture in Swedish schools and how teachers cope with it,* by Marianne Dovemark and Ann-Sofie Holm, draws on an analysis of empirical data referring to fifty-five teachers from primary school to upper secondary school level. Even though there were some differences in the studied teachers' working duties and assignments, all the interviewed teachers, without exception, expressed similar views that a pervasive and strengthened performative culture had gained ground in schools. In chapter 3 *The interaction between students and teachers in times of performativity* by Michalis Kakos, refers to an investigation of the changes in the professional roles and practices related to citizenship education (CE). Kakos highlights that the significant challenges that obstruct the implementation of democratic and participatory pedagogies do not relate to teachers' conscious choices and professional judgment but to embodied, unquestioned social practices and everyday interactions. Against this background Kakos discuses how performativity affects the interactions between students and teachers and how it shapes teachers' roles.

In chapter 4 *Building democratic professional relationship at school? Families, students and teachers in context* by José Ignacio Rivas and Analia Leite the analysis is focused on the teachers and their different personal and professional histories. In the authors' reflection group sessions, the teaching staff tended to adopt an initially paternalist and protagonist role that gradually changed and become more personalised and democratic spaces could be constructed. Chapter 5, *Primary school teachers' professional identity: an ethnographic study* by Juana M. Sancho, Fernando Hernández, Amalia Creus, Laura Domingo and Alejandra Montané, introduces a decolonising approach to nine primary school teachers' professional development in the first five years of their professional career. All the participant teachers observed that the relationship with pupils was the most rewarding aspect of their job. Chapter 6 ,*Tales from the field: student teachers' ups and downs in their socialisation process,* by Jose Miguel Correa, Luispe Gutierrez, Estabaliz Jimenez de Aberasturi and Asun Martinez, presents an empirical analysis contrasting two opposing cases of building teaching identity. The research highlights the emotional turmoil that student teachers go through. The authors argue that this is primarily because of their peripherality, as well as the means and strategies they must display so that this peripheral participation does not lead to disappointment regarding their teaching roles.

In chapter 7, *Raising the Standard: A research-based agenda for teacher education in England,* Alaster Douglas analyses the conditions for the current teacher education with a focus on the UK-context. The author emphasises the importance of challenging underlying assumptions and to teach students to think critically by embedding research-based agendas into both school-based as well as university-based teacher education courses. Chapter 8, *Discourses of performativity and effectiveness: Contesting and shaping teacher identity in a neoliberal world,* Lawrence Angus gives a critical perspective on the western world discourse and double logic on professionalisation and the contradiction: de-professionalisation. The author argues for a rational approach to learning and teaching where teacher identity should embrace a rational, democratic perspective in which students are regarded as contributors to a dialogical process. In chapter 9, *Professional changeability and technacy: The new professional raison d'etre,* Karen Borgnakke analyses case-studies focussing on the discourse practice and organisational strategies in the Nordic context where the demands of professional changeability are identified as a political credo going across the educational sector.

The background Network 19 — Ethnography — European Conference on Educational Research

The majority of the contributors to this book have been involved for a long time in Network 19 activities: i.e. the Ethnography network of the European Educational Research Association (EERA). This particular topic has been one of the topics discussed and reflected upon during many years within the network, through the work and initiatives of Bob Jeffrey, one of the book contributors.

Chapter 1

The governance turn, institutional embrace and the postmodern professional

Bob Jeffrey and Geoff Troman[1]

Abstract

The post-modern teacher in the UK is one that has been fashioned over the last twenty years. S/he belongs to a 'greedy institution' in which teachers embrace its values and reproduce them as well as adding value by contributing to a continuous reinvention of it. Their professional identity is now one that is isomorphic with the school, one in which status and professional expertise are bound up with the image of the institution in the glo-na-cal environment of global, national and local. Web sites proclaim the character of the school but also celebrate their local status while national league tables pin point their level of achievement locally and nationally. Their global responsibility is mirrored in their commitment to raising achievement for the labour market and the national economy.

The post-modern professional teacher is now a total teacher taking on everything and anything that policy demands as well as their own interests and values, for example contrasting performative and creative pedagogies. The commitment of the postmodern professional has been gained through the development of team work, distributed leadership and nurturing institutional career, through the necessity to take up dominant discourses of performativity and the survival of their institution in a market orientated environment. The postmodern teacher lives with continuing tensions, dilemmas and constraints of centrally influenced governance and even where flexibility is generated they face a constant striving to do the right thing. This chapter examines the life of the total professional who plays a major role in the development of the embracing institution.

---

1. Some parts of this chapter were included in the following publications.

Jeffrey, B., Troman, G., (2012) Governmentality in Primary Schools in the UK, in Jeffrey, B. and Troman, G., *Performativity across UK education: ethnographic cases of its effects, agency and reconstructions:* Painswick, E & E Publishing.

Jeffrey, B., Troman, G., (2012) The Embracing Performative Institution, *Journal of Organisational Ethnography*, 1(2) pp.195-212

Context

Andy Hargreaves (2000) identifies four ages of professionalism, the pre professional, the age of autonomy, the collegial and the post professional age or postmodern. The first age was one where students were treated as collective, stratified groups and educational practices consisted of traditional repetitive pedagogies dominated learnt from one's experience of it. The second, the age of autonomy, was one where the profession was established and pedagogic theories took hold. Teacher professionality was at its height and government took little interest in the curriculum or assessment procedures. The third age of collegiality followed the development of pedagogy and its support by locally interested teacher groups and Local Authorities who provided a professional career ladder for classroom teachers to become curriculum advisors and local inspectors. At the same time schools began to become more managerial, drawing together teachers in each school to develop school policies curriculum and pedagogy. It was in this context in primary schools, in the UK, that the new government intervention into professional activity became more prominent.

The period from 1990 to the present day for primary schools has been characterised as one in which there has been a drastic loss of autonomy and professional collegiality to be replaced by school managerial team work (Menter, Muschamp et al., 1997) to implement government directed centrally devised and controlled policies, practice and performance. In the early stages of the development of the postmodern professional teachers had become deliverers (Winch and Foreman-Peck, 2005), although the 'mediators' often adopted a principled infidelity, not fully adhering to the principles underlying the reforms and maintaining some of their own educational values (Wallace, 2005). However, exhortations to be more flexible, less rigid, more inventive and less timid were difficult to hear when grappling with the more dominant noise of accountability (Moss, 2005). Dispositions such as truthfulness, mutual respect, authenticity, courage and compassion were threatened by the values of the market place (Nixon, 2005).

There are now multiple versions of the post modern professional which apply to all teachers. Firstly, a restricted, bureau-professional form of professionalism where teachers are expected to function as experts in their own classrooms, but to work within bureaucratic frameworks laid down by their local authorities and administered by their headteachers (Reeves, 2005); a managerial form of professionalism in which teachers are constructed as closely supervised, rule following operatives and a new professionalism based on the notions of collaboration, knowledge sharing and problem solving seeing themselves as part of professional leaning communities (PLP) to expand capacity, act innovatively, to appreciate being valued, enjoying collective well-being, assisting aspirations and learning how to learn (Webb and Vulliamy, 2009).

Postmodern professionalism is a new version of professionalism in which a wide variety of public sector workers are expected to conform to a top down definition of organisational professionalism in which the government plays a distanced controlling role expecting self-control from its workers to professional behaviour that is defined by government, a no limit professionalism. It is both individualistic, competitive and bureaucratic at the same time. Occupational professional values which were, in the past, based on broad values established across the profession through theories of learning and professional association are now used to promote efficient management of policy and institutions. The marketing of institutional products connects professionalism to the organisation for which they work (Evetts, 2008).

Professionalism as efficient delivery emerged in the 1970s and was gradually incorporated into the postmodern form of professionalism we see operating currently. The prioritising of accountability through regular inspections and the publication of national league tables of achievement began to eliminate the essential element of stage two professionalism, that of ambiguity in which teacher judgement, according to context was valued and based on professional judgement. Management was incorporated into the professional role and the term bureaucracy marginalised as an inappropriate contemporary term but in essence postmodern professionalism reflected a bureaucratic approach focusing on career, entrepreneurship and the professionalism of management. Career and management have evolved as one. A teacher's role moved from professional dilemmas (Berlak, Berlak et al., 1976) to the management of problems. Management theories now permeate educational organisational cultures (Hoyle and Wallace, 2008).

However teachers are not passive in these processes of ethical drift (Cribb, 2008) just as they are not victims of policy shifts more generally. They are active ethical agents who continually have to negotiate the extremely dilemmatic terrain of contemporary educational practice, who have to reconcile conflicting ethical commitments, for example, commitments to inter-institutional collegiality and the survival of the particular institution in which they work (Gerwirtz, Cribb et al., 2006; Gerwirtz, Cribb et al., 2008).

Primary teachers have, it could be argued, had to make the most radical changes to their professional practice. Whereas secondary schools and Higher and Further education were always, to some extent, heavily influenced by achievement outcomes, in terms of professional and organisational status, post war primary schools were generally immune to these imperatives until the 1980s. They had developed professional values based on pedagogic principles during a renaissance of teaching and learning from the 1960s and the move towards a postmodern professionalism based on effective management of outcome was a direct challenge to their autonomy and pedagogically based practice of child centred education and activity based learning promoted during stage two of the development of educational professionality (Woods, 1993; Woods, 1995; Woods and Jeffrey, 1996; Woods, Jeffrey et al., 1997). Their compliance, incorporation, creative mediation, retreatism and resistance towards the introduction of the National Curriculum in 1989 are well documented (Osborn, McNess et al., 2000) but the emergence of the postmodern professional has taken time to become established as the demographics of school staff's gradually altered to include more teachers educated in the post professional age.

It is only now twenty years after the introduction of the National Curriculum and the beginning of Ofsted inspections and national testing that we can perhaps identify the characteristics of the new postmodern professional.

Theoretical Frame

This research is concerned with governmentality, the conduct of conduct and particularly with how teachers and learners seek to control their own conduct (Gillies, 2008). Postmodern professionalism exhibits social cohesion at the institutional level, rather than at the wider professional level but a cohesion that is both developed and appreciated by teachers in an institutional embrace (Jeffrey and Troman, 2012a). The educational policy arena is a complex fluctuating disarray of policy strategies, (Ball, 1998) e.g.: demanding performativity and at the same time encouraging creativity and flexibility enabling schools and teachers to act positively in the space between contrasting policies, but at the same time maintaining policy development through internalising these contradictions.

Ball's (2009) 'governance turn' identifies four sets of related changes taking place: in forms of government (structures and agencies); the form and nature of the participants in the processes of governance; the prevailing discourses within governance and a change in the governing of and production of new kinds of 'willing' subjects.

A major vehicle for governmentality is policy discourse (Ball, 1998). Central government educational policy texts have dominated schools in recent times from the National Curriculum, national assessment testing, inspection reports, Qualifications and Curriculum Authority (QCA) guidelines, national reports and the publication of school standards. These texts are written documents but they also contain values and beliefs about the role of education in society and the economy. As Ball (2008) notes, policy discourses privilege certain ideas and topics and speakers and exclude others, organise their own specific rationalities, making particular sets of ideas obvious, common sense and 'true' (p. 5). They mobilise truth claims and constitute rather than simply reflect social reality, 'Language is deployed in the attempt to produce certain meanings and effects' (Edwards, Nicoll et al., 1999), p. 620). Policies are very specific and practical regimes of truth and value and the ways in which policies are spoken about, their vocabularies, are part of the creation of their acceptance and enactment.

Methodology

This ethnographic research took cognisance of the structural influences in situations and the dilemmas, tensions and constraints under which primary teachers work and the way they manage and cope with their situations. To understand the complexities of what is happening we needed to employ a qualitative approach, which 'captures and records the voices of lived experience ... contextualises experience ... goes beyond mere fact and surface appearances ... presents details, context, emotion, and the webs of social relationships that join persons to one another' (Denzin, 1989: 83). Data needed to be collected within the school context, since experiences, perspectives and identities are strongly shaped by their context (Rosenholtz, 1989). Our ethnographic approach of spending time in the field using three different time modes — compressed, selective intermittent and recurrent (Jeffrey, 1999, Jeffrey and Troman, 2004)—ensured that we took into account the broad experience of teaching and learning and obtained a complex, rich analysis of how the creativity and performativity discourses interacted with the lives of those in primary schools.

Our theory of knowledge is a sociological approach that derives from empirically studies related to social theories and personal realities. We try to get to know the sub-culture of the classroom and school and take the view that people's personal realities and beliefs are embodied in speech and behaviours. The observations and analysis of the micro, we believe, is linked to macro discourses, policies and structures. We follow an interactionist sociology in which we see people carving out space despite the lack of formal power. In our ethnographic studies of teachers we asked: What problems do they face? How are they experienced? What meanings are given to them? What feelings are generated? Ethnography respects the empirical world penetrates layers of meaning and facilitates taking the role of the other by the researcher, an empathetic understanding, defining situations, and grasping the sense of process (Woods, 1996). We see ethnography is a relevant and appropriate methodology to support our Foucauldian theoretical frame.

Our ESRC research (RES-000-23-1281) examined the effects of two policy discourses—that of creative teaching and learning and performativity on the institution of the English primary school carried out in six schools in the mid 2000s. The general focus was how schools managed the twin policies of performativity and creativity and we found that a particular type of institution has developed to ensure success of both these and other relevant policies within a market context.

The database included fifty-two days observational fieldnotes, fifty-four recorded conversations with teachers and other significant adults and thirty-two recorded conversations with learners. We transcribed all recorded conversations with management, teachers, pupils and parents that we saw as being of theoretical significance.

The conversations probed areas such as:

> Perceived tensions between the creativity and performativity policies and the dilemmas and opportunities this creates for teachers, pupils and parents.
>
> Coping strategies used to ameliorate these tensions and dilemmas
>
> The educational professional identities being constructed in the context of the two policy imperatives.

The analytical methodology proceeded in the sequence: data collection—analysis—data collection—analysis. The process provided 'spiralling insights' (Lacey, 1976) as it sought to generate theory from the data using the method of 'constant comparisons' (Glaser and Strauss, 1967). Data storage, retrieval and analysis was supported by the use of the qualitative data analysis computer package Atlas Ti.

Changes in forms of governance—The institutional embrace

The first of Ball's characteristics of the governance turn—changes in the form of structures and agencies are encapsulated in the ways in which primary schools have had to respond to the market approach of government policy.

The *embracing institution* (Jeffrey and Troman, 2012) is not a *total institution* (Goffman, 1961) in which the inmates (teachers) were cowed in the face of the management and acted out resistances but more akin to the *greedy institution* (Coser, 1974) which demanded considerable commitment and one in which coercion was more subtle, for example aligning teacher commitment to raising standards with government policies although teachers disputed the means used by government to meet commitments. The *greedy institution* expected members to weaken ties with other social groups and give the institution their undivided loyalty, creating symbolic boundaries between insiders and outsiders, that is, as equally powerful as the physical boundaries of the *total institution*—disciplinary mechanisms (Scott, 2010). However, the *greedy institution* focusses on getting members to cut all ties with outside communities whereas the *embracing institution* has different objectives. It aims to create commitment to assist the institution's survival and development in a market place, to release members from innovative constraint for the benefit of the institution while retaining their enthusiasm for the institution's performative and creative objectives in the local environment. The *embracing institution* encourages teachers to take on more managerial roles, supervise each other, take responsible for various parts of the school organisation and curriculum often without extra pay or designated seniority. In this way the institution is continually reinvented with the collaboration and support of the inmates for institutional development and at the same time it benefits individuals as they develop careers and the institution. The *embracing institution* looks to embrace not only its members but the local community in order to maintain its market position and to that end, unlike the *greedy institution*, it develops an open culture.

The *embracing institution* works to develop open, collective, inclusive cultures in which there appear to be few centres of power but where power circulates freely by binding people together to develop the institution and its inhabitants. Central to the development of an institution in which everyone is embraced and each individual embraces the institutional discourses is openness, similar to Foucault's notion of freedom (Foucault, 1977)

The six primary schools, in our study, had an openness that burgeoned in the last few years. The performance of the teacher was a daily public affair, unlike the closed classrooms of the professional autonomous phase and its qualitative nature had changed.

> We don't have our door shut and we don't teach like that so much. We're a bigger team than it used to be when you were on your own in the classroom from nine to three. It's much more open and we encourage teachers to show us what they can do. (Carolyn, C-Yr.2)

This kind of open performance made the teacher more conscious of their public image, how they presented themselves (Goffman, 1959).

> In my last school I came in for a meeting with external visitors in a suit and the staff were surprised. So I asked the teachers about it and they said that I meet with important people that's why I wear a suit but when you meet with us you don't wear a suit because it appears we're not important. Well after that, I wore a suit every single day I taught the kids and I didn't wear a suit when I went to meetings 'cos I wanted to turn it on it's head. (Camile, C-HT)

Teaching had become a public affair. Even the private reports to parents were now virtually open with every parent knowing the school statistics on its SATs[2] performance, Ofsted assessments and children and parents talked openly with each other about the child's 'level' both in and outside the staffroom, the classroom and the school grounds (Jeffrey and Troman, 2012),

> We had an afternoon where we invited parents to look at SATs papers to encourage them to help their children'. (Carole, City-Yr.5)

Meetings often took place in public, not in the head's office, which in one of our schools was only used to house her two dogs, with the door open of course. One such meeting we noted was in the school café and included a DfES person and another meeting constituted six local headteachers.

2. Standard Assessment Tasks

Schools were not just willing to share information, but positively eager to share it.

It was not only the space that seemed open.

> On my second and third visits, I am left alone in the Head's office so that I can browse the curriculum and school policy folders. The Head welcomes the policy aspect of our research project; they have many visits from other schools, who are sceptical that this school's curriculum flow approach could work for them. She hopes that our project will serve to convince other schools of the viability of the curriculum flow approach, e.g.: Beacon Role—Leading Practice, see PNS—Excellence and Enjoyment—networking and sharing of good practice.
>
> (FN-H-8//1/07)

Schools were also open to the community and at the same time they established the school as an important community institution that was worthwhile supporting, developing and embracing,

> The Children's Centre in the school has picked up and is running the family therapy groups, PCAMS, the primary child mental health group, they're providing parenting through the family links programme. It's beginning to have an impact but it will slow. But it does fundamentally change things and certainly more schools are like us. When I appoint people the first thing I do is put them on the family links training.
>
> (HT-City)

Internally professional psychologists, welfare workers and inspectors or advisors and even researchers often sat at the back of a class making notes on classroom activities. Teachers were regularly formally observed by senior staff who monitored some aspect of the teacher's work and in some schools teachers observed each other in a form of professional reciprocity. There was more collaboration between teachers who often worked together planning a term's work for the same age group and joint activities often take place with two teachers working in the same room or the whole school worked on one project for anything from one week to six in which teaching ideas and strategies were shared and displayed. This open culture made hierarchical power less visible and appeared to show how horizontal power operated by focusing on the institution and less on hierarchical positions (Foucault, 1980). Everyone was embraced and everyone embraced the development of the institution.

Changes to the form and nature of participants—The post-modern professional

Balls (Ball, 2009) second characteristic of the governance turn—changes to the form and nature of the participants in the processes of governance—is exemplified in the development of institutional identities rather than broader pedagogically professional identities. Resentment to the 1989 reforms (Osborn et al., 2000) turned to embracement as the success and fate of the institution impacted more heavily on professional status, well being and self interests. Moral trajectories were mediated by an interaction context and narratives of change were collectively negotiated. In dramaturgical terms, mutual surveillance involved performances of obedience and role embracement: members sought to demonstrate the sincerity of their commitment to the institution, and manage the impressions they communicated to fellow staff (Scott, 2010). Performative regulation, a feature of the Reinventive Institution, (RI) (Scott, 2010) which aims to provide a space for reinventing identities, applied to the *embracing institution*. The RI inmate is both an actor who performs and a subject position defined by the sum of these performances. S/he is both agentically performative and constrained by the discipline of interaction.

Team Professional

Belonging to a team, the opposite of the lone professional of Lortie's (Lortie, 1975) 1975 study and the holistic individual/professional integrated identity of those in Jennifer Nias's 1990 study (Nias, 1989), is the major way in which a primary teacher's identity is now constructed (Jeffrey, 2002). Today's professional primary school teacher is a team player in open competition with other school teams but also part of a team that needs to present itself as a unified, creative, inclusive and effective managerial organisation, 'doing member' (Garfinkel, 1967).

> Being part of a team, getting to know adults as well is rewarding. It was very lonely when previously I was with just children all the time and then going home and having my own life. (Wanda, W-Yr.6)

Teaching in our research involved having more of a team role in the organisation of the school and using one's creativity to develop the institution.

In dealing with technologies of the self Foucault talks about how the self is governed, how we seek to control our own conduct so as to 'transform' ourselves (Foucault, 2000). Professional cohesion and good professional relations were essential to the development of the team approach.

> I find, in the staffroom, a display board entitled 'Staff Achievement Board', with some displayed certificates on which some members of staff have been commended for certain actions or for just starting a new role. All staff are encouraged to download a copy and to fill it in for someone they think worthy. It's all part of the team approach used in the school. The head has indicated that this is crucial and that staff are encouraged to do kind things for one another, such as get them a cup of tea, and not to make it that obvious. The TEAM approach 'Together Everyone Achieves More' is written in large letters above the main notice board and outside at least one classroom. (FN-C-26/02/07)

A dynamism existed in all our schools irrespective of SES status and often the low SES schools were the most dynamic and innovative attempting to make a difference.

> We're all striving for the same thing in this school, for the welfare and the education of the children, everybody from the people who serve the dinners, to the cleaners who sweep the floors and sort out the leaks in the boilers, to the office staff, to the teachers. It doesn't seem that there is a big hierarchy here of being a superior because you're the Head teacher or inferiority because you're a dinner-lady. (Christopher, C-Yr.3)

The team approach was manifest in the usual portrayal of photographs of all the school staff including support staff, kitchen and cleaning staff. These corporate teams reflected the modern commercial organisation in which everyone plays a part in the development and promotion of the cultural institution.

Nurturing institutional careers

One of most significant aspect of the embracing institution is the care it exhibits towards its members bringing them close to the institution's cultural life and development (Peters and Waterman, 1982).

> We do a lot of professional development, the courses and we have the resources to support us with changes of things which I think helps. We have specialists in to motivate us and I think that really does keep you going. We try to nurture each other and help each other and we're all very hot on family links and we do that with the class but we also try to do that with each other and support each other and have networks and have teams. (Carolyn, C-Yr.2)

This approach promoted,

> a huge amount of support in my NQT[3] year and particularly appreciated given the social and economic difficulties that the children live with here. If you didn't get it, it would be a disaster. That for me is the single biggest factor of teaching in this school and making it easier to teach in a different way. (Christopher, C-Yr.3)

Nurturing career development was an effective programme of induction and appeared to contrast with governmental policies and rhetoric that promised the weeding out of teachers for incompetence (Balls, Secretary of State for Education, July 2008).

Head teachers were not seen as overtly as decision makers but as people who frame and influence the conduct of conduct—the culture of the institution (Gillies, 2008).

> Why do I stay? I've got a Head who's very supportive, who allows me to do a lot of different things that maybe I wouldn't be able to do in another school, all the extra curricular things. I'm very keen on the health of the children and he is very supportive. If I want to do something to do with that he'll let me. So it's a combination of a nice school, lots of change happening in it all the time, lots of things going on and the supportiveness of the Head and the Deputy. (Imogen, I-Yr.5)

Another major aspect of the cultural development of the institution is the positive relationship between career guidance and counselling and flexibility of employees and their ability to function in flexible organisations. There is,

3. Newly qualified teacher

> a clear relationship between the employee's perception of being valued by the organisation on the one hand, and job performance, motivation, self-esteem and innovative behaviour on the other hand. The main reason for these positive effects is a social exchange process: 'When the organisation is good for me, I am good for the organisation'. These results suggest that career guidance and counselling for teachers can provide a promising platform for personal sense-making in relation to actual developments and changes that are taking place in schools.
>
> (Geijsel and Meijers, 2005: 427)

Distributed leadership

Flattened hierarchies have been more prevalent in primary schools since the late 1980s (Nias, Southworth et al., 1989) through forms of distributed leadership (Woods, 2004) in which teachers have taken specific responsibility for curriculum areas or other specific responsibilities and some of our teachers relished these new opportunities to become part of the management of the institution,

> I had a vague idea that I wanted to be more involved in the decision making processes and to get more of an overview of the school structure, how it works with the governors and self evaluation processes and those kinds of things that you always hear about in paperwork. I also wanted to understand a bit more about school curriculum plans and that kind of thing because I knew that I was doing interesting things in my classroom.
>
> (Mary-MM-Yr.2)

However, more recently, those remunerated responsibilities have become tied to a particular school or team interest, reducing the possibility of teacher's developing a subject career expertise such as literacy or maths over many years, so drawing people into the embrace of the institution.

> If a teacher is given a management point, that management point also comes with responsibility and accountability and because there is a pay range that the school decides as a collective, so everybody, all staff members know that if this member of staff is getting this pay point that they are responsible and this is the amount they will receive. Every school

> will make their own decision about what responsibilities and how much money that responsibility is given. So if you resign or go to another school that point is not going to go with you and it can be taken away during your time at the school. (Wilma, W-Yr.2)

Performative regulation (Scott, 2010) occurs where groups of people submit themselves to the authority of an institution, internalise its values and enact through them mutual surveillance in an inmate culture. Power operates horizontally as well as vertically, as members monitor each other's conduct, sanction deviance and evaluate their own progress in relative terms. The disciplinary gaze is not merely transmitted but reticulated: dispersed and refracted through an agentic network. Power is not only discursively constitutive but also interactively productive of new identities. The rituals of peer group interaction are central to this process and can be as important as the formal instruction they receive in motivating people to commit to an institution (Scott, 2010) instead of going it alone.

Distributed leadership drew teachers into the management of the organisation where their ownership could be seen through their commitment to it.

> I've learnt a lot from fast track about leadership. It's a programme with lots of new ideas in it that looks at things like distributive leaderships so you find out what peoples strengths are, find out what where the areas of development are, their weaknesses, help them to build up their weaknesses and play to their strengths. So it's a much more intrusive way of working rather than having a clear hierarchical structure where headteachers actually do this and everyone knows their own little box and they stay in it. It's a way of thinking about leadership, much more of a network which I think is very positive. (Mary, MM-Yr.2)

A school or organisational culture that promises some relief from the intensification of professional practice is likely to have volunteers taking up managerial courses and being creative about developing the school in order to gain managerial promotional posts.

The nurturing and distributive leadership approaches generated trust and again ensured that teachers become identified with the institution,

> It is the amount of trust she puts in me and she lets us make our own decisions because she trusts us, she knows that what decisions we make will be right and if it's something really important we will talk with her about that. (Hester, H-DH)

Team work and distributive leadership play a major role in constructing the new primary teacher professional identity which exploited talent and energy for the institution and enhanced commitment and dedication.

Change in the prevailing discourses of governance—Living in and with tension

The third of Ball's (2009) characteristics of change for a governance turn is the change to the prevailing discourse of professionalism that existed in earlier phases with the introduction of performativity and management dominated practices in the 1990s. The constraints we identified in the mid 1990s were concerned with central imposition of a National Curriculum, specific pedagogies examined by Ofsted, a prescriptive literacy and numeracy programme and the beginning of the influence of SATs (Jeffrey and Woods, 1998).

The current research shows a continuation of some of those constraints, the continuation of Ofsted inspections, albeit more frequent but less exacting and the extension of the influence on teaching and learning of SATs testing as well as the pervasive influence of soft progression performativity through the delivery of a curriculum, bounded and framed, by over two hundred learner assessments in the primary school (Jeffrey and Troman, Forthcoming).

> People seem to find a way to deal with things, you've just got to find a way haven't you? Because you have to work with the system, there are certain things that are in a system. You work with government, you've got power within a system, you have to work the system or you have to make the system work for you too, otherwise you end up banging your head against a brick wall. (Wei, W-Yr.2)

There was external pressure to test the whole school every year to ensure they got higher in the league tables, 'it's not something that the head or I, or anyone particularly wants but unfortunately it's the way it has to be' (Stephanie-W-DH), constructing organisational professionals (professionalism from above) as opposed to occupational professionals (from within the profession) (Evetts, 2005).

Their professional commitment to raise achievement results is seen in the welcome they give Ofsted to try to prove that they have been successful. This is more than professional surviving, this is striving professionality. Professional commitment underpinned this kind of professionality,

> Head teachers particularly have a tremendous impact on learning. I'm better equipped to do the job of headship here now than I was eight years ago because I've been here long enough for the parents, to have built up quite a deal of trust with me. They were quite slow to give their trust, in fact one parent said to me four years in, "you're a posh bitch but you're alright really". After taking a sharp sort of intake of breath I decided it was a compliment in the end ... It was a measure of just how long it takes to even start beginning to be accepted, really accepted by people on this estate. (Camile, C-HT)

Nevertheless the postmodern professional is living a balancing life with more dilemmas, tensions and constraints, a professional life full of risks, with some imperatives gaining ascendency over others, creating a fragmented existence (Ball, 2000). They see-saw between each new initiative or recurring imperative, living a professional life of highs and lows (Troman and Raggl, 2008), gaining psychic rewards and suffering psychic downturns (Troman and Raggl, 2008).

Postmodern professional identities are imbued with a wider range of emotions than in the autonomous phase of professionality (Jeffrey and Woods, 1997; Hargreaves, 1998) concerning success and failure, satisfaction and dissatisfaction, of well-being and dejection. Primary teaching has, postwar, been taken up by many responsible for child care because it enabled them to manage both childcare and a career and this still exists today although as beginning a family starts later nowadays, some are currently more likely to come from other careers first of all (Troman et al., 2008). The intensified nature of the modern primary teacher is more likely to cause parents to choose between the two,

> Well I'm quite pleased with how much I've developed in my career in just three years and that's a plus point with this school for the Head is very good at giving you a chance lead and helping you develop. But certainly I would like to get married. I'd like to have my own children but I can't imagine for one second being able to do this and have my own children. I'm sure people do but I certainly wouldn't be able to work in a school

like this where the children need a lot of my emotional side of me. I'm not sure if I could do that and have my own children. (Cecile, C-Yr.2)

Teachers accepted the situation and sought to manage living with tension,

> Obviously we have targets for all children in the school that's how it is, not that I always agree with these things but you do have targets and children are assessed to a certain level of a target and at the start of the year you have the previous years targets and you are expected to move them up. I have to bear in mind that you are not going to get every single child up to those targets and I have to know that as a teacher that that's not a failing. I have to accept that I'm not going to move every single child to that level and you have to know their limitations as well as your own. I think you need to know that performance is being assessed because we have performance and appraisals and we have to reflect on our practice and we need to know that what we are doing is working. (Harriet, H-Yr.6)

Performativity works in three ways: through a disciplinary system of judgements, classifications and targets towards which schools and teachers must strive and against and through which they are evaluated; second it provides sign systems which represent education in a self-referential and reified form for consumption; and thirdly it resides in the pragmatics of language (Ball, 1998). The testing culture has become part of a primary teacher's expertise and regular practice, whether they liked it or not,

> I think it's a good idea to use standardised tests, that you've some data that you can use and compare them with the teacher assessments. I think that's great but the way they use them by publishing them on the Net and using league tables puts so much pressure on teachers. It means that I'm teaching to a test for half the year and it means there's no time for all the other things that I'd like to teach, for laying the foundations and building optimistic and resilient kids, all the programmes that cater for that. (Witney, W-Yr.6)

An annual check on learner progress and indicating priorities for school and teacher targeting is now generally accepted.

> As Key Stage 1 Coordinator my job is to check and I say to my Key Stage 1 staff 'let's have a chat about how people are reaching their targets, how are we getting on and how many people in your class are meeting expectations, where they should be'. We'll discuss that and one may say 'no I'm really struggling with my middle group. We are constantly looking to see how people are getting on with our 'flying high' group—those who are near the class level and need extra help to get to it. I target them as soon as they came in and decide on my overall list as to where they should be by the end of the term. (Carolyn, C-Yr.2)

A second contrasting discourse—creative teaching and learning—emerged from the NACCEE[4] report of 1999 and it has been taken up by Ofsted as an educational 'good' (Ofsted, 2006). Schools have been active in constructing space for its development through creativity weeks (Troman, 2008) but the influence of the governance turn means that it has to take its place, in most schools, as subservient to performativity.

Although there is a tension between these two major policy discourses we can see two different kinds. There was a stable tension, a productive tautness between the two policies as teachers investigated how creative teaching and learning could assist the aims of performance, that of raising achievement, to ensure more effective learning, to encourage learners to persist through taking more control and ownership of their learning. This stable tension was also exploited by teachers to ensure that the experience of creative teaching and learning transformed not only the learner but a steadily improving level of achievement which had to be recorded regularly to assist progress. Attention to the performance of learners against National Curriculum attainment targets provided a discipline for creative teaching and learning activities, e.g.: the new literacy framework.

There was also a de-stabilising tension as the opposite processes of the two policies pulled against one another, stretching the relationship beyond resolution. There was then a tension between teachers' interests in handing over control and ownership and encouraging innovation and the need to maintain improving statistical returns for fear of reduced funding or public pillory. These pulled against one another threatening to snap teacher commitment.

The imprint of targets and levels was ubiquitous (MacBeath, 2005) and teachers struggled to develop cross curricula projects and more creative teaching,

4. National Advisory Committee on Creative and Cultural Education

> As I say I try, where I can, to integrate curriculum and I constantly try where I can. I'm always trying to alter my planning to bring that in but it's hard because like today's literacy lesson they have to be able to answer questions on the story in the manner of the SATs style. How do you make that creative and they have to be able to do it. I'm not helping them if I don't give them the skills or teach them the skills to be able to do that effectively. (Indra, I-Yr.6)

To integrate these two discourses into a pedagogic frame was very difficult,

> I felt a lot of pressure last year to maintain the SATs results at a higher attaining level but also to take on this creative curriculum that was being embedded in the school, linking and planning between subjects and making it enlivening and engaging as possible. I feel a lot more confident this year having had one year of successful SATs results under my belt and now I feel that I'm not going to have to answer too many questions about my teaching. However, I don't think I can do it together, I can't teach creatively and maintain high attainment for the results. It is difficult to keep the two things running in parallel. (Indra, I-Yr.6).

It was often a case of balance rather than integration, although one privileged school, in our research and some individual teachers managed to integrate performativity and creativity through smart teaching (Jeffrey and Troman, 2012). Strategic juggling of the curriculum became the norm,

> Sometimes on my weekly plan I get to Wednesday and I'll go 'We'll do this instead', but I know in my head that I've got to make sure that if that I've got to make sure I do that next week. It is an ongoing thing this. I still constantly think 'Oh I haven't really taught enough of that this term' because of what I enjoy teaching more There probably is a bias towards some things as opposed to other things, but I've obviously got to cover the other things as well. So I try to make sure I've got time for that as well. (Celina, C-Yr.3)

The postmodern professional is living a balancing life with more dilemmas, tensions and constraints, a professional life full of risks, with some imperatives gaining ascendency over others, creating a fragmented existence (Ball, 2000).

They see-saw between each new initiative or recurring imperative, living a professional life of highs and lows (Troman and Raggl, 2008), gaining psychic rewards and suffering psychic downturns (Troman and Raggl, 2008).

Postmodern professional identities are imbued with a wider range of emotions than in the autonomous phase of professionality (Jeffrey and Woods, 1997; Hargreaves, 1998) concerning success and failure, satisfaction and dissatisfaction, of well being and dejection,

> You just have to do it. You get frustrated, you do it and then you feel frustrated and then the results come out and you find that we got really good results and initially you go,'yay', and then you think'well, no, that's not really why I'm a teacher'. I'm not overly excited. I'm excited because the school has obviously done really well and certainly won't be put into special measures or anything, they'll probably get a pat on the back for their results. (Witney, W-Yr.6)

Primary teachers are now jugglers in this fast postmodern profession where the dominant culture is that anything is possible and everything has to be done,

> Once you start taking on other subjects to manage—it's a constant juggling act. That's the problem and I think that you have to realise early on as a teacher that you'll never—you'll never finish everything. You have to reach a point where you prioritise and you've done the things that needed doing that day. And I often find myself thinking right, this week I'm going to do dah, dah, dah and you only achieve one of those things because there's so many other things to take on (Cecile, C-Yr.2)

Schools and teachers are both living with a productive stable tension and living in tension as they grapple with these two contrasting policies. It is a tension negotiated by schools and teachers as they become familiar with the policies and they manipulate them to suit their situation and as they exploit the spaces generated by themselves and by the apparent loosening of central control (Troman, Jeffrey et al., 2007). Whereas the experience of professional tension in the post ERA period concerned changing roles and we identified a typology of differing reactions, the tensions experienced in primary schools today is between managing performativity policies that are integrated into the school system and seen as having some worth and the maintenance and integration of creative policies and pedagogies back into a structure heavily influenced by performance and performativity.

The dilemmas, tensions and constraints we identified as specific aspects of earlier phases of professional life (Woods, 1997) are now compacted all together in the everyday experience of post modern professionalism in the embrace of the institution and in becoming the Total Teacher, living in tension (Seddon, Billett et al., 2004). As Cribb (Cribb, 2005; Cribb, 2008) puts it,'These dilemmas are chronic and serious because ... there is no simple translation between institutional obligations and ethical obligations, between *doing my job* and *doing the right thing*'. (ibid. p.40)

Change in the governing of and production of willing subjects—Aspiring cultures

A governance turn needs, last of all, new kinds of willing subjects and the institutional embrace is critical in aiding the establishment of these subjects who gain new professional roles and are supported and developed by it. It is virtually impossible not to embrace many aspects of the dominant discourses such as performativity (Perryman, 2006) for the sake of the institution, for career and for professional identity. One of the main vehicles for the development of this commitment and identification is the discourse of aspiration.

The schools demonstrated an aspiring culture in which members held personal aspirations for career, for the learners, for their school and community and the values underpinning these aspirations were at the same time meritocratic, egalitarian and humanist. Our schools were littered with cultural and educational homilies exhorting members to think and act positively, to see learning as a comfortable but challenging journey made easier through self assessment and through co-operation with others, identifying mistakes as learning points and generally celebrating the joy of learning and education and downplaying authoritative power relations. These homilies were for adults as well, some of them placed in staff toilets. An aspirational culture was prominent throughout with a celebration of continual improvement.

Nevertheless the new aspirational culture had its satisfiers (Herzberg, 1971),

> I don't want to paint a false picture and say we're always happy because that's not true. There are days when I'm quite tired, especially towards the end of the term and you think 'oh goodness' but the majority of the time I think we are very positive and I think we're always willing to try

> new things and I think that's the key. We are a fairly young staff who have that energy and we feel comfortable with change. If you haven't been teaching as long then maybe you're willing to change. (Carolyn, C-Yr.2)

Promotion and challenges were daunting but welcome in this new 'can do' culture.

> It is a big job and it is a responsible thing to do. There are downsides to it but I think quite positive. Perhaps it's me in my innocence or my ignorance, I don't know. It's a big responsibility but I think it's one that I'm quite happy to take on. And I think I would do it very well. So that's just how I look at it really. (Vicky, V-DH)

Continuous improvement and a belief in the possibility of success was an example of how the conduct of conduct (Gillies, 2008) pervaded the school culture.

> The fact that Ofsted could drop in anytime means you have to always have it in place and always have to be motivated and keep things going and if you started some new initiative you need them to know that you can continue with it and if you've said on your school development plan and your school improvement plan that you're going to do it then it needs to be monitored and needs to be checked that we are doing it. (Cloe, C-Yr.2)

Challenges were a central part of the aspiring school cultures,

> I think targets for the school give people a bit of ambition, it does for me anyway, just to say you need to achieve this in this time, it's a bit more of a business psychology I think ... The moment it feels like you're on a treadmill it's time to change and to set yourself some targets to know where you want to get to and if you're ambitious enough, targets for head-teacher or advanced skills teacher or a SENCO[5], (Christopher, C-Yr.3)

A commitment to social justice strengthened the power of the institution and of those individuals who embraced these principles. Their commitment

---

5. Special Educational Needs Co-ordinator

was not just to maintain their league table position but to improve children's opportunities,

> Actually I want the test results improved as well so a child going on to secondary school can read and write. Actually we're genuinely worried about test results not because I care about where I am on the league table. If I can get my kids reading and writing, fantastic, I do all the old stuff. If I want to break this cycle of deprivation, one of the ways is to teach them to read and write so they can engage with other kids, so I worry about that. (Victor, V-HT)

Their aspirations were tied closely to the children's education although they accepted that the methodology was not perfect for all children.

> I don't see SATs as an imposition, it has to be done and we do it because all the children in the country do it. Actually some of the children, no lots of the children, enjoy the challenge, feel self satisfied with their results and I think it can be a good learning experience as well. Although this morning's lesson was quite dry and very, very much teaching to the test, there was speaking and listening in it, there were thinking skills in it. I read the story aloud and the children enjoyed listening to the story and they all engaged fully in the story, really, they were able to deduce information from it. These are all powerful skills to have and I think they are all important. The SATs aren't necessarily a bad thing, for as I say some of the children enjoy it, they feel quite motivated by it. You can see that this morning that they all want to do well, and they want to do their best and to work hard towards them. (Indra, I-Yr.6)

The discourse of improvement and challenge pervaded the whole culture, a postmodern form of governmentality.

> In fact one of the kids last week at Breakfast Club gave me the best feedback I have ever had. I want it written on my tombstone. I think it sums up best what you need to do and you do on a good day. She said, "I think you're like the Wizard of Oz Mrs Herbert because you educate our brains, you're kind but you give us courage". And I thought well, there you go there's a pretty good leg up that you need to give to your staff too as

> well. Give them the courage, give them the stamina but also give them a challenge. We mustn't see them as problems but give them the challenge and give them the support (Camile, C-HT)

The discourse of improvement, challenge and aspiration seeped into the life of all including the students. It is in this context of a culture of openness underpinned by a market discourse and of aspiration, a discourse that promotes the possibility of universal improvement and success through effort and a positive approach in which teacher's professionalism was being forged through the institutional governmentality.

We are seeing the institutionalisation of disposition where organisational policies determine the nature of professionalism (Søreide, 2007) as being flexible and totally supporting the survival and development of the institution to which the teacher belongs as the priority to determine professional aims and values. If the values of the institution coincide with teacher imported values such as social justice the morphology is united, if not then the teacher is bound to alter their disposition and identity to ensure their professional responsibility becomes synonymous with that of the institution's development.

Conclusion

Our conclusion from our research is that a primary teacher's postmodern professional life, is now one in which dilemmas are less pedagogic but relate to decisions about the extent to which they commit themselves and their identities to being a person-teacher in the mould explicated in the 1980s (Nias, 1989). Another professional dilemma is concerned with the use of creative pedagogies within soft performative practices (classroom target setting and assessment) and the extent to which they can employ creative policies and practices in the face of both soft and hard performative imperatives (SATs). At the same time there are still personal tensions being faced alongside constraints so the postmodern professional lives a teaching life of policy dilemmas, tensions and constraints.

Their professionality has been extended rather than restricted to areas of expertise (Hoyle, 1980), made more total, in which direct accountability to government via their school performance widened their focus of professional engagement and with the incorporation of managerial approaches, which now permeate teacher activity they now experience a professionally ambiguous role (Evans, 1994) or post-modern professionalism. This ambiguity is very different to that of the autonomy phase of professionalism when primary teachers' main issues were to do with classroom dilemmas focused on control, curriculum and societal issues. These were professional dilemmas faced by primary teachers in classes in which their professional judgment was paramount. The ambiguity faced by the teachers in our research concerned their interests in playing their full part in the survival and development of the institution of which they are a member in the local environment and developing a creative pedagogy. The situation was a complex one for both performative and creative policies have government support. Teachers' tensions over how to manage this situation is one that is replicated at a global level, where economic interests demand both creative and performative outcomes from institutions. Teachers private lives at the micro level have internalised the tensions of macro public policies (Mills, 1959).

Governmentality works at the micro level through examining local discourses, the kinds of power relations established and the emergence of agency through the strategic practices that Foucault (1980) maintains dominate local situations as Thrift (Thrift, 2000) notes, 'To govern human beings is not to crush their capacity to act, but to acknowledge it and to utilise it for one's own objectives' (Rose, 2000: 4). In this sense our research shows clearly the workings of governmentality.

Each of the postmodern professional identities—the managerial teacher, the creative teacher and the performing teacher—is a challenge to the self, to maintain and develop the former and to meet the challenges faced by external demands and the progression of their learners. They are both embraced by the institution, and they return this warmth by embracing the institution's values and imperatives while, to some extent, depleting the self, just as the teachers of the Nias era (1989) depleted the self through their personal commitment. The post-modern professional is both invigorated by and depleted by their institutional commitment. There are professional debilitating tensions and mixed emotions about their role of teaching, their passion for creative pedagogy and their commitment to improve the lot of their learners. There is some private performative anxiety in the face of performative failure and this affects their interest in professional care and educational development.

However, they have also developed a professional ease with their situation, an acceptance of their lot but a desire to maintain some control over it, a professional pride at any resulting performative progress and they maintain an interest in any professional progress and at the same they value the solidarity of values and professional aims in today's collective enterprises. They are imbued with the discourses of the day as they replicate the language and aims of the policy discourses, both performative and creative but they seek to manage any conflicts between them as best they can and at the same time act creatively to overlay them as the flexible opportunities present themselves. The amount of work and the desire to achieve difficult crossings are wearisome but challenging. They accept the fast moving situations and use their energy and commitment to manage them replicating the fast moving policy and economic global scene. Fast postmodern professionals for fast times—the Total Teacher immersed in the *embracing institution.*

References

Ball, S. (1998) Big policies/small world: an introduction to international perpectives in education policy. *Comparative Education* 34(2): 119-130.

Ball, S. (2008) *The education debate.* Bristol, Policy Press.

Ball, S., J (2009) The Governance Turn: Editorial. *Journal of Education Policy* 24(5): 537-538.

Ball, S. J. (1998) Performativity and fragmentation in 'Postmodern Schooling', in *Postmodernity and Fragmentation of Welfare.* J. Carter. London, Routledge: 187-203.

Ball, S. J. (2000) Performativities and Fabrications in the Education Economy: Towards the Performative Society? *Australian Educational Researcher* 27(2): 1-23.

Berlak, A., H. Berlak, et al. (1976). Teaching and Learning in English Primary Schools, in *The process of schooling: A sociological reader.* M. Hammersley and P. Woods. London, Routledge.

Coser, L. A. (1974) *Greedy Institutions: Patterns of undivided commitment.* New York, Free Press.

Cribb, A. (2005) *Education and health: professional roles and the division of ethical labour.* C-TRIP. Kings College, London.

Cribb, A. (2008). Professional ethics: whose responsibility, in *Changing teacher Professionalism: International trends, challenges and ways forward.* S. Gewirtz, P. Mahony, I. Hextall and A. Cribb: 31-42.

Denzin, N. (1989) *Interpretative interactionism,* (London, Sage).

Edwards, A., K. Nicoll, et al. (1999) Migrating metaphors: the globalisation of flexibility in policy. *Journal of Education Policy* 14: 619-630.

Evans, L. (1994) *The meaning of infant teacher's work.* London, Routledge.

Evetts, J. (2005) The management of professionalism: a contemporary paradox. ESRC C-TRIP Semianr Series. KIngs College London.

Evetts, J. (2008) The management of professionalism: a contemporary paradox, in *Changing teacher Professionalism: International trends, challenges and ways forward* S. Gewirtz, P. Mahony, I. Hextall and A. Cribb. London, Routledge: 19-30.

Foucault, M. (1977) *Discipline and Punish: The birth of the prison.* London, Peguin.

Foucault, M., Ed. (1980) *Power/Knowledge: Selected interviews and other writings.* New York, Pantheon.

Foucault, M. (2000) *Technologies of the self. Michel Foucault.* P. Rabinow. London, Penguin: 223-251.

Garfinkel, H. (1967) *Studiues in ethnomethodology.* Englewood Cliffs NY, Prentice-Hall.

Geijsel, F. and F. Meijers (2005) Identity learning: the core process of eduational change. *Educational Studies* 314: 419-430.

Gerwirtz, S., A. Cribb, et al. (2006) Changing teacher roles, identities and professionalism: A review of key themes from the ESRC C-TRIP seminar papers. . London Kings College London.

Gerwirtz, S., A. Cribb, et al. (2008) *Policy, professionalism and practice: understanding and enhancing teacher's work.* S. Gewirtz, A. Cribb. S. Gewirtz, P. Mahony, I. Hextall and A. Cribb. London Routledge: 3-16.

Gillies, D. (2008) Developing governmentality: Conduct3 and eductation policy. *Journal of Education Policy* 23(4): 415-427.

Glaser, B. G. and A. Strauss (1967) *The Discovery of Grounded Theory.* Chicago, Aldine.

Goffman, E. (1961). *Asylums*. Harmondsworth, Penguin.

Goffman, I. (1959). *The Presentation of Self in Everyday Life.* London, Penguin.

Hargreaves, A. (1998). The Emotional Practice of Teaching. *Teaching and Teacher Education* 14(8): 835-854.

Hargreaves, A. (2000). The four ages of professionalism and professional learning. *Teachers and Teaching,* 6(2): 152-182.

Herzberg, F. (1971). *Motivation-hygiene theory. Organisation Theory.* D. Pugh. Harmondsworth, Penguin.

Hoyle, E. (1980). Professionalisation and deprofessionalisation in education, in *World year book of education 1980: Professional development of teachers.* E. Holye and J. Megarry. London, Kogan Page: 42-54.

Hoyle, E. and M. Wallace (2008). Leadership for professional practice, in *Changing teacher Professionalism: International trends, challenges and ways forward.* S. Gewirtz, P. Mahony, I. Hextall and A. Cribb. London, Routledge: 204-214.

Jeffrey, B. (1999) Distancing research objects through the involvement of the self, In: A. W. Massey, G. (Ed.) *Studies in educational ethnography: Explorations in ethnography.* (vol. 2)Stamford Connecticut, Jai Press):163-182.

Jeffrey, B. (2002). Performativity and Primary Teacher Relations. *Journal of Education Policy* 17(5): 531-546.

Jeffrey, B. and Troman, G. (2004) Time for ethnography. *British Journal of Educational Research,* 30(4):535-548.

Jeffrey, B., Troman, G., (2012) Governmentality in Primary Schools in the UK, in B. Jeffrey, G, Troman. *Performativity across UK education: ethnographic cases of its effects, agency and reconstructions* (Painswick, E and E Publishing)

Jeffrey, B. and P. Woods (1997). Feeling Deprofessionalised: the social construction of emotions during an Ofsted inspection. *Cambridge Journal of Education* 26(3): 325-343.

Jeffrey, B. and Woods, P. (1998) *Testing teachers: The effects of school inspections on primary teachers,* (London., Falmer).

Lacey, C. (1976) Problems of sociological fieldwork: a review of methodology of 'Hightown Grammar', in *The Process of Schooling.* M. Hammersley and P. Woods. London, Routledge: 55-66.

Lortie, D. C. (1975) *Schoolteacher.* Chicago, University of Chicago Press.

MacBeath, J. (2005) Supporting innovative pedagogies: the role of school leadership. ESRC C-TRIP Seminar Series. Kings College London.

Menter, I., Y. Muschamp, et al. (1997) *Work and Identity in the Primary School: a post-Fordist analysis.* Buckingham, Open University Press.

Mills, C. W. (1959) *The Sociological Imagination.* New York, Oxford University Press.

Moss, G. (2005) The impact of literacy and performance pedagogies in primary teacher identities. ESRC -C-TRIP Seminar Series. Kings College London.

Nias, J. (1989) *Primary Teachers Talking*. London, Routledge.

Nias, J., G. Southworth, et al. (1989) *Staff relationships in the primary school : a study of organisational cultures.* London, Cassell.

Nixon, J. (2005) Good teachers? The integrity of academic practice. *London Review of Education* 2(3): 245-252.

Ofsted (2006) *Creative Partnerships: initiative and impact.* London, Ofsted.

Osborn, M., E. McNess, et al. (2000) *What Teachers Do: Changing Policy and Practice in Primary Education.* London, Continuum.

Perryman, J. (2006) Panoptic performativity and school Inspection. *Journal of Education Policy* 21(2): 147-161.

Peters, T. J. and J. R. H. Waterman (1982) *In search of Excellence.* New York, Warner Books.

Reeves, J. (2005) Inventing the chartered teacher:exploring the fractures opened in schools and authorities by enacting a 'new professionalism'. . C-TRIP Seminar—ESRC Seminar series. Kings College London.

Rose, N. (2000) *Powers of Freedom: Reframing political thought.* Cambridge, Cambridge University Press.

Rosenholtz, S. (1989) *Teachers' workplace,* (New York, Longman).

Scott, S. (2010). Revisiting the Total Institution: performative regulation in the Reinventive Institution. *Sociology* 44(2): 213-231.

Seddon, T., S. Billett, et al. (2004) Politics of social partnerships: a framework for theorising. *Journal of Education Policy* 19(2): 123-143.

Søreide, G. R. (2007) The public face of teacher identity—narrative construction of teacher identity in public policy documents. *Journal of Education Policy* 22(2): 129-146.

Thrift, N. (2000) Performing cultures in the new economy. *Annals of the Association of American Geographers* 90(4): 674-692.

Troman, G. (2008) Primary teacher identity, commitment and career in performative school cultures. *Britsih Journal of Educational Research* 34(5): 619-633.

Troman, G., Jeffrey, B. and Raggl, A. (2007) Creativity and performativity policies in primary school cultures. *Journal of Education Policy,* 22(5):549-572.

Troman, G. and A. Raggl (2008) Primary Teacher Commitment and the Attractions of Teaching. *Pedagogy, Culture and Society*, 16 ,(1): 85-99.

Wallace, M. (2005) Towards effective management of a reformed teaching profession. ESRC C-TRIP Seminar Series. Kings College London.

Webb, R. and G. Vulliamy (2009) Professional learning communities and teacher well-being? A comparative study of primary schools in England and Finland. *Oxford Review of Education* 35(3): 405-422.

Winch, C. and L. Foreman-Peck (2005) What do we mean by teacher's professionalism and professional knowledge? How useful are these concepts? ESRC C-TRIP Seminar series. Kings College.

Woods, P. (1993) *Critical Events In Teaching And Learning,*. London, Falmer Press.

Woods, P. (1995) *Creative Teachers in Primary Schools*. Buckingham, Open University Press.

Woods, P. (1996) *Researching the art of teaching:ethnography for educational use.* London, Routledge.

Woods, P. (2004) Democratic leadership:drawing distinctions with distributed leadership. *International Journal of Leadership in education* 7(1): 3-26.

Woods, P. (1996) *Researching the art of teaching: Ethnography for educational use,* (London, Routledge).

Woods, P. and B. Jeffrey (1996) *Teachable Moments: The Art Of Creative Teaching In Primary Schools*. Buckingham, Open University Press.

Woods, P., B. Jeffrey, et al. (1997) *Restructuring Schools, Reconstructing Teachers.* Buckingham, Open University Press.

Chapter 2

The performative culture in Swedish schools and how teachers cope with it

Marianne Dovemark and Ann-Sofie Holm

Abstract

School reforms implemented in Sweden in the early 1990s involved a shift from centralised norm-based management to decentralised management by objectives that imply 'soft governance'. Teachers' work is heavily prescribed by central government even though Sweden is said to have one of the most decentralised school systems in the world. This chapter draws on extensive empirical data that has been produced during the last ten years. It involves four separate research studies based on ethnographies, interviews and observations from among fifty-five teachers from primary school to upper secondary school level. Although there were some differences in their working duties and assignments, all teachers involved expressed similar perceptions of a pervasive and strengthened performative culture in school. The change not only involved increased workloads and stress connected to assessment and administrative work; it also implied that teachers were expected to marketise their schools.

Introduction

The teaching profession has been characterised by a loss of autonomy over the last three decades: professional collegiality has been replaced by government directed and controlled policies and the values of the marketplace. School reforms implemented in Sweden in the early 1990s involved a shift from centralised norm-based management to decentralised management by objectives that imply 'soft governance' (Hudson, 2011). Schools and teachers are regulated by evaluation and quality controls rather than direct control methods (Andreasson and Dovemark, 2013; Asp Onsjö, 2010). This chapter intends to illustrate and explore the performative culture in Swedish schools and teachers' strategies to cope with the expectations that have emerged of outcomes, efficiency and accountability. We ask the questions: how is the policy context understood and formed by teachers? and how have teachers' work and classroom practices changed to respond to the current policy context?

National research (i.e. Dovemark 2004; Lindqvist, 2002; Lundström and Holm, 2011; Nordänger, 2002; Strömberg, 2010) as well as international work in the field (e.g. Ball, 2003; Ball et al., 2012; Jeffrey and Troman, 2012) shows that there has been an intensification of teachers' work; actual teaching is only one of many tasks that now make up the working day. According to the Swedish National Agency for Education (SNAE, 2015), teachers' working conditions and an increased workload results in less time for preparing lessons and developing their professional competences.

The work of teachers is heavily prescribed by central government even though Sweden is said to have one of the most decentralised school systems in the world (Rönnberg, 2011, 2012). The Swedish Schools Inspectorate is an important body in controlling the prescribed policies and for reviewing school quality. The Inspectorate conducts regular supervision of all public and independent schools in Sweden, from pre-school to adult education, and the results and quality audits are frequently published in, for instance, Swedish newspapers and online league tables (e.g. siris.skolverket.se). Sweden thus follows other countries' (cf. Jeffrey and Troman, 2012) practice regarding 'quality enhancement' measurements, and is, as Angus argues in his chapter in this book, a part of global movements in education policy and teaching practice.

Performativity and ontological insecurity

The changing working conditions of teachers can in many ways be seen as related to inspections within notions of power: Foucault's (2000) knowledge, discourse and discipline. Inspections are primarily about gathering knowledge of schools and making judgements about them, and they are therefore intrinsically linked to power and can make teachers feel that performance is necessary as the consequences of failing an inspection are severe (Perryman, 2012; Rönnberg, 2014). Documentation becomes an important tool in meeting the Inspectorate's requirements and valuations of schools' outcomes and thereby their performance efficiency (SNAE, 2015).

Performativity in this text is defined as a culture that leads to performances that measure efficiency (cf. Ball, 2003; Jeffrey and Troman, 2012). Priestley et al. (2012: 87) express it thus: 'Performativity is not simply the demand for teachers to *perform* but more a pressure to perform in particular ways, most notably in terms of externally defined performance indicators.' Teachers must ensure that students achieve the kinds of grades that give their school the desired position in league tables. Such requirements stand in sharp contrast to a professional discourse on education, as they position the teacher as a curriculum deliverer and producer of performance statistics, rather than as a curriculum developer, a responsible professional and an agent of change. Priestley et al. (2012: 92) describe how the culture of measurement drives out a concern for what constitutes good education and that what follows is teachers distancing themselves from their personal values in order to 'play the game', a game that can take the form of fabrication: '... ethical practices lose out to performative pressures, as survival strategies lead to tactical and even cynical compliance.' Ball (2004) defines fabrication as 'versions of an organisation (or person) which does not exist (...) they are produced purposely to be accountable' (p. 224). Despite the fact that excellence and performance are objectives in cultures of performativity, Ball argues that it may produce the exact opposite effect. As monitoring and assessment consume more and more energy, teachers have less time for teaching. The logic stimulates 'plasticity instead of authenticity, self-worth and meaning' as Ball (2003) puts it (cf. Jeffrey and Troman, 2011; Larsson, Löfdahl and Pérez Prieto, 2009). The focus on standards in school in fact creates a set of pressures—a 'delivery chain'—that works 'downwards' from government via teachers to students. This 'deliverology' (Barber, 2010, cited in Ball et al., 2012: 76) becomes part of normal life in school through surveillance, monitoring, tracking, reporting and recording. Ball (2003) argues that the performativity culture leads to 'ontological insecurity' and 'inauthenticity' in teachers' practice and in their relationships with students:

> There is a flow of changing demands, expectations and indicators that makes one continually accountable and constantly recorded. We become ontologically insecure: unsure whether we are doing enough, doing the right thing, doing as much as others, or as well as others, constantly looking to improve, to be better, to be excellent. And yet it is not always very clear what is expected. (Ball, 2003: 220)

For the ontologically insecure person life is a state of perpetual anxiety (Ashman and Gibson, 2010: 6). Accordingly, when we are exposed to things outside ourselves that conflict with our idealised version of the world we feel a sense of ontological insecurity.

Contexts and methods

The data considered in this chapter was generated from four studies involving fifty-five teachers at ten different schools representing various educational levels (see Table 1). Two ethnographies were conducted, during the school years 2005/2006 and 2008/2009 respectively. The first one took place at two secondary schools (age, 13-16), the second at an upper secondary school (age, 16-18). On average, two to three days a week (full or half days) were spent in the field. Participant observations, interviews and informal talks/field interviews (Burgess, 1984; Hammersley and Atkinson, 1995) were conducted during lessons as well as during breaks. In all, 23 interviews with teachers were conducted during these ethnographies. The data used in the present chapter also includes semi-structured interviews with seventeen highly experienced (20 years or more) teachers at primary (age five to nine), lower secondary (age nine to thirteen) and secondary (age thirteen to sixteen) school level during the spring semester in 2007. Moreover, the empirical data involves semi-structured interviews with fifteen teachers at four upper secondary schools during the period 2012-2014. At two of these schools, observations and field interviews were conducted over ten-day periods.

Table 1. The empirical data: methodology and selection of teachers.

Methodology	Name of school	Year	Teacher category	Number of teachers
Ethnography	Pine school Fir school	2005/2006	Lower secondary/ secondary (age, 9-16)	13
Interview study	Sallow school Willow school Juniper school	2007	Primary and Lower secondary/secondary (age, 6-16)	17
Ethnography	Currant school	2008/2009	Upper secondary school (age, 16-18)	10
Interview study (partly involving observations)	Ash school Beech school Ridge school Oak school	2012-2014	Upper secondary school (age, 16-18)	15

In the present chapter we have chosen to mainly emphasise the voices of the teachers themselves. Observations in schools and classrooms have mostly been used as a basis and a confirmation of teachers' descriptions and the analyses made. All interviews were audio recorded, transcribed and analysed thematically.

Although the original overall purpose of the various studies differed somewhat, we have in this chapter specifically endeavoured to capture the dilemmas, tensions and constraints under which teachers work, and the way they manage to cope with their situation. In the following parts of the chapter we will present the findings under the themes: The culture of measurements and performativity; The frustration of assessing and documenting; Individualism rather than collectivism. All names of teachers and schools have been fictionalised in the text.

The culture of measurements and performativity

All teachers who were interviewed, regardless of school level, testified that their workload had 'increased tremendously' in recent years (as Siw, a secondary school teacher at Sallow school expressed it). The increased workload involved both the volume of direct engagement with students' school and curriculum development, as well as the costs in terms of time and energy in the work of performance, monitoring and marketing. Cecilia, with thirty-three years of experience from lower secondary school, illustrated her frustration two weeks into the semester in the autumn 2007 when rushing through the corridor, sighing: 'It really seems to be more important to document everything (what the students know or don't know) than to really know what their skills and knowledge are.' Cecilia illustrates how acquiring information, necessary for perfect control, consumes most of her time. She even added with emphasis: 'It [documenting everything] consumes all available time and energy!' Most of the teachers in our data sample expressed frustration about the issue of documentation (cf. Asp Onsjö, 2011). Hans, a primary school teacher at Pine, compared the current situation with what he used to do in the past as a teacher:

> Once [in the old days] we carried out projects for the sake of students and teachers … so we could be better off. It was about what we would do in the classroom. Now it's a lot of administration. Important things perhaps, but nothing that affects my students and me really. We [teachers] will now only produce written texts to put in a binder and keep in the bookshelf [in case of an inspection visit] … school plans, bullying plans, matrices, treatment plans and whatever …

Sara, a teacher at Fir secondary school, also stressed the differences between current development projects compared with those they used to do 'in the old days … those were all related to the life within the classroom.' The notion of just 'constructing different documents' (Hans, Pine) and 'producing all those paper products' to be delivered 'at a possible inspection' (Lars, Juniper) was strong. The management of performance was clearly orchestrated by the threat of inspection. Lars was one of the few teachers who openly and clearly showed a distrust of the inspections. He had had previous experience of the School Inspectorate quality audits, and expressed the view that 'it was only a control on an administrative level.' He criticised the Inspectorate and pointed out that the inspectors only check that 'different documents are available [in a binder] at school' rather than 'stay at school for some time' and 'get the opportunity to see how it works.' The inspectors were only interested in 'their piles of paper' he said, and highlighted short-term instrumental goals driven by performativity which several other researchers have documented over a long period of time (cf. Jeffrey and Woods, 1998; Lindgren, 2014). Unlike Cecilia, Lars seemed quite unconcerned about the inspections. He did what was required of him, but at the same time it was a kind of cynical compliance: 'I produce what they [the Inspectorate] want … it really has nothing to do with the real life in the class room.' Lars seemed to operate on two parallel tracks: one track concerned 'the life in the class room', the other concerned 'the production of all different documents' the Inspectorate expected. In a situation where performative pressures lead to tactical and even cynical compliance, Lars played a game (cf. Priestley et al., 2012) that took the form of fabrication (Ball, 2004). Unlike Lars, Ruth (Sallow) who represents a majority of the studied teachers' expressed opinions and experiences said she felt managed and controlled:

> There are so many things we have to do … all these evaluations is one example … evaluations nobody cares about … you just have to do them because they are supposed to be done.

Britt (Ridge) below, also expressed doubts about their benefits:

> And I don't know to what use they [the evaluations] are … they just disappear … do they just go into a pile of papers? (…) I don't know. Who got all the evaluations? What was done to them?

The evaluations and inspections made teachers insecure and many of them expressed a sense of pressure: 'Whatever I do, somebody is going to judge me.

Everything I do is measured.' (Ruth, Sallow). The requirement of performativity made Ruth question her own identity as a teacher:

> Nowadays it's only about maximising the performance in different subjects … all other questions … questions about life and democracy … you have to shut it out of the class room … it really makes me feel bad.

Her distance from her own personal values was clearly linked to the requirements of performativity (cf. Jeffrey and Troman, 2011; Lundström and Holm, 2011). According to Ruth, the culture drove her concerns away from what constitutes good education (cf. Biesta, 2010; Priestley et al., 2012) and what the curriculum actually still demands in terms of fostering citizenship and inclusion.

Cecilia, Lars, Hans, Rita and Ruth were interviewed during the school years 2005 to 2007. They expressed a common view that evaluations and documentations had increased over time, and many of them questioned to what practical use. A similar pattern is also seen in our recent studies, but we also identified an increasing conformity in parallel to a kind of resistance. Maya, one upper secondary teacher we met at Ridge school during the school year 2013/2014, expressed it in the following way:

> I always have the feeling that you do a lot of things, but you don't really know why or if it leads to anything. (…) and there are goals and progress, and you have to demonstrate it all (…) and there will be no time. Things are just added and added all the time. And you do a lot of new things … but actually there isn't a real intention behind it … and you get no time for it … (…) then you go to yourself and prioritise what you want to prioritise. Because you can't take anymore (…) you just can't stand it.

Maya expressed a feeling that she had had enough of control and demands. Her strategy seemed to be to run her own race. One of her colleagues, Arne, expressed the same attitude. He pointed out that 'you can't only focus on the ranking-lists [you have to have your own agenda as well]', and so did Inez, a teacher at Currant. Other teachers claimed that the demands of documentation not only put pressure on teachers but also 'stole time from principals' (Britt, Ridge), who were 'overloaded by all [of the] administrative tasks like evaluations to be printed' (Arne, Ridge). In addition, many of the teachers complained that the evaluations were often quite ineffective, since they were rarely followed up.

Teachers delivered evaluations time after time, but they did not seem to see any point in doing them when they were not used to enhance teaching practice. Obviously, all the teachers studied were involved in the 'delivery chain' (Barber, 2010, cited in Ball et al., 2012: 76).

The frustration of assessing and documenting

The interviewed teachers all spoke about major changes regarding increased demands and reduced influence and support in their professional lives. 'All work can always be done better', they argued. One example came from Lisa, a secondary teacher at Sallow. She described the real and substantial pressures of trying to live up to all the expectations and requirements she felt she had to face:

> We must get all students to pass ... and that really is up to us [teachers], both parents and students ... and the boss demands us to get students to pass ... and it is a huge burden ... I work more than one-hundred per cent ... I go into work and teach almost all hours ... [instead of doing preparations] ... without any extra payment of course.

The public discourse about school quality (cf. Andreasson and Dovemark, 2013) puts strong pressure on Lisa to get all students to pass. This was a recurring dilemma of a large majority of the studied teachers, especially among those who taught the older students. Time after time we met teachers who were frustrated and talked about 'difficulties to make up assessment criteria' (Signe, Willow), how they should be interpreted and what would be deemed a pass or not. Rita (Sallow) also expressed this. Once when we met her she had failed six of her students. She said that 'they had not achieved the goals', and she was sure that she had 'assessed the circumstances correctly.' But she was still very frustrated and worried about what her boss and her colleagues in her team would both think and say. Moreover, she was concerned about what parents in the neighbourhood might say when the local media published the statistics on students' ratings. It would appear that 'we don't meet the mission', as she expressed it. Rita became insecure and blamed herself; the problems came down to the individual even though they could plausibly be seen as structural.

The rating system made many of the studied teachers feel deeply insecure. Vanja, a teacher at Willow school, considered that the grading took a 'tremendous amount of extra work'. A contributing factor to this was the requirements to produce written evaluations that 'demanded precise formulations'. Vanja expressed worries about how the formulations were going to be interpreted by different stakeholders—students, parents, receiving teachers and officials. Ingrid, a teacher at Juniper, said it was 'the worst thing with the job nowadays':

> I think it's horrible to find the right words (...) it's absolutely the worst thing I do, that is to write down reviews ... and these reviews are supposed to be sent to parents so they can read them before we meet ... and it really is even worse when you know parents are going to read them ... no ... I think I might suffer a breakdown just thinking about it (...) it really is insurmountable!

To formulate and document assessments was 'a horrifying job' for most of the teachers we spoke to. Peder at Juniper explained how important it was to write in a way 'so nobody could misunderstand it.' He also complained over how much time he had to spend and 'all the energy you have to invest' in the process of assessments:

> It takes quite some time to write all these evaluations. I have to prepare myself hours in advance ... I sit down in front of the computer. The most important thing is to be extremely clear [about what you mean]. It really has to be absolutely clear ... so that the one [teacher] who has the development dialogue with the parents should not have to read between the lines ... and have to interpret the text ... you can't write 'he or she is pretty good' ... you can't do that ... if you write 'pretty good' than it really isn't good at all ... if you interpret it in that way ... then either the student reaches the goals or he doesn't.

Peder tried to transform the complex social process of assessing a student into simple, interpretable words. However, as previous research indicates, it is an extremely challenging task to try and write something that can only be interpreted in one way; indeed, such an apparently simple task may not be possible at all. Furthermore, Selghed's (2004) and Tholin's (2006) research shows both how teachers interpret the same criteria differently and how the way in which assessments are conducted can vary considerably.

To assess knowledge and skills in different subjects, as well as understanding the curriculum's demands on abilities and competences such as critical thinking, creativity, communication and problem solving in 'realistic situations', were perceived as 'time-consuming' (Rita, Sallow), and even, according to Lars (Juniper), 'absolutely impossible'. Anna (Sallow) told us about her dilemmas and the insecurity she felt when handling assessments; she said she had to 'go through the assessments time after time'. Even though she invested a lot of time, energy and work in the job she realised that the assessment was not fair anyway, which of course compounded her sense of insecurity and made her feel guilty in relation to her students, parents and colleagues. Anna told us about one of many occasions when she struggled with her work:

> You know solutions in maths ... when you are supposed to assess their [the students] ways of expressing themselves with mathematical language (...) I really can get mad ... last Sunday I was sitting with one of those sensible tasks they get (...) I had assessed all of the tasks and I had decided that I had completed [the assessments] ... and then I started to think 'oh ... it was such a long time since I started' ... I had had seventy [students to assess] and I started to think 'you have to check how you started the assessments' and then I thought 'Oh God! Did he [one student] only get passed?'... and then I started to go through all the assessments again ... when I had done that I wanted to go through again and again. Honestly I could go on for ages ... but then you have to come to the end ... it's [assessing] much more difficult than it used to be.

According to Anna, she could spend an endless amount of time assessing and grading students' work and exams; but whatever she did it never seemed enough. She constantly felt guilty even though she 'spent twenty-four hours a day' on her work. Several teachers in our studies expressed this sense of inadequacy and insecurity. Stina at Juniper also mentioned dilemmas and the time-consuming nature of the work when assessing: 'It really takes time and energy to assess students' ability and to analyse cognitive abilities in a legally certain way.' Stina also felt that assessing was 'never really fair' and as a consequence suffered a troubled conscience. These observations follow Black et al. (2003) who have examined the situation in the UK. They claim that the 'new' way of assessing requires a great effort by the teachers, and teachers in general feel uncertain when assessing students in relation to given objectives and criteria. In addition, according to the SNAE (2013, 2015), teachers primarily work alone in assessment situations, which also contributes to their feelings of inadequacy and insecurity. A kind of 'ontological insecurity' (Ashman and Gibson, 2010; Ball, 2003) appeared when 'work could always be done better' (Anna).

In the interviews, teachers expressed a common view that assessments and evaluations had become a 'natural part' of their work. Course evaluations were described as part of daily life by the interviewees. Karina (Oak) told us about a new phenomenon at her school. She was expected to predict what grades her students would get, based on how they were expected to meet course objectives. Karina was frustrated: it was time consuming and she felt like it should be done just for the sake of 'reporting something'. The reason for this, she said, was probably connected to the wider economy:

> I think it's about money, if I'm to be completely honest (...). I don't think it's about how we should support our students ... it's more about, I don't know ... but my feelings are ... you [the school] want to be able to present some good numbers [and marks]. And especially now ... it's a pretty harsh climate in the media about [free] schools and there are a lot of inspections and such like.

Karina, who worked at an independent school, expressed reservations about the need to 'estimate or predict students' performances'. She perceived 'good numbers' as a kind of fabrication and explained:

> Pedagogically I think it's pure suicide ... If I'm supposed to predict how many students are going to achieve the goals before the course has started or ended, then ... as a teacher ... I really have failed. I suppose as a teacher you restrict your students by low expectations and demands ... it really will be a self-filling prophecy there.

Our data contain many such expressions of resignation. Teachers working at Ash upper secondary school in a deprived suburb told us that they neglected some of their administrative work, such as documentation and assessments, in order to 'survive'. Tore explained to us:

> We know the reality we live in, we know which students we have. So, of course we do not stare blindly at this [ranking system, rating statistics]. We can't compete with the high-performing schools anyhow (...) It is part of our reputation that students have low grades at this school.

His colleague, Paula, added that the local media coverage of ranking lists increased the pressure on the Ash school teachers as it signalled that they were poor teachers: 'We don't get the top grades here and then [journalists think] we are lousy and they even accuse teachers of not being able to do their job.'

Individualism rather than collectivism

To handle all of the demands of assessment and evaluations some of the studied teachers told us that they colonised colleagues' time, space and work. The pressure of being compared to other schools and teachers, the knowledge that the importance of the school's reputation was in many respects simply related to grades and nothing else, made teachers force themselves to compete with each other to get 'as much time as possible together with their students' (Carl, Fir). Lisa at Sallow school told us that she 'felt compelled to chase her students', in effect to create 'time and space for private education' to be sure to get students to pass:

> Well then … I can sneak in to a [another] lesson (…) if they [the students] haven't passed in my subjects … if they haven't passed in biology for example (…) then I take the opportunity to … give them extra tasks and even try to give them exams (…) There is no other time [than other colleagues' lessons] … I really can't take an ordinary lesson [one of mine] because then they of course lose my review … it becomes in a way a vicious circle … it's escalating all the time.

Lisa felt simply compelled to 'steal time' from colleagues' lessons to ensure that students could pass in her subjects. Teachers found themselves caught between different loyalties when they partly colonised colleagues' space and time. Many teachers expressed uncertainty about their relationships with students as they sometimes found themselves being, as Mia (Fir) expressed it, 'far too kind'. Mia realised that the pressure to get all her students to pass secondary school made her 'pilot them to a passing grade'. She went on: 'We can find out from the national tests that students had no knowledge or skills at all [even though they got passes in my subject].' Mia felt insecure and blamed herself, she suffered from 'a bad conscience' and worried about how her students could manage their upper secondary education in the future if already during secondary school she 'had been too kind and let students pass.' She did not only feel guilty about the students who she had 'fooled about their capacity'; she also expressed regret for those colleagues at upper secondary level who she had 'cheated' when she 'delivered students who really didn't have the right capacity for those programmes' they had chosen. It would seem that Mia had adapted her behaviour and internalised the performative norms on how to cope with expected standards and demands. The way various stakeholders put pressure and demands on her, made her feel insecure and she invariably ended up blaming herself.

A majority of the studied teachers, regardless of when they were interviewed, stressed how the teaching profession had changed fundamentally. The striking references to 'stealing time' quoted here exemplify how collectivistic work and collegiality in school has to some extent disappeared in favour of individualism. Teachers also mentioned the increasingly isolated nature of their work (cf. SNAE, 2013, 2015), and admitted they did not dare 'to invite colleagues into the class room' anymore:

> You don't want to show how bad you are ... you don't ask colleagues [for help] ... you pretend you are able to do everything (...) Today, no one asks how to do things [to help each other]. (Maya, Ridge)

The isolated nature of the work and the pressure of appearing as a good, clever and skilled teacher made teachers compete instead of collaborate. Arne, an upper secondary teacher at Ridge, expressed concerns about what could actually happen within a group of colleagues. He had, at the time of the interview, over thirty years of teaching experience and had seen how teachers had been badly treated:

> Actually ... it has not been evident to colleagues or the school management to support and help [those who have been badly treated] (...) We're supposed to help students, but how often are we talking about helping each other?

Accordingly, through the various studies, we can see how the demands of performance and documentation have compelled teachers to work at the expense of colleagues' time and effort, and for this they blamed themselves. The culture of measurement (Priestley et al., 2012), realised through, for example, performance reviews, has resulted in a greater range of teachers' behaviour and social lives being made public. Teachers became anxious and insecure, and even blamed themselves for working too much:

> I know that … I've always been really bad [at limiting my work]. I have no self-preservation … it [work] swallows me up and I do everything that they [school leaders] require … and I [always have worked hard] … I can't say no [when somebody asks me to work more]. (Maggy, Sallow)

According to Maggy it did not seem to matter how she behaved; whatever she did, she was still torn between demands from parents, school leaders, colleagues and students. The measurement culture and the controls placed upon them (exercised through marketing and the relentless demands for excellence) affected the studied teachers in various ways. Everything—they are told—can always be done better! When the decision is left to the individual to decide whether something is good enough or not, ontological insecurity becomes a fact (Ashman and Gibson, 2010; Ball, 2003). This was, in particular, strongly expressed in relation to assessment and grading, but also (mainly in the study conducted in 2012-2014) in relation to marketisation. In these later interviews the upper secondary school teachers described how the increased competition between schools had contributed to an even greater workload and pressure (cf. Lundahl et al., 2013); the intense demands to market and promote their schools took time from their ordinary teaching duties. Karina (Oak) expressed her concerns over these issues:

> When I, as a teacher, have to leave my classes in order to promote the school (…) then I feel 'this can't really be my working mission.' Actually, I really love to talk about my school but I don't want to leave my students [without teaching].

Too much time was spent on marketing, promoting and evaluations according to many of the interviewed teachers. They expressed frustration that they could not keep up with the most important tasks—that of teaching and supporting their students' learning. One teacher even pointed out that the system was 'exploiting teachers', and that the teaching profession had become 'proletarianised' in various ways. Karina (Oak) added that teachers risked becoming 'a product you just can throw away when it's consumed.' Some teachers felt defenceless against the way their schools based the individual salaries on students' evaluations of teachers. This shift in power relations between students–teachers (i.e. customers–sellers) made the teachers dependent on being on good terms with their students (cf. Lundström and Holm, 2011).

The pressure on teachers from various stakeholders made many of them anxious and concerned about their relationships with students. Ali, who had recently started his employment at Ridge school, told us that the tight time schedule at his new school made it difficult for him to keep up with students in need of extra support. Ali compared his current working conditions with the ones he previously had at a smaller school with fewer students:

> It's not that we as teachers don't care about how students are doing here at Ridge school, but the fact is that we do not have time to solve problems! And there is also another school culture here [compared to the other school]! I'm running from one classroom to another ... [pretends to speak to a student who asks for his attention in the corridor:] 'I don't have time to talk to you. I know you have a problem, and you cry, but I recommend you to go to a counsellor instead because I have a class in five minutes, I have to take care of thirty students ... so I can't stay here and console you ... because I have thirty other [students waiting for me] and if I'm not there in two minutes they will leave [and go home].

Ali illustrated the dilemma many of the studied teachers expressed, namely how to handle the balance between helping students in need of immediate support and the more performative teaching duties. For Ali, this dilemma became more evident at his new school where the time schedule was more compressed and teacher–student relations more distanced. Teachers seem to act in 'particular ways' and in doing so distance themselves from their personal values (Priestley et al., 2012: 87); a kind of inauthenticity among teachers appeared (cf. Ball, 2003).

Discussion—efficiency rather than honesty

This chapter discusses the performative culture in Swedish schools and how teachers cope with it. We have touched on the strategies they use to meet the rigorous expectations of outcomes, efficiency and accountability, and explored how the policy context is understood and formed by teachers.

In writing this chapter, we have drawn on extensive empirical data that has been produced during the last ten years. Four separate research studies based on ethnographies, interviews and observations made among fifty-five teachers from primary school to upper secondary school level in Sweden were used during the course of research. Although there were some differences in their working duties and assignments, without exception all of the teachers interviewed expressed similar views that a pervasive and strengthened performative culture had gained ground in schools. This profound change did not only involve increased workload and stress connected to assessment and documentation work (cf. Andreasson and Dovemark, 2013; Asp-Onsjö 2011; SNAE, 2013, 2015); it also implied that teachers were expected to marketise their schools (Lundström and Holm, 2011). The pressure to recruit students was in particular mentioned by teachers at upper secondary level. This might be related to the overall increased competition between schools in the Swedish upper secondary school market over the past few years (Erixon Arreman and Holm, 2011; Lundahl et al., 2013).

The findings also show an increased pressure on teachers as a result of constantly being observed and assessed. Perryman (2012: 48) describes this as a state of 'panoptic performativity'. And it seems that many of the teachers we met have internalised the 'gaze' and now tend to be 'self-regulated' (Jeffrey and Troman, 2012). The teachers argued that the 'struggle of visibility', involving activities such as documentation and reporting for ranking lists, consumed time, money and energy at the expense of what they perceived as the 'core' activity of teaching. Satisfying the 'gaze' from outside (for instance by delivering different evaluations) sometimes overshadowed professional judgements. If more and more energy is consumed by evaluating assessments and completing documentation, then there is a risk of devoting less time for teaching and maintaining healthy relations with their students (cf. Ball, 2003; Lundahl et al., 2013). Several of our studied teachers were concerned that they repeatedly felt compelled to prioritise documentation, assessment and evaluation at the expense of socialising with students. This confirms that market logic risks stimulating plasticity rather than authenticity (cf. Larsson, Löfdahl and Pérez Prieto, 2009). In Ball's (2004) terms it might be described as a 'process of social transformation' (p. 25) in which the meaning and experience of education—as well as what it actually means to be a teacher—has fundamentally changed. According to our data, the position of teachers has changed over the last few decades from a relatively autonomous profession, where the focus was squarely on 'the work with students in the classroom' as Hans in our study expressed it, to more atomised, service-oriented workers in a business context where focus is on accountability and documentation (cf. Lundström and Holm, 2011). In a situation where documentation, assessment and evaluation have, according to our studied teachers, become a normal part of everyday school life, teachers have clearly become a part of the current 'deliverology' (Barber, 2010, cited in Ball et al., 2012: 76).

As active and ethical agents who continually negotiate within their educational practices, the studied teachers used various strategies to cope with the demands imposed by the performative culture (cf. Jeffrey's chapter in this book). Many adapted and did the best they could to decode the expectations and play the game (cf. Perryman, 2012), often meeting the Swedish Schools Inspectorate's requirements. They responded to the testing and measuring culture, and fabricated and produced texts 'to be put in a file'; they were acting 'purposely to be accountable' (Ball, 2004: 224). Complex social processes, such as the task of assessing, for instance, critical thinking and creativity, were transformed into simple words, figures and categories for judgement (cf. Andreasson and Dovemark, 2013). Some teachers became cynical, and due to the fact that it was not always clear what was expected of them many expressed frustration; an ontological insecurity appeared (cf. Ashman and Gibson, 2010). Teachers were unsure whether they were doing enough, doing the right thing, doing as much or as well as others, and in this competitive situation were constantly looking to improve, to be better, to be excellent (Ball, 2003: 220).

In Sweden, as in many other countries, what it means to teach and what it means to be a teacher has changed dramatically in the last few years as a result of far-reaching educational policy reforms (Ball, 2003; Ball et al., 2012; see also Angus and Jeffery in this volume). According to Ball (2003: 217), educational policies and reforms have not only been made into tools for imposing technical and structural change on organisations; they have also been employed as mechanisms for reforming teachers themselves and consequently changing what it means to be a teacher. In short, the technologies of reform have actually produced new kinds of teacher subjects. The teachers interviewed for this study clearly illustrate this process and demonstrate some of its unsettling ramifications.

To sum up, our studies indicate that deep changes have recently taken place within Swedish teaching. The current debate in the media, among politicians and teachers' unions highlights the emerging 'teacher crisis' in Sweden (*Dagens Nyheter*, 2014; *Lärarnas Tidning*, 2014a, b). The constant denigration of Swedish schools over the last years has resulted in the teaching profession being held in much lower esteem than was previously the case; furthermore, widespread reports of the massive increase in teachers' workload and stress (ETUCE, 2012; SNAE, 2013, 2015) have led to severe difficulties in recruiting student teachers. More than a third of practising Swedish teachers do not expect to work as teachers until retirement, and the number is even higher among younger teachers (*Lärarnas Tidning*, 2014a, b). That the 'policy epidemic' (Levin, 1998) and the 'terror of performativity' (Ball, 2003) have stuck their claws into the lives and work of Swedish teachers is certainly borne out by the findings of our study.

References

Andreasson, I. and Dovemark, M. (2013) Transforming Insecurity into a Commodity: using the digital tools Unikum and InfoMentor as an example in Swedish education, *European Educational Research Journal*, 12(4):480-491.

Ashman, I. and Gibson, C. (2010) Existential identity, Ontological Insecurity and Mental Well-being in the workplace, *Lancashire Business School Working Papers*, 1(3):2-19. ISSN 2040-4158.

Asp-Onsjö, L. (2011) Dokument, styrning och kontroll i den svenska skolan [Documentation, monitoring and control in the Swedish school], *Educare*, 2: 39-56.

Ball, S. (2003) The teacher's soul and the terrors of performativity, *Journal of Education Policy*, 18(2):215-228.

Ball, S. J. (2004) *Education for sale! The commodification of everything?* King's Annual Education Lecture, 2004, University of London.

Ball, S. Maguire, M. and Braun, A. (2011) *How schools do policy. Policy enactments in secondary schools,* London and New York: Routledge.

Black, P., Harisson, C., Lee. Marshall, B. and William, D. (2003) *Assessment of learning: Putting into practice,* London: Open University Press.

Burgess, R. (1984) *In the field. An introduction to field research.* London: Allen and Urwin.

Dagens Nyheter [Daily News] 2014. Många lärare tröttnar snabbt på sitt jobb [Many teachers get quickly tired of their jobs], (19 November, 2014)

Dovemark, M. (2004) *Ansvar—flexibilitet—valfrihet: En etnografisk studie om en skola i förändring* [Responsibility, flexibility, freedom of choice. An Ethnographic Study of a School in Transition], PhD Diss. University of Gothenburg.

Erixon Arreman, I. and Holm, A-S. (2011a) Privatisation of Public Education? The emergence of independent upper secondary schools in Sweden, *Journal of Education Policy*, 26(2):225-243.

Erixon Arreman, I. and Holm, A-S. (2011b) School as Edu-business: Four 'serious players' in the Swedish upper secondary school market. *Education Inquiry*, 2(4):637-657.

ETUCE. 2012. *El European Region—Activity Report 2010-2012,* European Trade Union Committee for Education Brussels.

Foucault, M. (2000) Governmentality. in J.D. Faubion (ed.*), Essential works of Foucault, 1954-1984. Power,* Vol. 3. New York. The New Press.

Hammersley, M. and Atkinson, P. (1995) *Ethnography. Principles in practice.* London and New York: Routledge.

Holm, A-S. and Lundström, U. (2011) Living with the Market Forces: Principals, perceptions of market competition in Swedish upper secondary school. *Education Inquiry,* 2(4):601-617.

Hudson, C. (2011) Evaluation—the (not so) softly-softly approach to governance and its consequences for compulsory education in the Nordic countries, *Education Inquiry,* 2(4):671-687.

Jeffrey, B. and Troman, J. (2011) The construction of performative identities, *European Educational Research Journal*, 10(4):484-501.

Jeffrey, B. and Troman, G. (eds) (2012) *Performativity in UK Education. Ethnographic cases of its effects, agency and reconstructions*, E and E Publishing.

Jeffrey, B. and Woods, P. (1998) *Testing teachers: the effect of school inspections on primary teachers*. London: Falmer Press.

Larsson, J., Löfdahl, A. and Pérez Prieto, H. (2010) Rerouting: Discipline, Assessment and Performativity in Contemporary Swedish Educational Discourse, *Education Inquiry*, 1(3):177-195.

Levin, B. (1998) An epidemic of education Policy: What can we learn from each other? *Comparative Education*, 24(2):131-141.

Lindgren, J. (2014) Grund grund för bedömning? Dilemman i 'inspektionsträsket' [Basis for assessment? Dilemmas in the 'inspection swamp']. *Utbildning and Demokrati* [Education and Democracy], 23(1):57-83.

Lindqvist, P. (2002) *Lärares förtroendearbetstid* [Teachers' confidence working hours]. Diss. Malmö University.

Lundahl, L., Erixon Arreman, I., Holm, A-S. and Lundström, U. (2013) Educational marketisation the Swedish way. *Education Inquiry*, 4(3):497-517.

Lundström, U. (2012) Teachers' perceptions of individual performance-related pay in practice: A picture of a counterproductive pay system. *Educational Management Administration and Leadership*, 40: 379-391.

Lundström, U. and Holm, A-S. (2011) Market Competition in Upper Secondary
Education: perceived effects on teachers' work. *Policy Futures in Education*, 9(2):193-205.

Lärarnas Tidning [Teachers' Newspaper] (2014a) Många kommuner är dåligt rustade för att möta lärarkrisen [Many municipalities are poorly equipped to meet the teacher crisis]. (12 November, 2014).

Lärarnas Tidning [Teachers' Newspaper] (2014b) Allt fler unga lärare överväger att lämna yrket innan pension. [Increasing numbers of young teachers consider leaving the profession before retirement.] (12 November, 2014).

Nordänger, U-K. (2012) *Lärares raster. Innehåll i mellanrum* [Teachers' breaks. Content in the interspace]. PhD Diss. Malmö University.

Perryman, J. (2012) Inspection and the fabrication of professional and performative processes, in B. Jeffrey and G. Troman, (eds.) *Performativity in UK education. Ethnographic cases of its effects, agency and reconstructions*. 41-66. E and E Publishing.

Priestley, M., Robinson, S. and Biesta, G. (2012) Teacher agency, performativity and curriculum change: Reinventing the teacher in the Scottish curriculum for excellens? in B. Jeffrey and G. Troman, (eds.) *Performativity in UK education. Ethnographic cases of its effects, agency and reconstructions*. 87-108. E and E Publishing.

Rönnberg, L. (2011) Exploring the Intersection of Marketisation and Central State Control through Swedish National School Inspection. *Education Inquiry*, 2(4):689-707.

Rönnberg, L. (2012) Reinstating national school inspections in Sweden—The return of the state. *Nordic Studies in Education*, 32(2):70-80.

Rönnberg, L. 2014. Att ta inspektionen i egna händer—hur lokala aktörer använder Skolinspektionen [Taking the Inspection into their own hands—how local actors use the Schools Inspectorate]. *Utbildning and Demokrati* [*Education and Democracy*], 23(1):85-106.

Selghed, Bengt (2005) *Betygen i skolan* [The grades in school]. Stockholm: Liber

Strömberg, M. (2010) *De första sex åren. En studie av fyra lärares professionella utveckling med en yrkeslivshistorisk ingång* [Teachers' professional everyday life—a national survey of school teachers' use of time]. PhD Diss. University of Gothenburg.

Swedish National Agency of Education [SNAE]. (2013) *Lärarnas yrkesvardag—en nationell kartläggning av grundskollärares tidsanvändning* [Teachers' professional everyday life—a national survey of teachers' use of time]. Rapport 13:1326. Stockholm: Fritzes.

Swedish National Agency of Education [SNAE] (2015) *Grundskollärares tidsanvändning: En fördjupad analys av 'Lärarnas yrkesvardag'* [Teachers' use of time. An in-depth analysis of the 'Teachers' professional everyday life']. Rapport 417. Stockholm: Fritzes.

Tholin, J. (2006) *Att kunna klara sig i ökänd natur. En studie av betyg och betygskriterier—historiska betingelser och implementering av ett nytt system* [Being able to cope in unknown nature. A study of grades and grading criteria—historical conditions and the implementation of a new system]. PhD Diss. University of Gothenburg.

Chapter 3

The interaction between students and teachers in times of performativity

Michalis Kakos

Introduction

The last decade has seen a renewed interest by the educational research community in interactionist approaches for the study of social phenomena in education. This interest which has been largely led by linguistics (see for example: Castanheira et al., 2001; Rampton, 2006; Graff, 2009; Frelin and Grannäs, 2010) has claimed that human interaction and the notion of negotiation are at the heart of the processes which lead to the construction of institutional roles and practices. The study which is presented in this chapter has followed this suggestion, and has attempted to respond to Vanderstraeten's call for 'the school class to be understood as an interaction order' (Vanderstraeten, 2001: 275).

The aim of the study was to investigate the changes in the professional roles and practices and the challenges related to the implementation of citizenship education (CE), a subject which has advocated the use of participatory learning and democratic pedagogies aiming to 'equip students with the knowledge and skills needed for effective and democratic participation' (QCA, 2010). The case examined by this study was the interaction of teachers and students in the process of incorporation of the subject in the English Secondary curriculum. By focusing on this case, the study has highlighted that some of the most significant challenges that obstruct the implementation of democratic and participatory pedagogies do not relate to teachers' conscious choices and professional judgment. Instead they embody unquestioned social practices which become expected and therefore are reinforced through everyday interactions. The study has pointed out how these practices relate equally to institutionalisation or professional roles and to the ways that performativity shapes modern educational discourse (Kakos, 2012a and 2012b).

This has not been the first study which identified these issues. Concerns about the incompatibility of the educational discourse to the one that a (democratic) political education should aim to introduce to schools have been raised even before the introduction of citizenship education. Outlining his early concerns, Pring had described the dominance of a 'business-like' discourse in modern education and had pointed out that 'The shift in the language of education—the changing metaphors and analogies—brings with it a shift in how we see the relationships between teacher and learner, and between teachers and those who organise the education system—indeed, how we perceive the political framework within which teachers are asked to relate to their pupils and to what are now referred to as stakeholders' (Pring, 1999: 73-74).

Apple has also described the processes of 'conservative modernisation' and the effects of marketisation of education (Apple, 2000; 2001) while Ball has identified market, managerialism and performativity as the three policy technologies driving the modern education reform. Quoting Rose (1989), and effectively echoing Pring's views, Ball has pointed out that 'education reform brings about change in our subjective existence and our relations one with another' (Ball, 2003: 217). Ball is concerned about how this reform affects 'one's social identity' and focuses on the role of performativity to study 'the subjectivities of change and changing subjectivities which are threatened or required or brought about by it' (Ball, 2003: 217). His definition of performativity is apocalyptic of the processes behind this shift of subjectivities:

> Performativity is a technology, a culture and a mode of regulation that employs judgements, comparisons and displays as means of incentive, control, attrition and change—based on rewards and sanctions (both material and symbolic). The performances (of individual subjects and organisations) serve as measures of productivity or output, or displays of 'quality', or 'moments' of promotion and inspection. As such they stand for, encapsulate or represent the worth, quality and value of an individual or organisation within a field of judgement. (Ball, 2003: 216)

Performativity as in Ball's definition reveals some hidden processes which allow the embedment of the modern managerialist, market-driven educational reality in the subjectivities of those involved in it. In this way it operates as a useful conceptual tool for the description of the turn of educationalists to 'enterprising subjects' (Rose, 1989; in Ball, 2003: 217) living in conditions of constant evaluation, surveillance and self-surveillance and in that way it explains the paradox of the construction of inflexible performances within an apparently flexible and 'devolved environment' in education. Ball points out that such conditions and the profound change on teachers' subjectivity lead to the development of an 'ontological insecurity' (Ball, 2003: 220). In this context, 'both the interactions and relations between colleagues and those between teachers and students are affected' (ibid, p. 224).

The focus of the argument in this chapter is not far from being a response to Ball's observation. The discussion will start with a presentation of the conceptual framework of the study. Reflecting on Ball's conceptualisation of performativity I will then attempt to provide an interpretation of the concept when this is approached intersubjetively before moving on to present how such approach shaped the method of the study. In the findings section I will discuss how performativity affects the interactions between students and teachers and how , by doing so, it shapes teachers' roles. The discussion will focus on the analysis of teachers' descriptions of their interaction with students as one based on a 'contractual agreement' the terms of which are closely related to performance and outcomes. Key role in the understanding of the ways that the contract operates is the role of an invisible audience which monitors teachers' performance, stripping from teachers the ownership of their interaction with their students. In the concluding section I will point to the limitations of this analysis to offer a complete explanation of teachers 'ontological insecurity' and teachers' alienation from themselves (Ball, op. cit., p. 215). Attempting to address these limitations I will suggest that this alienation may be more appropriately attributed to conditions which are not associated with performativity but are inherent in schooling and are more closely associated with the institutionalisation of their interaction with students. It is the vulnerability produced by this institutionalisation that may be exploited by performativity and which strips teachers from the ability to re-establish connections with their role, even when conditions become appropriate to facilitate this.

The conceptual framework

Drawing from interactionism theories, the development of the framework for this study is based on the adoption of the view about human interaction as a process which depends on the mutual contribution of the participants, who are 'taking the role of the other, thinking about one's own communication, interpreting the acts of others, as well as considering both the expectations and the directions of others' (Charon, 1995: 150). in agreement with Charon's observation the study's approach towards the concept of interaction has recognised the significance of the expectations that students and teachers have from each other, from themselves and their engagement in this interaction. The framework also recognised the significance of the role-taking and role-reversal which refers to the process of interpretation of each other's acts and the consideration of each other's expectations, directions and perspectives (Blumer, 1969; Charon, 1995). Expectations and role-taking are two of the key elements of the framework of the study. A third element which is only implicit in Charon's definition is the concept of social power which, when taken into account, suggests a view of interaction as constant negotiation (Kakos, 2008). I will consider this by turning to intersubjective conceptualisation of human interaction.

From an intersubjective angle, human interaction is more than an encounter of social roles. More fundamentally, interactions are the fields in which subjects emerge. 'Subjects (as conceptualised by philosophers like Heidegger (1962)), cannot be viewed as pre-existing, known entities, but they need to be understood [...] in process, unfolding or folding up, being done or undone, in relation to the other, again and again' (Davies, 2006: 436). As Butler points out 'while [...] subjects appear, at least at the level of the everyday or commonsense, to precede their designation, this apparently pre-existing subject is an artefact of its performative constitution' (Youdell, 2006: 515). The birth of the subject is located within the process of the disavowal of its dependency to the discourse within the subject exists, a discourse which 'we never chose but that, paradoxically, initiates and sustains our agency' (Butler, 1997, in Davies, 2006: 427). As Davies notes, 'the agentic subject disavows this dependency, [...] because the achievement of autonomy, however illusory it might be, is necessary for the accomplishment of oneself as a recognisable and thus viable subject' (Davies, 2006: 427). Davies' observation about the process of disavowal of the subject's dependency brings up the link between autonomy, recognisability and viability of the subject. Indeed, central in Butler's conceptualisation of subjectivation is its contextualisation within a social milieu and the process of recognition of the subject by other subjects (Butler, 1997). It is within this intersubjective context that subjects are recognised and therefore constructed. Such intersubjective understanding of the subject lies very close to Levinas's suggestion: 'For Levinas, our very subjectivity [...] is a function of an existentially prior responsibility: one becomes an 'I' by being subject to the other' (Chinnery, 2003: 10). A 'dynamic, inter-subjective, constructed moment by moment through social interaction, and, at the same time, subject to existing ideologies and perceived social constraints' (Mayes, 2010: 195).

Mayes' observation effectively summarises the significance of the role of power in understanding human interaction and highlights that such negotiation does not concern only the interaction between subjects but the interaction of the subjects with external forces and constrains. Moreover, seen in the context of this study, Mayes' observation with regard to the role of the ideologies in framing human interaction could be interpreted as an implicit suggestion for performativity to be viewed as ideology. In the next section I will briefly discuss an intersubjective interpretation of Ball's description of performativity before moving on to show the particular ways that the key elements of the study's framework (role-taking/role-reversal, expectations and power) have shaped the methods for data collection.

Subjectivation and ontological insecurity

Ball's comment on the change of subjectivities being brought by educational reform brings the discussion about performativity closer to its conceptualisation by Butler (Butler, 1993). It does so by raising the issue of the formation of the subject within a particular context. For Ball this context is performativity as a culture which affects individuals. In that respect Ball seems to adopt the view about individuality preceding subjectivation. Within his argumentation subjectivation seems to be a 'process that transforms individuals into subjects' (e.g. as in Simons and Masschelein, 2010). For Butler the context within which the subject is formed is a 'discursive practice that enacts or produces that which it names' (Butler, 1993: 13). Butler names this practice as 'performative' but the term does not bear Lyotard's connotations that Ball's conceptualisation has (Ball, op. cit., p. 226) but it is derived from the debate between Derrida and Austin on the nature of language and its relationship to the world (Youdell, 2006). Butler sees the birth of individuality (and the sense of autonomy) as inseparably linked to the process of subjectivation and recognises that subjection as integral element of this process.

The difference between Ball's and Butler's descriptions of the relationship between individuality and subjectivation implies also a difference in the cause of the 'ontological insecurity'. Ball locates this cause in the inauthenticity of teachers' performances which are 'played up' as a response to the new calls deriving from the educational reform. In that respect Ball acknowledges the history of their subjectivity, the memory of their subjecthood as it was constructed within discourses with distinctively different value systems and he associates their ontological insecurity to a 'values schizophrenia' that they experience (op. cit., p. 221). Indicative of this is the opening phrase of the quote from the school teacher who appears in Jeffrey and Woods' (1998) book Testing Teachers and which Ball refers to in his article: 'I don't have the job satisfaction now I once had working with young kids ...' (Jeffrey and Woods, 1998; in Ball, 2003: 221).

For Butler on the other hand, 'while [...] subjects appear, at least at the level of the everyday or commonsense, to precede their designation, this apparently pre-existing subject [and therefore, I would add, the memory about the previous existence] is an artefact of its performative constitution' (Youdell, 2006: 515). Within such conceptualisation of subjectivation the ontological insecurity could be located in the process of the subject's disavowing of its dependency to the discourse which 'we never chose but that, paradoxically, initiates and sustains our agency' (Butler, 1997, in Davies, 2006: 427). As Davies notes, 'the agentic subject disavows this dependency, [...] because the achievement of autonomy, however illusory it might be, is necessary for the accomplishment of oneself as a recognisable and thus viable subject' (Davies, 2006: 427). However, not all processes of subjectivation and therefore not all claims of autonomy or disavowals of dependency lead to ontological insecurity. There must be something that enters to the impromptu constructed memory of the subjects that causes the insecurity that Ball recognises.

I suggest that we are justified to assume that the ontological insecurity to which Balls refers could be the result of the simultaneous emergence of two subjects which battle over the same individuality. In such case the source of the ontological insecurity might lie in a process of simultaneous submission (and resistance) of the subject to two conflicting systems of power, representing two different agencies or two conflicting systems within the same agency. In the latter case a government could support the marketisation of education while simultaneously appearing as engulfing and promoting values which are being actually intimidated by marketisation. The support to educational agendas arguing for personalised learning or aiming to 'instil character in pupils' (DfE, 2014) within an educational discourse which replaces authentic social relations with judgemental relations and eradicates the value of individuals as persons (Ball, 2003: 224) could be viewed as an example of this. In the case that we want to examine teachers' ontological insecurity as the result of their subjection to the demands of two conflicting agencies we might be able to recognise that performativity could be in conflict with a broadly and historically shared (albeit often implicit) understanding of what constitutes 'substantive teaching practice' (Hardy and Lewis, 2016) and what education is about. The quote from another teacher in Ball's article (2003: 222) can be an example of this, 'Education has traditionally been about freedom. But there is no freedom any more. It's gone'.

Methodology and Data Collection

The complexity and depth of the study of human interaction steered tentatively the design of the study towards the ethnographic tradition. Evidence was collected within a total period of four months through traditional ethnographic tools including thirty-four hours of observations of citizenship education classes, interviews with forty-three students and fifteen teachers. The observations allowed the witnessing of the implementation of citizenship education and of the ways that relevant teaching methodologies were applied. Due to the fact that citizenship was implemented as a cross-curricular subject, the observations allowed the building of an understanding of the diverse ways in the methods of the subject's implementation (in academic and non-academic subjects) and offered cases which were then further explored in interviews with participants. Semi-structured interviews supplied evidence about participants' understanding of each other's expectations, their perspectives regarding each other's definitions of the situation and generally about their subjective experience of their interaction with each other (Blumer, 1969; Charon, 1995). All teachers involved in the delivery of the citizenship education curriculum were invited for interviewing. In their interviews the investigation targeted not only their perspectives with regard to the interaction but also their views about the position of citizenship education in the school curriculum, and about the challenges and opportunities that exist for introduction of participatory methodologies in modern schooling. Student participants were selected from citizenship education classes and most interviews took place directly after such classes. Data about their age and academic group was collected and analysed in correlation to their responses.

Finally, four group interviews with students were carried out which followed the observation of a set of role-plays. These role plays required the construction by students and their engagement in staged situations that are possible to occur in the school. These activities allowed students to represent their views on teachers' perspectives of the roles that both, students and teachers hold, their understanding of teachers' views regarding the application of power and of teachers' expectations from the interaction with the students (Kakos, 2008).

The site for this study is Hillcliff is an 11-18 mixed comprehensive school situated in a sub-urban area of a city in the North of England and at the time of the study it accommodated a population of about 1,100 students.

Discussion

In presenting the analysis of the evidence from this study I will argue that the implementation of citizenship education has highlighted teachers' struggle to balance their interpretation of Government's and public expectations from schools with a view of their profession and of education in general which they seem to be aspired to attain but at the same time associate with an utopia. In this struggle, teachers seem to have lost the ownership of their interaction with students and also to a degree the ownership of their own role, an observation which relates to the alienation that Ball refers to (ibid). However, it is not clear the extent to which this is solely the result of performativity discourse. The inflexibility in the interactions with their students which does not allow teachers to implement participatory teaching methods seems to be compatible to the business-like discourse but is seems to be dictated by conditions which seem to be common not only among performativity-driven educational institutions but institutions in general. Trapped between institutionalisation and performativity it is not surprising that teachers seem unprepared and unwilling to take up opportunities that are on offer to engage with interactions with their students that are in line with the ideals that they allegedly hold.

The embarking point for the development of the above argumentation in this chapter is the phenomenon of'depersonalisation' of the interaction between students and teachers. I will then show how this depersonalisation strips the ownership of the interaction from the interacting parts and allow for it to be redefined in line with the terms of an imposed contract. Denouncing the terms of this contract and simultaneously following it, teachers allow agents which are external to the school to script the terms and to take ownership of the contract. By representing a performativity—informed understanding of education, these agents appear to impose a performance-driven model of teaching and of professionalism in education.

The particular observation about the depersonalisation in education and of its effects on the implementation of participatory and democratic pedagogies is not new (see for example Watkins, 2008). The study offers support to this observation. In describing the difficulties in incorporating participatory pedagogies in his lesson and allow open dialogues in the classroom, one of the teachers points out that his interaction with students.

> ... tends to be, hmm ... very, very rigid—you know, you are the teacher, they are the class. It's hard to ... get close to them ...
>
> (Interview with Mr Tess, Head of History).

The rigidness and distance that Mr Tess refers to seems to be detected also by students, especially those in lower ages. For the older students the experiences are somewhat different:

> ... there's got to be that barrier and they've got to know where that barrier is and that is the ideal. The gap gets close when you get older students, you can lighten up because you don't necessarily need the discipline.
>
> (Interview with Ms Koun, Drama teacher)

Explaining the reasons why the gap with younger student is greater, the History teacher points out that younger students

> ... are not mature enough [...]—they can't read the teacher—[...] I think young ones often find it much harder to read the point at which ... you've moved away from being ... relaxed and friendly to become more formal. (Interview with Mr Tess, Head of History).

The ability to 'read the teacher' and students' familiarisation with practices is also recognised as a sign of maturity by students:

> ... it's like ... when ... it's like ... they have been here longer and they ... they know how the school ... the rules and stuff, they know ... It's like ... that ... you see that you are not as when you were in Y7 ... you change. You become more mature . Interview with Raya, Y9 student

Raya however, points out that this kind of maturity is associated also with an invisible hierarchy in the school community:

> [There is an hierarchy in the school] ... the head teacher-deputy—teachers—sixth formers—pupils, it's like that, but like ... the older you are, in the year, so probably like ... Y10 they are higher up than Y7.
>
> (Interview with Raya, Y9 student)

Raya's observation suggests that school community may be structured in a way that bears similarities with structures of various other institutions. In explaining these hierarchies and the power of 'old timers' it is perhaps more effective to link maturity with the process of subjectivation to institutional power and with the internalisation of the institutional principles and values. This internalisation justifies the subject's position and directs it in demonstrating behaviours that maintain the subject's status and therefore support the current dominant scheme (Foucault, 1992). Intrinsic in this process is the acceptance by rulers and ruled of the principles that are used to justify the traditional forms of institutional power. One of the most powerful justifications in the context of educational institutions is the association of power and control with learning. Aaron's view of the kind of role that he wishes his teachers to assume in order for a good relationship with them to be established is illustrative of this:

> *Aaron*: ... hmm ... just being normal, not like a teacher.
> *Interviewer*: 'Being normal –not like a teacher'?
> *Aaron*: [he laughs] Yes, like ... be a normal person, just ... don't have the relationship as a teacher and a student ... have a relationship ... like ... a friendly relationship. (Interview with Aaron, Y9 student).

Evidently, for Aaron the expected (although not ideal) relationship between teachers and students is one that does not allow teachers to present themselves as 'real people'. This depersonalisation, however, seems to serve a purpose and to be dictated by the circumstances in which teachers perform their role:

> [Teachers] have to be like that; otherwise they would not be able to teach and we would not learn.
> (Notes from group discussion, Drama exercise 1, Y9)

This has not been the only instance in which students associated the rigidness of their interaction with teachers and teachers' control with learning. Aaron might seem to wish for personalised interaction but he also knows that such interactions might not be appropriate for schools. In an opportunistic discussion about the introduction of a new stricter behaviour policy Alex gives us a glimpse of his school-based expectations:

> *Interviewer*: It seems that this system helps parents and teachers to have better control. ...
> *Alex*: Yes.
> *Interviewer*: Is this a good thing?
> *Alex*: I think so, yes.
> *Interviewer*: Why?
> *Alex*: Because, hmm... students can't do what they want, and if they do what they want, they don't learn, so ... I want a good job, where I can get money, and, so... I have to learn. (Interview with Alex, Y8 student).

The suggestion that the attainment of students' goals require the handing in of the control of their actions to teachers and Aarons' differentiation between the ideal interaction with teachers and the kind of interaction that he expects to have may indicate students' simultaneous subjection to two conflicting agencies: one is performance-driven and the other can be associated with a view of education as an opportunity for humanistic, personalised interaction. Evidence from this study indicates that the resolution of the discrepancy lies in a hierarchical order of students' expectations from the interaction with teachers and from the school in general. This hierarchy of expectations allows teachers of non-academic, therefore 'less significant' subjects to deviate from the norm and to develop personalised relationships with their students. However, such interaction seems to be exceptional and not appropriate for all subjects:

> *Lilah*: PSE [Personal and Social Education]. PSE is like that. ... And Art, is a bit like that.
>
> [I would like to] have more PSE lessons, not the other lessons to become like PSE ... It / you cannot have like ... Science like that. You don't learn the same things. (Interview with Lilah, Y10 student).

Moreover, such personalised interactions are not necessarily linked with the students' understanding of the school's *raison d'être*. Implicit in the construction of this hierarchy is students' hierarchical understanding of the subjects that emerge from their experience in education. By considering their interactions with teachers (and the role of the school in general) as purpose-led (where this purpose is informed by the discourse of marketisation) students seem to experience schooling as alien to their personhood but a necessary experience which allows access to the goods that their performance within the market discourse has to offer. In that respect it can be argued that the depersonalisation of the interaction between students and teachers is facilitated by the institutional conditions (rules and rituals, large classes etc.) but the justification of its functionality lie currently within the dominant views about the role of education and in the expectations that the interacting parts hold and possibly more particularly in students' expectations. Alex's remark which relates education with employment indicates that marketisation is embedded in the construction of these expectations.

The association between education and employment in Alex's quote indicates also that in this 'contractual agreement' students' institutional role occupies the position of the 'client' who 'buys' teachers' services. Alex's claim indicates that the offer of such services resembles at best an authoritarian guidance by an expert and, at worst to a passive 'delivery' of a process (i.e. the lesson), the effect of which 'happens' to the students. This raises questions about how students perceive their role in the school and the scope of their active participation. Most importantly it raises the issue of ownership over the social reality which students co-construct with teachers. Besides, on that basis it could be assumed that this ownership might lie solely on the side of teachers, who are the 'service providers' in this contract. The validation or rejection of the assumption and the ownership of the interaction will be examined at this next part of the discussion.

The lack of ownership, and the ways that the terms of the 'business contract' which guides the interaction between students and teachers are agreed, is described in more detail in some of the teachers' interviews.

> *Interviewer:* How would you describe an 'ideal relationship' between students and teachers'?
> *Mr Webb*: Well, we've got certain [...] work to complete ... I say "right [...] I'll make a pact with you, that I make the lessons interesting and I'll try to make the lessons fun, when I can, and if we are doing any assessments or tests you'll know in good time, and if possible I'll actually make sure that you are aware of what we have to cover for those [...] and what I'm asking for is co-operation and ... to be co-operative.
>
> (Interview with Mr Webb, Head of Geography).

Mr Webb argues for a model of interaction between students and teachers which is described as 'cooperative'. His call for cooperation does not suggest an active role for students but a role that offers the least possible obstructions to the performance of the teachers' role. Importantly, Mr Webb points out that the terms of this contractual agreement have been determined by 'specifications' which do not seem to be in his or in students' control. Moreover, his views reveal that the imposition of these specifications and the responsibility to follow them and to complete 'the work' is shared between students and teachers. Indicative of this is that he places himself and the students in the same side of the agreement. What Mr Webb seems to take for granted is students' opposition to these 'specifications' and their alignment with himself and with others who oppose but obey the content of the contract. However, this may be a false assumption since students' expectations, as we have already seen, may in fact be better attuned to these specifications than Mr Webb assumes. From such point of view the imposed specifications seem in fact necessary to guarantee that Mr Webb will respond effectively to students' expectations.

Not taking into account the relevance of students' expectations to the imposed specifications, Mr Webb describes the contractually formed interaction between teachers and students as a performance based on a 'pre-written script'. This view, shared among teachers in Hillcliff High suggests also that those who are responsible for the writing of this script as well as the 'audience' of the performance are constituted by three groups: the school's management team (and more specifically the Headteacher), the Government (and the Ofsted inspection teams) and the students' parents. Teachers suggest that their interaction with students is monitored and affected by the priorities, directions and expectations of these three groups which operate at a distance from the actual settings in which students and teachers interact. The distance that separates students and teachers from those invisible groups is evident not only from the physical absence of members of these groups from the classrooms, but also from the lack of any reference in the evidence supplied by teachers regarding the influence that they can have in these groups' actions and decisions. This is evidenced particularly when teachers discuss the role of the management team:

> I think the management is more ... concerned about results ... as they are on paper / than they actually are in producing ... students(?).
>
> (Interview with Ms Wales, Head of PSE)

The government seems be seen in a similar role:

> I mean [...] where do we get the balance between producing well adapted students who can contribute ... socially ... and sort of ... conform ... and actually getting the kids with the result that the Government want to have. (Interview with Mr Web, Head of Geography).

It seems therefore that the 'invisible audience' are those who provide the script that guides teachers' performance and are the same who hold the authority to evaluate this performance. In this context teachers' interaction with students does not lead to the outcomes that teachers seem to value and wish for. However, I think that one would find it difficult to choose the best option between the two possible educational outcomes described by teachers in the quotes above ('producing well adapted students' and 'getting the results that Government wants'). Both possibilities appear as forms of 'production', equally missing the 'freedom' in education that the teacher in Ball's article longs for or allow the development of truly pedagogical relationships (Todd, 2014: 232). It is important also to note that teachers seem to recognise that a 'discrepancy of productions' does not exist (only) between the imposed priorities and those which they are personally aspired to. Another discrepancy is located between two sets of expectations simultaneously imposed by the invisible audience. In Mr Webb's case, one set of expectations seem to be closer to his own aspirations but it still does not seem to gain his support since he considers them as impossible to be attained within the current educational reality.

Teachers' resolution of the discrepancies in their roles bears similarities and differences to students' resolutions. The similarity is the possibility that at a personal level teachers seem to denounce the professional role which emerges from their performativity-driven, school-based interactions. The difference is that unlike students, teachers seem not to be able to find a long term solution to the resulting dissociation from their institutional roles, experiencing what Ball recognises as 'ontological insecurity' (ibid). The quote from Mr Webb indicates that the reason for this might not lie in any memory of their past performances as professional educators but in the fact that unlike students, they are directly subjected to what they consider as conflicting expectations of the 'invisible audience', to two mutually incompatible performativities (Kakos, 2012).

However, the perceived incompatibility would not have the impact that it has if teachers did not internalise in their role the incompatible expectations in their interactive performance. They do so because they seem to consider as an aspect of their professional responsibility to subject themselves to the power of this audience and to interact with students from within the role that emerges from that subjection, despite the impact that this might have on the quality of their interaction. By doing so, and by not claiming ownership over this role, they are left with no means to guide and evaluate their performance. Consequently, this is left to those who own the subject (i.e. the audience) and it is those whose demands are used to evaluate this performance against, further reinforcing their dominance over this performance. In that way, teachers' interaction with students from possibly the only means which could potentially lead them to unification with their personhood, becomes the major link of the chain which ties them down to a professionally alien role. I suggest that it is this interactive process what could be described as performativity.

Conclusions: Subjectivation and surveillance: the interactive construction of professionalism in performativity

Performativity as 'technology and mode of regulation' (Ball, 2003: 216) is often placed by relevant literature within a triangle formed by: (a) the government and the State (with its agencies); (b) marketisation and the public as a community of consumers; and (c) the teachers as agents and at the same time victims of its imposition. In this chapter I have attempted to present a view of performativity from a standpoint located within the space constructed by the interaction between teachers and students. Viewed from that angle, performativity appears as a construct that emerges from this interaction rather than imposed upon it. Such understanding of performativity provides the space for a discussion about the relationship between the kind of performance that performativity promotes and the subjects performing it.

Drawing from the evidence generated by this study, the discussion has described the interaction between students and teachers as a business-like contractually-managed one. The terms of the contract seem to be drawn in a way that leads this interaction primarily towards the support of students' expectations and aspirations which are related to academic and professional goals and are located outside the school (access to Higher education and professional career). This indicates a rather utilitarian, fixed-term contractual relationship between students and the school and consequently with teachers. Described differently, this suggests that students' expectations (as element of the interaction between students and teachers) relate to a goal which is to be satisfied outside this interaction. The expectations that they have from their teachers are secondary expectations in that they are understood and evaluated on the basis of the extent to which they allow this interaction to be worthwhile. For teachers on the other hand, the terms of this contract are suggested by the expectations of an 'invisible audience' which measures the value of this interaction in terms of its impact on students. Therefore, the expectations that lead teachers' performances are located within this interaction but the measurement of the value of this interaction is external to their role since it does not take into account their own satisfaction from performing it.

For students, the development of a utilitarian relationship with the educational interaction hosted in schools seems to lead them to disengagement from it on a personal level. However, by aiming towards long-term, out-of-school gains, they are able to come to terms with their (obligatory) investment in time and energy that their compulsory education requires. The end of school brings their performance to a tragedian catharsis which coincides with the death of a subject which young people have learned to live with (but not necessarily reconciled with) during their school years. However, the situation is rather different for teachers.

Teachers too seem to experience a bipolar relationship with their institutional subject. However, this is not experienced by them either as temporary or as serving a goal located out of this interaction. Particularly for teachers who seem to value personalised interactions with young people, teaching might be a rather frustrating experience of an intensive interaction in which they are meant to serve as professionals but struggle to find the gains from it on a personal level. If the subject emerging from such interaction is alien to them, then the reconciliation with it since it is not located in time it may not be located anywhere.

In the context of such analysis, the question about the ownership of teachers and students' interactive performance reveals a vacuum. This vacuum puts in question the position of the teachers and students as each other's 'significant others' (Hargreaves, 1972) and reveals the role of the 'invisible audience' which monitors, evaluates and effectively owns their mutually constructed social situation. Literature seems to recognise in the role of this audience the manifestation of performativity and in its invisibility the ultimate form of surveillance. It is down to this audience that teachers operate in conditions of 'panoptic performativity' i.e. the 'regime in which ... the sense of being perpetually under surveillance leads to teachers performing in ways dictated by the discourse of inspection in order to escape the regime' (Perryman, 2006: 14).

Evidence from this study offers some support to this but points out that teachers and students develop different kinds of relationship with this audience. Moreover, it points out that the involvement of this audience in the interaction between students and teachers comes hand in hand with the dissociation of teachers and students (as persons) from the institutional roles which they perform. However, it suggests that it is not always clear whether the invisible audience is the cause of this dissociation or if it is conveniently placed within the vacuum of the ownership of the interaction caused by this dissociation.

Evidently, teachers' frustration in their battle with performativity and their memories of a different past advocate the validity of the first interpretation. However this chapter has shown that while teachers long for the performativity-free past, they simultaneously resist and reject educational policies which seem to be in tune with some of the principles of that past. Of course this might be because these policies are equally imposed and further limit teachers' freedom or because they are a source of frustration since they cannot be successfully implemented in a performativity-driven educational discourse. From such point of view, educational agendas which bring notions such as democracy (such as citizenship education) and personal might be equally responsible for teachers' ontological insecurity as marketisation and performativity. Indeed it would be interesting and important to investigate these assumptions and the justification of teachers' scepticism towards such policies. However, even in the case of validation of such assumption what will still remain unanswered is a question about the 'degree of freedom' that we are prepared to recognise in teachers' professional role. Such question would turn the discussion from the modern conditions in which schools operate to the essence of schooling and its institutional nature. In such case the discussion would aim to explore whether a school-based educational interaction which allows greater freedom to teachers in designing and implementing curricula and educational policies could lead to improved quality of educational provision, where this quality is defined in ways that oppose to performativity (i.e. in terms of personalised interaction, ownership, ontological security). Such discussion should turn our attention to the past and to evidence drawn by studies conducted before performativity became included in educational vocabulary. In such case we should notice that depersonalised interactions (Woods, 1979), role conflicts (Wilson, 1962) and role strains (Hargreaves, 1972) are inherent in teachers' role. Moreover, if the discussion turns to other possible grounds on which teachers justify their practice, Hargreaves' reminder of Cox's list which includes Tradition, Dogma, Prejudice and Ideology (Hargreaves, 1996), might suggest that the imposition of criteria from the Government might not be the worst possible option.

In light of the above, I think that an alternative suggestion about the roots of teachers' ontological insecurity should bring up the question about the reasons that prevent 'freedom' (as in Ball's article) from being developed within school discourses. In a course of thought suggested by Althusser (1971) such explanation should lead to the perception of the school as an Ideological State Apparatus (ISA) and of performativity as the current Ideology. As effectively Althusser has shown, subjects are established within ideologies and these ideologies are realised within ISAs (1971, pp. 169-171, 184). This does not suggest of course that individuals operating within a certain ideology (i. e. performativity) are unable to recognise this ideology and even denounce or resist to it. In a recent study Harber and Lewis have illustrated how this leads teachers to 'doublethink' data associated with their performance, 'where data were simultaneously denied and deified, and delivered in complex and contradictory ways' revealing 'contradictory logics within a field of schooling practices, in which there seemed to be at least some evidence of teachers' representations of student (and teacher) performance being constituted at the expense of more substantive teaching' (2016: 11). Perhaps Butler's observation that denouncement and resistance is necessary for the recognition of the subject offers some explanation of this while Althusser would recognise this as the struggle in ISAs which is a manifestation of the class struggle (1971: 185). From such point of view, teachers' memories of a glorious creative past can be seen as a statement of this resistance to this ideology through the mythicisation of another one, also available for subjects to resist to but which does not actually operates outside other similar ISAs. If the aim is to (re)establish education's liberating force through a sense of engagement and seeking of personal fulfilment, our attention should not be turned to the ways that policies are imposed or negotiated but before that, to the reasons that education is often reduced to a school-based, policy-driven, outcomes-seeking, institutionally-defined performance.

References

Althusser, L. (1971) *Lenin and Philosophy*, London: Monthly Review Press.

Apple, M.W. (2000), Can Critical Pedagogies interrupt rightist policies? *Educational Theory*, 50(2): 229-254.

Apple, M.W. (2001) *Educating the 'Right' way: Markets, standards, God, and inequality*, New York: Routledge Falmer.

Ball, S. (2003), The teacher's soul and the terrors of performativity, *Journal of Education Policy*,18(2): 215-228.

Blumer, H. (1969) *Symbolic Interactionism: Perspective and Method*, Berkley: University of California Press.

Butler, J. (1993), *Bodies that matter: on the discursive limits of 'sex'*, New York: Routledge.

Butler, J. (1997), *The Psychic Life of Power: Theories in Subjection*, Stanford, CA: Stanford University Press.

Castanheira, M. L., Crawford, T., Dixon, C.N., and Green, J.L. (2001) Interactional Ethnography: An Approach to Studying the Social Construction of Literate Practices, *Linguistics and Education*,11(4): 353-400.

Charon, J. (1995). *Symbolic Interactionism: An Introduction, An Interpretation, An Integration*, London: Prentice Hall.

Chinnery, A. (2003), Aesthetics of surrender: Levinas and the disruption of agency in moral education, *Studies in Philosophy and Education*, 22(1): 5-17.

Davies, B. (2006), Subjectification: the relevance of Butler's analysis for education, *British Journal of Sociology of Education*, 27(4): 425-438.

Department of Education (DfE) (2014) Measures to help schools instil character in pupils announced. Online: www.gov.uk/government/news/measures-to-help-schools-instil-character-in-pupils-announced Accessed 1 April, 2016

Foucault, M. (1997), The ethics of concern for the self as a practice of freedom, in: Rabinow, P. (Ed): *Michael Foucault. Ethics subjectivity and truth*, New York: The New Press.

Frazer, E. (1999), Introduction: The idea of political education, *Oxford Review of Education*, 25(1) and (2): 5-22.

Frelin, A. and Grannäs, J. (2010), Negotiations left behind: in-between Spaces of Teacher-Student Negotiation and Their Significance for Education, *Journal of Curriculum Studies*, 42(3): 353-369.

Graff, N. (2009), Classroom Talk: co-constructing a 'difficult student', *Educational Research*, 51(4): 439-454.

Hammersley, M. (1990), *Classroom Ethnography*, Buckingham: Open University Press.

Hardy, I. and Lewis, S. (2016): The 'doublethink' of data: educational performativity and the field of schooling practices, *British Journal of Sociology of Education*, DOI: 10.1080/01425692.2016.1150155

Hargreaves, D. H. (1972), *Interpersonal Relations and Education*, London: Routledge and Kegan Paul.

Hargreaves, D. H. (1996), Teaching as a Research-based Profession: Possibilities and Prospects, London: Teacher Training Agency.

Kakos, M. (2008), *The interaction between students and teachers in Citizenship Education*, Thesis (PhD), University of York.

Kakos, M. (2012a). Embedding citizenship education: An ethnographic tale of Trojan horses and conflicting performativities, In: *Performativity in the UK Education System: Theory, Policy and Practice*, ed. B. Jeffrey and B. Troman. London: Tufnell Press

Kakos, M (2012b) Four questions from England about the compatibility of citizenship education to modern schooling. In: Palaiologou, N. and Dietz, G. (Eds) *Mapping the Broad Field of Multicultural and Intercultural Education Worldwide: Towards the Development of a New Citizen*. Newcastle upon Tyne: Cambridge Scholar Publishing

Mayes, P. (2010), The discursive construction of identity and power in the critical classroom: Implications for applied critical theories, *Discourse and Society*,21(2): 189-210.

Perryman, J. (2006), Panoptic performativity and school inspection regimes: disciplinary mechanisms and life under special measures, *Journal of Education Policy*, 21(2): 147-161.

Pring, R. (1999), Political education: relevance of the humanities, *Oxford Review of Education*, 25(1) and (2): 71-87.

Rampton, B. (2006), *Language in Late Modernity: Interaction in an Urban School,* New York: Cambridge University Press.

Simons, M. and Masschelein, J. (2010), Governmental, Political and Pedagogic Subjectivation: Foucault with Rancière, *Educational Philosophy and Theory*,42(5) and 6: 588-605.

Todd, S. (2014) Between Body and Spirit: The Liminality of Pedagogical Relationships, *Journal of Philosophy of Education*, 48(2): 231-245.

Vanderstraeten, R. (2001), The school class as an interaction order, *British Journal of Sociology of Education*,22(2): 267-277.

Watkins, C. (2008), Depoliticisation, demoralisation and depersonalisation—and how to better them, *Pastoral Care in Education*,26(1): 5-11.

White, P. (1999), Political Education in the Early Years: the place of civic virtues, *Oxford Review of Education*, 25(1) and 2: 59-70.

Wilson, B. (1962), The Teacher's role—A Sociological Analysis, *The British Journal of Sociology*,13(1): 15-32.

Woods, P. (1979), *The Divided School*, London: Routledge and Kegan Paul.

Youdell, D. (2006), Subjectivation and performative politics—Butler thinking Althusser and Foucault: intelligibility, agency and the raced-nationed-religioned subject of education, *British Journal of Sociology of Education*,27(4): 511-528.

Chapter 4

Building democratic relationships at school? Families, students and teachers in context

José Ignacio Rivas, Analía Leite and Pablo Cortés

Abstract

This chapter relates to part of an investigation about the school experience of teachers, students and families. It analyses how you can build a democratic model of a school community from school experiences of these three groups. In this chapter, we focus on the teachers and the type of relations that they build from their different personal and professional histories. We inquiry if it is possible to create a system that goes beyond the technocratic approaches and individual educational practice, enabling a collaborative framework. To do this we employ narrative strategies and discussion groups in a primary school and one high school.

The confluence of the different experiences of teachers brings out the various views about educational practice that each one of them holds. The questions about gender, power relationships, the sense of knowledge, the social and cultural values, the vision on childhood and youth, assumptions on learning, are some of the issues that generate controversy in the relationship between schoolteacher mates. Often, the networks of personal relationships and professional affiliations that are generated in the school environment screen these different views. Beside this, these different views provide a way to build the school community regarding diversity, respect and the conflict.

Introduction

This chapter is the final part of the research study: *School experience, identity and community: collaboratively researching to transform educational practices.*[1] The work has been carried out over four years in three school institutions in the provinces of Malaga and Almeria: one primary school, one secondary school and one rural school that covers primary education and the first two years of secondary education.[2] The objective of this study is to analyse the school experience of

1. Project SEJ2007-60825/EDU under the [Spanish] Ministry of Education General Research Directorate's National Research Plan.
2. The Spanish education system provides for primary education from 6 to 12 years-

teachers, students and families in these centres, so as to promote strategies to construct democratic communities out of a deliberative impetus shared by all three collectives.

Our research is set out in three phases: phase one focuses on the construction of the subjects' narration about their own school experience as students and pupils (in the case of the teachers and families) as well as their current experience in the schools in which they form part. This narrative process was carried out using successive interviews with each subject individually. Phase two entailed a process by which the stories were given back to the different collectives at group meetings in which the narratives were analysed and discussed. This phase saw advances in the interpretation of the subjects' experiences, both from the research team's point of view and from that of the subjects themselves. These meetings were open and participation was wider than just the subjects with which the narrations were created. Phase three, the last phase, entailed holding reflection groups in which teachers, students and families all took part together. These were carried out during the last academic year with an approximate periodicity of one per month, although each centre had its own dynamics to this respect. Joint discussion groups are yet to be held in the three centres with other collectives involved in the education system.

This chapter focuses on this last phase, and on the teaching staff's perspective, particularly at the secondary school in which the research was carried out. We understand that each centre has its own distinguishing characteristics according to the different levels of education they deal with, and we are aware that secondary education has a more complex situation in the light of the current climate of education reform and change.

The development of this study is structured in three parts. First, there is a presentation of what the reflection groups were like, as regards the procedures that were raised, participation, focus groups, etc. The second part covers the three focal points resulting from the group work and which deal with the difference between the groups, the hierarchy in the relationships and the sense of educational success through effort. The third part will presents a discussion about these results, raising questions about the meaning of school knowledge, the construction of deliberative communities and the change in teachers' professional perspective.

---

old, compulsory secondary education from the age of twelve to sixteen, and post-compulsory secondary education from the age of sixteen onwards.

Stages for debate: reflection groups

In this research project, reflection groups were proposed as a strategy to create a meeting point between collectives, in which they can discuss their own school's experiences and the possibilities of transforming their reality. Consequently, the interpretations that have previously been made, both by the research group itself and in the collective and individual feedback sessions, are held up for public scrutiny in these sessions. The aim here is to procure a meeting point between subjects from different bodies that enables shared reflection channels to be established in order to define the changes in the school's dynamics. It is clear that the possibility of modifying the reality from a strategy that is limited both in time and its institutional scope, is not going to represent a radical and profound change. It is more a case of enabling a space for dialogue that provides elements to evaluate the everyday workings of the school and that affects set individual and/or group views. Perhaps the most important change entailed bringing together collectives that generally act in different, sometimes even opposing arenas in the same place.

Four monthly meetings were arranged, each with its own particular focus. These focuses arose, as we have mentioned above, out of the narrations and corresponding feedback. The most relevant questions that came out of this preliminary process, and which constituted the most important points of reflection, were then selected. These were:

1. Subject: What is expected of the centre: what is required of it and how each of the actors in the school work, what are the expectations?
2. Subject: How do the participants understand the purposes of the school. What is the school for each of the participants?
3. Subject: How are differences at secondary school lived?
4. Subject: How can it be improved: strategies.

In the four sessions, the meetings were attended by teachers, students and families. Some of the people attending the meetings had participated in the preliminary phases of our research. In the case of the teaching staff, there were five teachers who took part in all four sessions and a further five who only participated in part. They came from different departments and levels of education: History, Chemistry, Biology, English, Physical Education, Philosophy, Latin, Business Studies and Psychology. The students were the collective with the highest participation and six students regularly attended the four sessions, with this figure reaching nine at one session. In this case, they came mostly from

Compulsory Secondary Education, but there were also some students from Years 12 and 13, and from Vocational Training courses. The families were the group with the lowest participation, although there were between two and five members at all the meetings.

All the meetings were recorded on video and audio, and the participants were later sent a summary of the meetings so that they could make any relevant additions of their own. Likewise, a document was drawn up for each meeting with a script including the main questions for each focus, in line with previous phases. This document also included some information about these different contents, so they had their own voice to back up the categories in question. These voices were from different bodies but anonymity was respected in all cases.

The meetings lasted between one hour and an hour and a half, and they were held to coincide with the most suitable school times to ensure the majority could be available.

Lastly, we should point out that there was quite a smooth participation by all those attending, although the teachers were the group that took up most of the time in the interventions. The research coordinator acted as moderator in all the meetings, with the clear instruction to open up participation as far as possible to the largest number of those present, which proved to be harder than envisaged in some cases.

Professional challenges in today's schools: Profession, culture and democracy

From the reflection groups, as well as from the narratives about the teachers' school experience, we can see that there is a constant dialectic between what MacEwan (2011) calls 'the two genealogies of teaching'. In other words, there is one technique that is more method-based, and another that is more centred on the relationships between teaching staff and students. There is a technocratic view against a relational view. This view corroborates the results obtained in previous research into professional culture in secondary education (Rivas et al., 2003), in which a vision of teaching based on transmission of content is revealed.

As this author shows, these two tendencies in the way of conceiving teaching and the work of teachers have been the stage for historical confrontation, but also, undoubtedly, both personal and professional confrontation. Throughout the teachers' narrations, it is easy to distinguish how, in a large part of said narrations, these two tendencies form part of the ways in which the teaching staff talk about their work. In secondary teaching, a technical orientation prevails over the relational, although there are constant references to the students and the families as part of their work. As we will see later, the latter's response to classroom activities is important when it comes to 'motivating themselves' in their work. So both perspectives live side by side in teaching, although the technical side proves dominant. In fact, the way in which these relationships are conceived has a hierarchical nature that reinforces the method-based view.

As MacEwan (2011) describes:

> One is regarded as originating as a response to the changing conditions of human affairs and typically views the relationship of teacher to pupil as asymmetrical and dependent on the prior condition of a prescribed teaching method. The other conception of teaching, deriving from Plato, views teaching and learning as interconnected—as arising in a productive relationship, a form of intimate association in which teacher and pupil are bound together in a mutual effort to bring about their own improvement. (p. 137).

Two questions stand out in this matter. Firstly, they are different ways of institutionally responding to school activity. In other words, they originate in institutional contexts that entail a certain mandate in the teaching work. Furthermore, as Najmanovich (2010) reminds us, they represent two different models of knowledge and society.

> ... the human tasks of teaching and learning have taken on different forms depending on our conception of knowledge, the technologies of word and the means of communication we use, the styles we adopt in our relationships with others, the values in play, and the ways in which teaching-learning practices are institutionalised in each society, as well as the networks that join them and pass through them. (p.6).

In short, teaching work takes place in a community space, although its action in the classroom takes place in solitude, and it is representing ideological, political, social and personal options with which the teaching staff, one way or another, forms a relationship. Consequently, the transformation of professional models takes place insofar as the institutional and collective commitments are generated.

This idea gives meaning to the three focal points that constitute our perspective on the professional relationships of teachers. The option that secondary teaching has historically made around a curriculum- and technical-based model sets the conditions for developing teaching work and the relationships that they establish as a collective, but also with the other players in the school context: families and students or pupils.

These three focal points would be the following. Firstly, the way in which teachers relate in groups that represent different ways of approaching their job, whether through personal, political, social or professional affinities. Secondly, the inherent conflict in school relationships both within and between each body. Thirdly, the values that come into play in the teachers' performance

Birds of a feather flock together: Difference, diversity and action

The reflection groups see the different collectives come together, and with this, a setting emerges that is characterised by the diversity of positions and different perspectives, which (at least a priori) appear to represent different ways of acting in the school environment. We have mentioned diversity and difference, as they entail two different processes. On one hand, there is a variety of different groups, with a range of motivations and interests, that live together in the school space. On the other hand, these same groups compete to maintain their own positions on a stage that is also political, so the differences, not just the variety, are a fundamental part of school life. So, we find an interactionist perspective (diversity) living side by side with a socio-critical and political perspective (difference) to express different dimensions of the relationships.

From a global point of view, the teaching staff, students and families have different and controversial positions. The experience narrated in the three collectives reveals the different bodies have a certain isolation with regard to the others, which leads to complex situations. When the collectives meet up, it is easy to perceive the teaching staff in a prominent position as regards the family and students. Their action moves between paternalism and authority, setting the guidelines in the proposed lines of dialogue.

Furthermore, with regard to the teachers themselves, there are different groups maintaining contrasting positions. As we have seen in a previous research study (Rivas et al., 2003), these groups function in isolation from each other and there is often no communication between them at all. They operate like islands within the school itself, with little or no communication between them. The possibility of them meeting up in situations such as the reflection group are an opportunity to get to know each other, which does not usually happen in the school's everyday life, whether because they belong to different levels, specialities, departments, etc. or whether because they represent different ideological positions.

So we can speak of the presence of hegemonic groups facing other dominated, or at least marginalised, groups. To this effect, the most hegemonic stances are those that represent the set models, both from a political, cultural and educational point of view. Undoubtedly the most hegemonic position (invisible in many cases, but this does not make it less real) is that held by the educational administration and, in this case, the groups that act as its emissaries. The references to the administration as the body that regulates school life are common, and place most of the groups in a position of opposition or as victims. The idea that there is a set line of action appears in the different phases of our research among the teaching staff. As one teacher states:

> The teaching staff may share some of the responsibility, but we have been working as volunteers for many years now. The real changes, though, come from 'above', from the authorities; with money and a proper plan. However, there are too many changes in the education system: constant changes in laws, decrees, royal decrees ... the Government should show the education system more respect. There is a lack of stability and a consolidated education system.

This casual organisation, following the works of Maffessoli (1990), could be said to be of a 'tribal' nature, as it represents an element of professional and personal identification, and the same could be said of the situation with families and, particularly, with the students (Weiss, 2009). According to this proposal, a certain sense of belonging is created, which goes beyond a mere academic or administrative attachment. Professional performance, ways of understanding and acting with regard to the curriculum, have a lot to do with this group belonging, setting up shared comprehension systems. For example, in this sense, the manner in which different ways of acting are set up is significant, as the teachers themselves declare, regarding whether the teaching takes place in a Secondary group or in a Diversification group.[3] In the latter case, one of the teachers explains, "the students receive more personalised attention and they

---

3. Diversification is the name given in Spain to the group of students who have learning difficulties or problems, and it operates in parallel to the Compulsory Secondary groups.

appreciate that attention". You could say that "being a teacher of ..." implies different ways of doing things.

Hargreaves and Macmillan (1995: 1996) already pointed out what they called a 'balkanised culture' in secondary school teaching. That is, working 'in small sub-groups of the school community, as is the case with secondary school subject departments' (1996: 236), and this generates a fragmentation of knowledge and makes it difficult for the teaching staff to collaborate with each other. For example, the teachers in the reflection groups made comments to the effect that established their differences with primary education, or between the different levels of education. Without a doubt, education centres are institutionally shaped to strengthen this professional culture. In fact, practically the entire school life is fragmented in different ways: groups from self-contained classrooms, different courses, levels, departments, areas, teaching categories, subjects, and so forth. Each of these represents different ways of affiliating members of the school community and, undoubtedly, also members of the teaching staff. These affiliations also act as platforms for teaching action.

A comment made by one of the teachers is particularly significant,"... everyone does it here, you have to let go a bit ... I'm telling you, this is the first time that I'm teaching like this, so, if everyone's following the text book, I'm not going to be any different, because afterwards, next year, they're going to have to follow the text book." Cooperation within the particular group, as Hargreaves and MacMillan (1996) explain, becomes a professional stance of defence or affirmation; therefore, it may be in conflict with positions defended by'others'. In this way, the manner in which people take up a position regarding teaching, mediated by belonging to a group, reduces the problem to one of professional legitimisation of the teaching staff (Beltrán, 2010) and, in any case, to an academic or didactic controversy. This pushes other collectives out of the limelight, turning them into mere receivers of the defended stances, and removing them from forming part of the decision, as would be the case in education in a particular cultural and social community. In other words, the greater the concern for the differences in the collective, the fewer the possibilities to take other collectives into consideration.

We think that this situation is not a question of'bad intentions' on the teachers' part. On the contrary, most teachers express concern for the students and the effects of their work, although the aforementioned paternalism still exists. As we indicated before, the institutional set-up plays an important role. In this case, we must point to the continuance of the modernist education project on which western education systems are based. In short, it is the success of the technical, method-based tradition over the relational tradition based on particular individuals and situations. The school institution, now more than ever, is built on concepts such as efficiency, efficacy, quality and excellence, which, according to Habermas (Habermas, 2000; Najmanovich, 2010), require the system to be valid, regardless of the context. The growing centralisation of education systems, with a greater impact of the decisions made by the education administrators, and broader powers for managing centres, would be clear examples. Educational matters, such as cultural proposals and those related to knowledge, give way to bureaucratic and technical matters.

This institutional set-up and the responses given by the teaching staff represent an obstacle for working jointly and collaboratively to achieve the educational objectives. On the contrary, we have to think of the school institution as a diversity of purposes, of the different 'tribes' that comprise the institution, but which are linked to one single reality. Families, students and teachers, on one hand, and within each of these collectives, make up different groups that act according to different purposes.

It is relevant in this case to look at the questions raised by Dubet and Martuccelli (1998) about how it is possible for schools to train social agents to toe the line and at the same time train them to be autonomous and critical beings. It is impossible, then, to speak of the school institution as a simple process of socialisation. With regard to this tribal set-up, something takes place that these authors define as 'subjectivisation'; i.e. the development of a personal subjectivity that recognises the 'other' as different. The problem is whether this is contrary to or in collaboration with a political dynamic of community as a space for personal construction (Hernández, 2010).

Making the 'other' visible to the 'others' as part of my own personal construction can be a good way to make progress in changing the teaching profession. As one of the teachers claimed, "what we are lacking is the human side of education, as the academic side is already resolved." Despite the dominant technical tradition, the teaching staff undoubtedly feels the absence of personal relationships to construct other ways of doing things.

What the boss says goes: hierarchical relationships in the school experience

The relationships that unfold in schools is the second of the focal points that developed out of the reflection groups, and which is clearly connected to the previous point. The 'tribal' system with which the schools work entails peculiar ways of inter-relating. In this case, the model that most stands out in the reflection groups is the hierarchical model: the teachers feel subjected to the administration's logic, but in turn exercise their authority over the students and the families, who between them are also subjected to their prevalence positions. The fact that the school institution continues to be faithful to the bureaucratic and rational model of modernity is a key factor in setting this dynamic.

This relationship, in the school agents' discourse, is also marked by the idea of respect. In fact, it is the main point of argument of the three collectives, although with different meanings for each one. It is undoubtedly the basis of democratic values in social relationships, but in the framework of a hierarchical relationship, it is not always understood in a horizontal way. In the case of teachers, respect is clearly joined with authority, as is the case with successful students and many of the families. One teacher, for example, argues:

> There would have to be a certain credibility in the authority of people who love you, who teach you and help you towards a wonderful future, and this is not channelled.

As can be seen, respect is required for the authority that they represent, due to its institutional position, which is a common theme in all the meetings. The paternalism that we mentioned in the previous section would be an example of this. There is a new, yet constant, element in the argument: the notion of future. The promise of bigger and better chances of social and professional success serve as an argument to justify the teaching that is offered at this moment in time. It is irrelevant whether this makes sense for the students or not. In this way, the teaching-staff demands a certain attitude when the students enter the class; they have to want to learn and make the most of the lesson. This brings us once again to the method-based tradition, as it does not question the teaching models, but rather it demands that the student accept those models as being useful for their future.

The problem now is that the relationship of authority has changed as regards what could have been their school experience. As one teacher eloquently expressed, the "what did the teacher tell you?" has changed into the "what did you say to my son/daughter?" So the teachers feel that the school authority has been broken as a moral reference point for family and students, and this represents a change in the school's duty: we have gone from 'moral authority' to 'dissatisfied customer'. This results in a feeling of loss of support for their work, as 'when there is some kind of sanction, we find the parents looking for a way to excuse their children.' The family-school continuity is lost and the latter ceases to be a moral reference, something that did not happen in the past.

In any case, it is clear that this demand reflects a hierarchical-type relationship, as we mentioned before: the teaching staff set the standard, according to their professional status, and the family and students must collaborate to make it work. The problem is that society does not follow the same rules, as they continually mention, but rather other systems of values and relationships are being developed. These are seen as an obstacle to their work, insofar as they do not coincide with the values inherent in the type of school system we have, and not as new possibilities to develop. Hence the conflict appears to be practically guaranteed.

Therefore, relationships, authority and values are the three dimensions with which we handle the hierarchical order of the school institution. We are, however, seeing how they highlight the chain of power, as Foucault (1996) mentions, that circulates around the institution and operates through its wide-ranging bodies and groups. The teachers believe that the students are there to learn so that they can be someone in life, but at the same time they feel that they are subject to the administration's authority. The chain of power extends insofar as there is a certain asymmetry in relationships between the subjects, due to the different roles that each one has to play in the institutional operation.

Once again the modernist mandate emerges in the interpretation, as deep down there lies a principle of 'obligation' or 'duty' to study as the only way to ensure progress and social transformation. The redemptionist idea of education, analysed in different ways, upholds teachers' idealisation of their work, and acts in a rational-bureaucratic system that regulates and establishes the places (different and often conflicting) that each one should occupy. This means that one cannot think in terms of the 'different and significant other' on which to construct subjectivism and democratic relationships. This does not have anything to do with the teachers' interest, dedication and professionalism, but with institutional construction.

We could say, following Rockwell (2001: 49-50), that teachers have the power that the institution gives them, and that they develop in most of their educational activities, in accordance with institutional legitimacy (school and academic). So a learning or an initiation in the 'social rules of the game' takes place, which acts, according to what is revealed through the teachers' expression, on the students' participation in school work. This is undoubtedly the space in which the relationships between teachers and students are negotiated, and where the different roles and social positions are defined. For example, the different references to the teachers to the effect that 'they do not impose themselves' are significant, showing that the teaching staff are poorly valued professionally by the school's social environment. The successful students clearly express that if the teachers knew how to impose themselves, there would not be such disorder in the classroom and those who do want to study would not have to waste so much time. The way in which Dussel and Caruso (1999: 199) analyse teachers' authority is relevant here, as they are attributed a particular position in transmitting a society's culture, which awards them power and authority that goes beyond them as mere individuals.

It is interesting to note that this aspect occupies a lot of time in the reflection group, which gives an idea of the value being placed on this topic by all parties. Without a doubt, and once again following Rockwell (2001), teaching and knowledge, in terms of historical and rational demand, is the least questioned and is where the teacher's authority finds its most genuine space for expression. In the teachers' own words, "you can't change what you have to teach": the administration makes demands, the students need a minimum, etc. This is the reason why it is also the most controversial space, when some of their principles can be subverted. In the case of Spain, a significant point is the conflict that arose from allowing students to go on to the next level even though they had not passed all their subjects, and this is repeatedly referred to by all the protagonists in this research study. For example, one mother points out:

> Yes, I think that we felt like we were in a … system, you know? I mean, like we were part of a set of rules and that was what had to be done… Nowadays, I think it's entirely the opposite with kids these days, if they can't be bothered, nothing happens to them. That has to change too, because kids can't … you have to obey the rules, and I think that's it, not too much, not too little.

Once again this is interpreted by the teaching staff as respect: "without respect there is no education," one teacher claims, "but trust has to be earned day by day." Their authority may be questioned insofar as their decisions can be questioned, although from our point of view, it can also be questioned if the students do not feel committed to, or involved in the tasks they are doing. That is why the loss of meaning, on a social level, which is currently being felt with regard to school and what it can offer as a real project for the future, is one way or another questioning the work of teachers. The teachers themselves are aware of this situation:

> School failure is due to a lack of motivation; the students feel that the school has no meaning once outside it, what possibilities are open to them to do something? Society demands some things, and school demands others. Society and school walk along different paths, even regarding their values. School has to provide a solution to the problems being raised.

The situation is complex and this is experienced by all sides, although school is still viewed according to its hierarchical rational-bureaucratic model, so the possibilities to construct a community are increasingly more complicated. It would be necessary to think about reciprocal, rather than hierarchical, relationships in which respect is a premise that goes in both directions. The different role that each one plays in the institution means that some set purposes and procedures and others act as blind recipients. Furthermore, the teachers themselves, in that their functions are reduced to those of mere manager, as we mentioned before, are also blind recipients of decisions beyond their control. Consequently, the line of respect is broken or questioned at different points along the way.

Paths of glory: for success through effort

In the two previous points we feel that there is an underlying topic that is also in line with the modernist ideal with which we are constantly evaluating the school institution. We are talking about effort as a guarantee to achieving school success and, therefore (as regards a project for the future) social and professional success. This is unquestionably one of the main themes arising out of the teachers' discourses and statements, as well as those offered by the other collectives. It also appears hand in hand with early school leaving figures regarding compulsory secondary education in Spain, which currently stands at around thirty per cent. This fact accentuates the sense that the school has lost its meaning for today's students, or at least, their lack of interest.

The discourse in this point begins with the mutual expectations between teachers and students. The general feeling is one of disagreement and discontent, and this is related to the difference in objectives that are in play. Although the teachers expect the students to enter the classroom with an attitude of learning and making the very best of the time, the students expect the teachers to offer dedication and hard work, as well as a willingness to innovate, covering a variety of options. The students are demanding enough among themselves, between the 'successful' ones and the 'unruly', as we mentioned previously.

This results in a search for school spaces in which the students (or at least 'those who want to study') can work and achieve success. This is a concern that is also shared by the families, who see how their children are finding it hard to survive in certain classes. One mother says:

> When there's a good atmosphere in the classroom, the conditions are there for all the children to make progress. If you are in a good group, there are more possibilities to achieve success; if you are not in a good group, the possibilities of failure are higher.

Once again we can place this situation in the historical legacy of the modern school as it has turned out. On one hand, segregation into groups means different possibilities, partially at random. On the other hand, the search for homogeneity, through a rational-bureaucratic system, generates different responses depending on the individual settings and subjects. It is in this context that effort acquires significance: effort is the value that remains to demand, after the process of homogenisation that makes everything equal, and after the idea of a subject being a bearer of capacities, as we will see below.

Following this logic, success would come through a 'culture of discipline' or 'of order'. In the terms of the mother mentioned above, this would be the same as achieving order in the classroom. With order, in the teachers' opinion, it would be possible to generate 'work habits' that would ensure the students have the possibility of success. This coincides with the contributions made by the research studies conducted by Rudduck and Flutter (2007). The result is that the means become the end, and habits and order become more important than the learning of content itself. As one teacher points out, "if they give their all, I pass them". Although this gives an idea of the teachers' responsibility and their concern for the students, it also reveals the existence of a certain 'protocol of behaviour', that supposedly predisposes or guarantees learning. How are these protocols established?

The method-based tradition once again raises its head. Given a protocol that is 'legitimised' by the curriculum and/or the tradition of the teaching culture, the moral responsibility falls on the students, leaving the institution and its representatives out. Each one is responsible for their own actions and, therefore, for the future that they ensure for themselves. So, just as we spoke about teachers having set ways of doing things, we can also talk about the students' set ways of behaving, which guarantees school success. As we presented in another work (Rivas et al., 2010), the exposure and public sanction of school acts operates as a moralising and control element for students' behaviour. A job 'well done' or 'badly done' is publicly presented as a regulation of group conduct.

Some teachers have helped us interpret this moral scenario:

> They are set in a discourse of disability, and this is false, because the student has not worked hard enough, how long do you spend on daily study? ... give me figures, how many hours a day do you spend studying? ... If you do not know what you are capable of, how far you can go, putting all your strengths into it, you could give more if you put your mind to it, other kinds of circumstances are a different story ...

> It requires discipline, effort; it is not as easy as sitting down and listening to a lecture.

> You have to change, you need an extra push, and that's where we come in, tomorrow without fail.

There is a certain idea of subject and knowledge that is represented in these expressions: a certain innatist perspective of the subject (bearer of a certain type of capacity) and a stratified and univocal knowledge. Declarations such as the following are common: "they could do more if they wanted to"; "I'm not very good at studying (or at maths, or history....)"; "Studying's not for me ..."; "I don't like studying ....". In short, there are those who are good at it, and those who are not; there are subjects that students like, and others that they do not; there are hard sciences and soft sciences... The previous idea of 'I don't want to study' (lack of interest or loss of meaning of school) is seen to transform into an idea of capacity, 'Studying's not for me' 'I'm no good at it'. A principle that is related to will is resolved in the form of capacity. If willpower is a problem in the subject's commitment to certain ends, capacity is an innate predisposition that the subject has and which gives him or her certain possibilities. At least as a discourse, the equation is both appealing and dangerous.

From the moral point of view that we are proposing, the historical modern mandate of the right to education acts as an element of coercion over the students.

The right to education, as a historical conquest, becomes an 'obligation to study', as social coercion. In this way, the students are reproached for not valuing something that is the result of a centuries-old collective effort.

From our point of view, this brings up the comparison between a rationalist-universal model and a contingent and placed model. The right to education is not the same as accepting a homogeneous and single form of education, particularly when society is different now to when the format was founded, which would be a way of newly colonising the students' awareness as citizens (Rivas, 2010).

In the series of paradoxes in which the teachers move, we feel that there is a certain recognition of this confrontation, particularly when they claim: "What is lacking is the human side of education, because the academic side is settled"; or, "brilliant students are not brilliant for academic reasons, they are brilliant as people". The regulation of the education system through curriculum and rules solves the academic problem, in the peculiar way in which it has done so, but there is still a real need to give a different dimension. Maybe this new twist should modify the resolved academic side, as in some way, it is responsible for the absence of all things human in everyday education.

Some elements for debate

The three focal points raised show us a situation that is not really conducive to the development of community in educational institutions. Difference as confrontation or isolation, hierarchy and authority as a form of relationship, and the teacher's role as manager, all create a complex scenario that is politically conflictive and educationally biased. There is an underlying vision of knowledge as standardised disciplines and protocol-based ways of acting, which represent major obstacles to transforming the school reality. As Contreras y Pérez de Larra (2010) asserts:

> Knowing is something that happens to us insofar as it transforms us; it is what happens to us as a result of what we have lived; it is something that moves us inside and that generates new frameworks of understanding through which we can live, feel and think about the world and reality; something that opens us up and shows us the possibility of new experiences; it is an experience in that it happens in us, but also the fruit of what is left of it. (...) *If data is not acquired through experience, there will be stored data, but not knowledge; there is no genuine knowledge if the data is not acquired through experience, through something that transforms us.* (54)

Some proposals are advancing towards what we could call collaborative professionalism, which includes a range of collectives in the running of the school (Hargreaves, 2000; Hargreaves and Godson, 2006), as is the case with the learning communities, professional learning communities, etc. What is important about all these is that they do not think of the teachers independently and in isolation from the other collectives. It is not a question of technical order to be resolved from a certain professional training. Education is a matter of a social, political and cultural nature that can only be resolved through its commitment and involvement with the subjects and the contexts in which they act. To this effect, Rudduck and Flutter (2007: 22) drew our attention to the need to not keep the non-formal education system separate from our inside world and that not only means that we modify our perceptions of the young people we are teaching, but also the suppositions that keep traditional structures and relationships in their place.

In the reflection group sessions we felt that a relevant process was created that had a bearing on this change. However, as we have mentioned previously, the teaching staff tended to adopt an initially paternalist and protagonist role, gradually other voices began to be heard that enabled us to filter many of the opinions expressed. In some cases, the students or families even contradicted some of the teachers' preconceptions, and vice versa, which was new to many of those present. Although the tendency is for each collective to stick to its own, this type of space for expression generates and constructs the educational institution to promote democratic spaces. It is clear, in principle, what each collective wants. Little by little they become more personalised and gradually the more personal or minority stances also take their place. The aim is to break away from the authority of the body with horizontal sessions, where the narrated experiences acquire their own value to the detriment of a hierarchical perspective.

The path, as is the case in the global society, must travel through new ways of understanding and managing democracy, breaking away from established positions and opening up new channels of collaboration from a horizontal perspective, from respect (understood as reciprocity in actions) and decision. This means advancing towards what we could call 'communities of discourse or dialogue', just as we speak of discourse or radical democracy as a transforming political model. As Gale and Densmore (2007) point out, in this perspective the power lies with people, and it is not something that can be had, but rather something that can be exercised. Consequently, it breaks away from the patrimonialist conception of politics and participation, taking the decisions to the hands of the subjects, even where this brings discrepancy and difference.

References

Beltrán, F. (2010) El currículum formal: legitimidad, decisiones y descentralización (The formal curriculum: legitimacy, decisions and decentralization). In Gimeno, J. (Comp.) *Saberes e incertidumbre sobre el curriculum (Knowledges and uncertainty on curriculum)*. Madrid: Morata, 205-220.

Dubet, F. and Martuccelli, D. (1998) *En la escuela. Sociología de la experiencia escolar*. (On the School. Sociology of school experience) Buenos Aires: Losada.

Contreras, J. and Pérez de Larra, N. (2010) *Investigar la experiencia educativa* (Researching educative experience). Madrid: Morata.

Dussel, I. and Caruso, M. (1999) *La invención del aula. Una genealogía de las formas de enseñar (The invention of the classroom. A genealogy of the ways of teaching)*. Buenos Aires: Santillana.

Foucault, M. (1976) *Vigilar y castigar. Nacimiento de la prisión (*Discipline and Punish: The Birth of the Prison). Mexico: Siglo Veintiuno.

Foucault, M. (1996) *Genealogía del Racismo* (Genealogy of Racism). La Plata: Altamira.

Gale, T. and Densmore, K. (2007) *La implicación del profesorado. Una agenda de democracia radical para la escuela* (Engaging Teachers: Towards a Radical Democratic Agenda for Schooling). Barcelona: Octaedro.

Hargreaves, A. (2000) Profesionales y padres: ¿enemigos personales o aliados públicos? (Professionals and parents: personal adversaries or public allies?). *Perspectivas 2000*; 2: 221-134.

Habermas, J. (2000) *La constelación posnacional. Ensayos políticos* (The Postnational Constellation: Political Essays). Barcelona: Paidós.

Hargreaves, A. and Goodson, I. (2006) Educational Change Over Time? The Sustainability and Nonsustainability of Three Decades of Secondary School Change and Continuity. *Educational Administration Quarterly*, 42(1), 3-41.

Hargreaves, A. and Macmillan, R. (1995) The balkanization of secondary school teaching. In L. Siskin and J. (Eds.), *The subjects in question*. New York: Teachers' College Press, 141-171.

Hargreaves, A. and Macmillan, R. (1996) La Balcanización de la enseñanza. Una colaboración que divide (The Balkanization of Teaching. Collaboration that Divides). In A. Hargreaves (Ed.), *Profesorado, Cultura y postmodernidad. Cambian los tiempos, cambia el profesorado* (Changing Teachers, Changing Times: Teachers' Work and Culture in the Postmodern Age), Madrid: Morata, 235-263

Hernández, F. (2010 ed.) *Aprender a ser en la escuela primaria* (Learning to be in the Primary School). Barcelona: Octaedro.

Maffesoli, M. (1990) *El tiempo de las tribus. el declive del individualismo en las sociedades de masas* (The Time of the Tribes. The Decline of individualism in Mass Society). Barcelona: Icaria.

MacEwan, H. (2011) Narrative Reflection in the Philosophy of Teaching: Genealogies and Portraits, *Journal of Philosophy of Education,* 45(1), 125-140.

Najmanovich, D. (2010) *Epistemología y Nuevos Paradigmas en Educación. Educar y aprender en la sociedad-red* (Epistemology and New Paradigms in Education. Educate and learn in Net-Society). [Online]. Rizoma Freireano, 6. (Available 2010 May 13) http://www.rizoma-freireano.org/index.php/epistemologia-y-nuevos-paradigmas-en-educacion-educar-y-aprender-en-la-sociedad-red--dra-denise-najmanovich

Rivas, JI., Leite, AE., Cortés, P., Márquez, MJ. and Padua, D. (2010) La configuración de identidades en la experiencia escolar. Escenarios, sujetos y regulaciones (Identity configuration in school experience. Settings, individuals and regulations), *Revista de Educación*, 353, 187-209

Rivas, JI. (2010) Descolonizar la educación. Transformar la práctica docente desde una perspectiva crítica (Decolonizing education. Transforming the Teaching from a critical perspective). In P. Aparicio (Ed.), *El poder de educar y de educarnos. Transformar la práctica docente desde una perspectiva crítica (*The power of educating and educate ourselves. Transforming the Teaching from a critical perspective). Xátiva, Valencia: Ediciones del Crec, 57-72.

Rivas, J.I., Sepúlveda, M.P., Rodrigo, P. and González, E. (2003) *La cultura profesional de los docentes de enseñanza secundaria* (The Professional Culture of Teachers in Secondary Education) Available 2016 http://procie.uma.es/images/pdf/culturaprofesional.pdf

Rockwell, E. (2001) *La escuela cotidiana* (Everyday School). Mexico: Fondo de Cultura Económica.

Rudduck, J. and Flutter, J. (2007*) Cómo mejorar tu centro escolar dando la voz al alumnado* (How to improve your school (Giving pupils a voice)). Madrid: Morata.

Weiss, E. et al. (2009) Jóvenes y Bachillerato en México: el proceso de subjetivación, el encuentro con los otros y la reflexividad (Young people and high school in Mexico: subjectivisation, others and reflexivity), *Propuesta Educativa*, 32, 83-94.

Chapter 5

Primary school teachers' professional identity: An ethnographic study

Juana M. Sancho, Fernando Hernández, Amalia Creus, Laura Domingo and Alejandra Montané

Abstract

This chapter builds on a project aimed at describing, analysing and interpreting the notions, representations and experiences related to the professional identity of primary school teachers in their first working years. We explore five of the nine micro-ethnographies based on these five teachers' personal accounts about their school experience as students, their initial professional development and the first steps of their professional careers. These narratives were enriched with the observation of their school practice and the analysis of relevant documents and artefacts. The text firstly makes explicit the research project background. Secondly, we discuss the ethnographic dimension of our study. Then we make a primary approach to the contributions of these ethnographic cases to the understanding of what it means to become a teacher in the contemporary world. Here we pay especial attention to the relationship established with our collaborators.

The research in context

From the important number of education reforms carried out in the last fifty years a recurring theme emerges, which is proving to be hard to address. Teachers (and educators in general) seem to find it especially hard to change their beliefs about what teaching and learning means, their ideas about children and youth, and what characterises good teaching practice (Sarason, 1990; Fullan, 2007). In the last few years, this finding has aroused a growing interest in exploring the situations, processes, experiences and perspectives linked to how teachers constitute and negotiate their professional identity (Clandinin and Connelly, 1995; De Gee, 200; Sfard and Prusak, 2005). Taking into account that in the contemporary, globalised, multicultural and multilingual, highly technologised, post-capitalist, liquid, volatile, uncertain, complex and ambiguous world (Castells, 1996, 2012; Boltanski and Chiapello, 2005; Bauman, 2006, 2007;

Johansen, 2007; Sennet, 1998; 2012), the constitution of professional identities can no longer be approached from the perspective of modernity (Giddens, 1991).

In this context, the main aim of *The construction of the professional identity of primary school teachers during initial professional development and the first years at work*[1] project was to describe, analyse and interpret the notions, representations and experiences related to the professional identity of primary education teachers. The project, while taking into account the complete learning life of participating teachers, particularly focused those dimensions and concepts that stem from the initial professional development and the first few years of schoolwork. We also envisioned this research as a way to provide an orientation for the policies and practices of both initial and in-service teacher's professional development, in order to contribute to the development of a teaching profession capable of acknowledging the educational possibilities and facing the challenges and obstacles of today's society.

The specific objectives of our research relevant for this text were:

To contribute to the development of research-based knowledge about the complex processes underlying the constitution of primary school teachers' identity during the initial professional development and the first years of schoolwork.

To describe, analyse and interpret the interdependence and influence of the discourses, representations, experiences and practices underlying the constitution of primary school teachers' professional identity.

To provide evidence-based results that can inform and contribute to the decision-making processes of:

(a) those responsible for the policies and practices of initial and in-service teachers' professional development;
(b) schools that take in new teachers; and
(c) new teachers themselves, who are at a crucial moment in their professional lives.

The ethnographic dimension

In this project we introduced a decolonising approach to teachers' professional development. For authors such as Tuck and Yang (2014: 238) social science research has traditionally been a 'settler of colonial knowledge, nothing less

1. Part of a larger project, *The construction of the professional identity of pre-school teachers during initial training and the first years at work* (MICINN-EDU2010-20852-C02-02).

and nothing more'. Hence, the need to humanise research with a decolonising practice that incorporates participants in reflecting and collaborating throughout the research process, building 'relationships of care and dignity and dialogic consciousness-raising for both researchers and participants' (Paris and Winn, 2014, p. xvi). And our decision to implement an inclusive research perspective in which those who tend to be the objects of other people's inquiry become somehow agents in the implementation process ensuring that issues that are important to them are addressed and their views and experiences properly included (Nind, 2014).

Regarding the methodological design, the project envisioned several distinctive phases. The first one, which is the basis of this chapter, consisted of developing nine micro-ethnographies based on experiential accounts and observations of nine primary school teachers in the first five years of their professional career (see table 1). This evidence was complemented with the analyses of relevant documentation and artefacts, some of them provided by our collaborators.

Curt Le Baron (2006) characterises micro-ethnography as the study of small parts of the experience or segments of the daily reality of a person or group. Micro-ethnographic studies share the features of long-term ethnographic studies such as fieldwork, observation, interviews, etc., but focus on a topic, site or community for a shorter space of time. This does not mean less rigour and effort in the process of gathering evidence and analysing and interpreting them. In fact, in our project, it entailed the following up of nine teachers for between four and six months through various in-depth interviews, observations in the workplace, collecting and analysing materials, artefacts (pictures, text, etc.) and initial training programs. This approach added complexity to the notion of fieldwork, making it an intricate symbolic line that allowed movement through personal experiences to professional practices, articulating what is socially produced and individually experienced (Jeffrey and Troman, 2004).

In this context, in-depth interview techniques were the lever to reconstruct with these teachers their views, representations and meanings about their ways of understanding professional identity, experiences and practices during their initial education as teachers and the first years of work. These interviews allowed us to place, contrast and explore the meaning granted to their becoming teachers; the representations and discourses about childhood, teaching and learning, school discipline; and the relationships with their teachers, colleagues, educational authorities, pupils, etc. They also allowed us to reconstruct how they incorporate the pedagogical routines and to explore how they negotiate their teaching practice with their previous ideas about education acquired as students and student teachers (Sancho and Hernández, 2014).

Table 1. Characterisation of five of the teachers' focus on the micro-ethnographies.

Name	Type of University	Type of school/ contract	Teaching experience	Degrees	Researcher
Jenny	Public	Public/semi-urban -Substitute: ⅓ of day	1 year	- Teacher Education Diploma: Physical Education - Master in Research in Didactics, Teacher Professional Development and Assessments	Fernando
Mireia	Public	Public/rural -Full-time (substitute)	2 years	- Teacher Education Diploma: Infant Education[3]	Alejandra
Xavi	Private	Public/semi-urban Substitute: ½ day. Responsible for a class.	2 years	- Teacher Education Diploma: Primary Education - Master in Research in Didactics, Teacher Professional Development and Assessments - PhD candidate	Juana M.
Marta	Public	Public/urban Full-time (permanent)	5 years	- Teacher Education Diploma: Special Needs Education (SEN) 3 - PhD candidate (about to finish her dissertation).	Amalia
Eva	Public	Public/semi-rural - Full-time (permanent)	5 years	- Teacher Education Diploma: Primary Education - Master in Psychopedagogy	Laura

The second resource used in this phase of the study was the ethnographic observation. We observed these teachers' practices, their school context and culture. These observations included pictures taken by the researchers or the teachers themselves, and whose meaning was discussed with them, and allowed them and us to re-place and re-signify the narrated experience. From the ethnographic description of schools, we obtained significant scenes of meaningful practices. Norman Denzin (1997: 207-208) refers to the term 'scene' when speaking about the interpretative assumptions structuring poetics and narrative texts. These scenes were the ones captured by the researchers and were made up of certain events that attract their attention in relation to the focus of the study. Then the text reconstructing the scene was given back to the collaborating teachers to start a new conversation and reflect upon what was said in the text. A strategy that avoided us researchers being the only ones to set the meaning and prevent us from colonising teachers' voices.

These in-depth interviews and the observations carried out in the teachers workplace allowed us to develop a typology of the ethnographic notion of field made up of knots, loose ends, people, situations, places, artefacts and emotional spots. More specifically, the ethnographic dimension of this chapter has to be found in research aspects such as:

> The researchers used field notes as a basis for writing a text, which could well be considered a field journal that was shared with the teachers. Sharing this text favoured a relationship of accompaniment that contributed through reflection and resonances to generate knowledge experiences 'about oneself, about others and the everyday life' (de Souza, 2011: 46). In our case, it contributed to reveal the gist of our research: how and by what means teachers constitute their sense of being professional?
>
> The loci where meetings took place were important because they mediated the relationship. We described and placed these different settings in the ethnographic accounts.
>
> We organised this phase of the research around a series of narratives that made up the meaning of the researcher-researched relationship and allowed us to connect the focus of the study: how scenarios, people, rules, experience—from which each teacher makes sense of the kind of teacher they would like to become are articulated.
>
> An important part of the job of the researcher was observing individuals in the workplace. This took place over one or two days. This entry in their working milieu for contextualising what they said and did was another essential element of the ethnographic study.
>
> Finally the process of writing placed a good deal of attention to emerging knowledge about the meaning of being (becoming) a teacher.

All those aspects connect to the Jeffrey and Troman's (2004) view on the following ethnographic research principles:

> Taking place over an extended time span to grasp a fuller range of empirical situations to be observed and analysed and to allow for the emergence of contradictory behaviours and perspectives. Time in the field, alongside time for analysis and interpretation, allow for continuous reflections concerning the complexity of human contexts.
>
> Considering relations between the appropriate cultural, political and social levels of the research sites and the individuals and groups/ communities' agency at the research sites.
>
> Including theoretical perspectives in order to:
>
> 'Sensitise' field research and analysis
>
> Provide an opportunity to use the empirical ethnographic research as an interrogator of theory.
>
> Develop new theory.

Based on our ethnographic work, the following section provides five short accounts on the main elements involved in the constitution of our collaborators' professional identity and on the key events that marked these teachers' experience in the path that led them to become (or not) the kind of teachers they would like to be.

A micro-ethnographic study of the research on novice teachers' identity

The length of time the researcher spends in the field or devotes to building the relationship with the subjects is one of the fundamental aspects of ethnographic research. As mentioned, time in the field, alongside time for analysis and interpretation, allows continuous reflections concerning the complexity of human contexts. This fact, together with the adopted inclusive research perspective, led us to start the following ethnographic narratives by referring to how the relationships with collaborators were established.

Being a teacher as a question of building caring relationships with pupils. Fernando-Jenny

In the case of Jenny (Fernando), a teacher in her first working year, the research relationship spread over a period of six months. During this time they held several meetings (at the university because it was the place where she was enrolled in a graduate program and was very convenient for her; in the journey between her school and the train station of the village where she lives and in a cafeteria in Barcelona). Fernando also visited the school where she worked (and years ago was a primary school pupil) to study the institution, her teaching practice, and her relations with other teachers and her third grade pupils. They also maintained a good number of exchanges by e-mail and several telephone calls. Fernando took pictures of her school settings and she sent him several pictures taken by her. They shared two texts written by her about issues related to her work as a novice teacher. In addition, he sent her several documents to read on issues that emerged from their conversations, such as integrated curriculum and inquiry-based topic work, pedagogical relationship, learning for understanding, etc. All together this shaped Fernando's ethnographic study, led to a fuller range of empirical situations to be observed and analysed, and allowed for the emergence of contradictory behaviours and perspectives (Jeffrey and Troman, 2004).

Jenny majored in physical education in the primary teacher training college. However, her first job was as a substitute of a classroom teacher. This meant she had to teach all curriculum subjects and put aside her specialisation before the emerging demands or necessities of the schools where she was sent. When she and Fernando started their research meetings, she was sharing the role of a third grade classroom teacher with another substitute teacher, besides teaching physical education to other groups. Under these circumstances, she perceived her mission as school teacher as:

> not to teach content ... what I like is to guide them, because pupils also teach me things. I try to understand them, see what is going on with them, where their motivation is ... I don't know how to explain it ... accompanying them in their processes.

Jenny draws her position as novice teacher by pursuing a caring relationship with pupils in the first place. This could be, in part, because she was highly influenced by one of the teachers of the graduate program she was pursuing, who dealt with the relevance of creating caring relation experiences in the teaching and learning process. And in part because at the beginning of her teaching career she was aware that 'there are many things you don't know' and, maybe, the idea of offering and creating positive and caring relationships could be the point of confluence for both teachers and students. In any case, in her vision of becoming a teacher the building of caring relationships played a relevant role.

> There are things I care about, like establishing ties with the students. The teacher who comes and only says negative things ... So I appreciate the approach to them and I think I have the awareness that this is all that matters.

Teaching, in Jenny's perspective, was a question of affection and mutual recognition.

> Relationships between people are important. The key is how I interact with the students. It's about listening to the other, asking yourself how you can help, and how s/he can help me.

The teacher Jenny was replacing was on maternity leave, and returned to the classroom in the last week of the school year. For this reason, Jenny finished the relationship with her pupils in a quick, upsetting and agitated manner. However, she had no choice but to understand the meaning of teaching job insecurity and its impact in her professional identity, and just said, 'It is part of the many things of what learning to be a teacher means'.

The wish of becoming a primary school teacher. The need to communicate with others.
Alejandra-Mireia

Mireia (Alejandra) was in the second year of her teaching career. She lived in a small town of two-hundred and fifty inhabitants and worked in rural schools in her region. Alejandra maintained a research relationship for over four months from their first contact. Initially, they met in her town, and the first sessions were oriented towards seeking the meaning both of them considered underling the research project and the recreation of their own personal experience in school contexts. Mireia thus had the opportunity to narrate her vital experience of being a schoolchild in this small town, as well as her principal memories of her life as a student. She also brought in images of her childhood, of the rural school she attended, of her university studies and the beginning of her schoolwork.

They carried out five face-to-face meetings and exchanged several e-mail messages. Alejandra also went with her to her rural school, with a total number of eighteen male and female pupils. Alejandra considers that the school context had relevantly marked her ethnographic viewpoint: a small town, the trip to the school in which Mireia works, the curving rural road, and the mountains.

All this contributed to configure something special and to establish difficulty for continued face-to-face communication, increasing the intensity and time given to each meeting.

Mireia lived in the village where she was born. There she attended the rural primary school until aged eleven she went to a larger town for her secondary education. Later, she studied a teaching degree at the University of Barcelona. In her imagination, from her early childhood years, she had always wanted to be a teacher, and therefore this was a key element in the constitution of her professional identity: the vocation. Standing out clearly in her two first years of professional activity was an interest in establishing a positive relationship with both the pupils and the other schoolteachers, thereby configuring communication as a mainstay or core value of her professional development. Another element standing out as a recurrent node was freedom. Mireia felt her professional identity develops more positively in a context in which she can decide and feels free to act and relate with others. She considered this fact as one of the most relevant when comparing her experience with the two schools she had worked in. Another element that should not be forgotten is the context in which she was learning to teach: the rural environment. In this context, the type of relationship and communication among stakeholders (teachers, parents, pupils, and town) is developed via patterns and characteristics quite different of those found in urban zones. Here, everything and everybody are much more interconnecting, anything occurring in the school can transcend its walls and any social event can have an immediate effect on school life.

Mireia did not locate in her primary and secondary school or university learning experience special signs or marks influencing her way of learning to be a teacher. She stated that she learnt following the trace of her own errors in order not to repeat them, and that she based her professional development on confidence in herself, the pupils and her school colleagues. She was happy with her life and doing her work. She openly transmitted her happiness to her pupils and colleagues and it was apparent that this made up an important part of her professional identity.

The fight for educational freedom. Juana-Xavier

The formal research relationship with Xavier (Juana), in the second year of his teaching career, went on for over six months. Before that, Juana met him briefly in a graduate program and spoke to him about the possibility of participating in this research project. As soon as he learnt about the focus of the study, he showed great interest. They held five in-depth interviews, exchanged several e-mails and telephone calls, and Juana spend a whole day at the school he was working in throughout the school year. Four of the meetings, by his choice, took place in the University of Barcelona. In the first one, following the negotiation document Juana had sent him by e-mail, they made explicit their understanding of the scope and aims of the project, the mutual duties, responsibilities and possible benefits. This was followed by an open-ended conversation about his views on education, his expectations and first disappointments as a young teacher. In the negotiation process, Juana made it explicit that this was overall an educational research project. That meant, according to John Elliott (2006), that its main aim was to have a positive impact on the professional development of our collaborators. Xavier clearly understood this research dimension—in fact, it was a fundamental point for him to offer us his time and effort—and in every meeting he came with questions about different aspects of his teaching experience looking for Juana's advice or for relevant literature.

In the second interview he gave Juana a detailed autobiographic account of the crucial moments (positive or negative) of his whole life—first as pupil (infant education, primary, secondary university) and then as teacher—which he identified as having an impact in the on-going construction of his professional identity. The third meeting, held in his school, was devoted to reflecting upon the role he was performing there and the uneasiness he often felt when facing the distance between the kind of teacher he would like to be and the one he believed he was by having to follow under the school guidelines. The fourth one, again at the University, revolved around the meaning given to several pictures Juana took from his school, the ones he selected from his experience as a school pupil and the artefacts (a history book with lots of notes) he considered fundamental in his becoming a teacher. In the final one, Xavier and Juana revised the ethnographic account.

During Juana's visit to his school, she had the opportunity of interviewing the head teacher who described the mentoring system the school had for new teachers. She also attended a coordination session Xavier had with the teacher of the parallel group of the same grade, and was able to see all the school facilities and observe Xavier's teaching practice. She had also access to Xavier's *Facebook* and *Twitter* profiles and the blog were he discusses educational issues. He also writes articles in a local paper and Juana had the opportunity of reviewing them.

Xavier thought of the development of his professional identity as a way of becoming the kind of teacher he would like to be. He calculated three distinctive pillars in the constitution of his professional identity. He tracked the first one as far back as his infant education. He went to a rather progressive infant school with a pedagogical project based on children's activity, desire of learning, capacity of choice and freedom. The second, after a rather unconventional educational record, was to be found in a teacher who taught him history in the baccalaureate. He located the third, in his initial professional development as a teacher in a private university of catholic background and with a reputation for promoting progressive educational views. Going to the university was not his first choice, but he managed to get the most out of his learning experience at this institution.

These three pillars of reference were shaping his idea of school: a place to develop the possibility of being in an atmosphere of freedom. Knowledge: an endless network where meaning is giving through topic work or project-based learning. Children: human beings with a high capacity to learn. Teacher: somebody eager and able to transmit knowledge and foster students' passion for learning.

However, up until now, his working experience was far from these ideals. In the first school he worked after graduation, all the teaching practice was organised through worksheets. Therefore, the room for the teacher's creativity and capacity to develop his own pedagogical ideas was very limited. Nevertheless, he found a narrow gap in one of the subjects he had to teach: Music. In the Spanish curriculum, Music in general has very little academic value and can be a good place to try out innovative teaching ideas. Xavier took advantage of this place to try out his progressive pedagogy; and the experience, in spite of the circumstances, was rather satisfactory.

During his second teaching year, he was working in the primary school where the ethnographic observation was performed. Xavier expressed many mixed-feelings about his teaching experience there. He worked only part-time, but was the teacher responsible for one of the groups, which meant he had to follow up their progress, organise parents meetings, etc. He was happy to be able to perform these important educational tasks, but had the impression that by not being able to be there the whole school day he could miss something important from his pupils. On the other hand, the school had a progressive pedagogical past, a system of welcoming new teachers that theoretically was eager to listen to their ideas, and a coordination system that, again in theory, helped new teachers to do their job better. Nonetheless, Xavier did not feel his ideas were considered and contemplated the coordination system more as a surveillance to make sure nothing changed rather than as a way of helping newcomers to become better teachers. Xavier's uneasiness was clearly shown in one of the observed lessons where he had to teach a given content in a given way with which he did not totally agree. In fact, most of the pictures Juana took from different parts of the school (always with no students) evoked in him concepts of routine, repetition and lack of meaning. The only spot in the school where he felt he belonged was the orchard. The school orchard was the only place that gave him a feeling of freedom.

Going (from and) beyond students' contexts and experiences. Amalia-Marta

Regarding Marta (Amalia), in her fifth working year and specialising in children with special educational needs (SEN), some contextual factors were relevant to the organisation of the fieldwork. When Amalia invited Marta to participate in the research she had just started maternity leave for her third child. This particular situation had important consequences for managing the research time. For instance, they needed to match the meetings to the narrow periods of time when Marta had someone to stay with the children, usually her mother or husband. These moments were usually at the end of the day for two or three hours in some place near her house, normally a local coffee shop, where she could easily walk to. Because Marta was not in the school due to the maternity leave, they agreed to divide the fieldwork into two stages. A first set of in-depth interviews about her professional career as a teacher and, once she was back in school, Amalia started the ethnographic observations followed by a second set of interviews.

Marta's participation in the research happened through several comprehensive meetings. In these meetings, the negotiation process took place and Marta spoke at length of her experience as an SEN teacher. She spoke about her experiences as school and university student, about her first teaching experience and the relations she established with her pupils. This all served to give sense to the kind of teacher she was becoming. The gaps between the meetings with Marta were filled by virtual exchanges. Thus, beyond the interviews, other kinds of research evidence gained significance: text and images that Marta was sending by e-mail. Short stories written from a reflexive position, where Marta rebuilt and shared with Amalia some critical moments in her teaching career.

Due to Marta's special circumstance the research relationship followed a particular rhythm. Perhaps when some of our colleagues have already finished the ethnographic observations we will start them at Marta's school. However, the relationship built with her through alternative places and times out of the framework of the institution seemed to make room for conversations that might not occur if the interviews had been set in her workplace. In this sense, the time and space in which we set this first stage of the fieldwork had an important role in the researcher process.

For Marta, the relationship with the students has always been the most important feature of her professional identity, of her way of learning to become the kind of teacher she would like to be. Talking in perspective about her career, her professional knowledge construction process always appears connected with the boys and girls to whom she has been linked with as an SEN teacher.

> The most important thing for me was to establish a relationship supported by a constant and very personal desire to be with them at all times, despite their difficulties and resistances to learn and to listen and respect me. Then I wonder: 'how could they not behave like this when they have no food at home, when their father arrives home drunk, or when their parents are in jail?' What I have learned sharing my time with these children is to look beyond these difficulties. To look at each and every pupil focusing in the precise moment we're together, when and where we are right now.

Learning to be a teacher, then, is, from Marta's perspective, to make every day a physical and emotional effort and, above all, to establish a constant dialogue with her.

> How do I do it? Am I doing well? Have I been sufficiently attentive to everyone?

As researchers, we wonder about the role Marta's colleagues have in the constitution of this dialogue (Padilla Petry, 2014), as Marta's reflections seem to revolve around herself and the children, "her children". She told Amalia that other points of view were important to her, that she really appreciated the possibility of sharing doubts and experiences and of finding other ways of seeing and valuing her work. However, she has not always found these opportunities.

The importance of mentoring.
Laura-Eva

Eva (Laura), in the fifth year of her teaching career, was working in a rural school, but not an isolated one because it is well connected to a big city. This school was the place where Laura carried out fieldwork for her PhD thesis, and she thought this was a relevant contextual factor. Just when we started this research, Laura had completed the fieldwork for her thesis in Eva's class. She spent three months there and the established personal bond that had important consequences for our study. They had had many conversations on their mutual interest in education before discussing her participation, and they knew each other well.

In the six-month period that Eva participated in our research, they had five meetings. These meetings were on the terrace of a bar near the school, a very pleasant place for both of them. The first time they got together in relation to this research Laura explained to Eva its focus and objectives and they negotiated the terms of her participation, the process and the work patterns. In the second, they had a long conversation in which Eva talked about her university. The third meeting was about a text Laura wrote about the content of the second meeting; they shared it and had a brief talk because they did not have enough time. The fourth was the last school day; it was an extensive dialogue about her early years as a teacher. After exchanging several texts and reflections by e-mail, in the last meeting, they discussed the final ethnographic account.

Laura had been observing Eva's class for three months; had shared her reflections about her teaching and learning experiences; and spent a day per week at her school throughout the school year. This was a magnificent starting point for easily finding the space and time needed for our research.

In this process, Eva pointed out several key situations that have contributed to the shaping of her professional identity. At first, she spoke about her initial professional development at the teacher-training college. In particular, she referred to the third year that consisted of teaching practice at school. She emphasised the crucial role of the internship mentor of the school.

> I learned to give importance to these small details I had in mind as a teacher.

Eva was convinced that the good teaching experience with this tutor had very much to do with the kind of teacher she was becoming. Eva and Laura kept talking about her initial professional development as a teacher. She referred to the subliminal nature of learning (Mlodinow, 2012) when acknowledging that there are other kinds of learning not immediately apparent but which leave an important mark along the way. For example, she referred to the importance of some university teachers she had had.

They talked about her experience in several schools (twenty in her first year). She highlighted the importance of the school where she was working for the constitution of her professional identity. It was her second year at the same school. It was a school with an innovative educational project and she was very happy because she felt she was learning a lot every day and was in the position of becoming the kind of teacher she wanted to be.

Concluding remarks and perspectives

The constitution of a professional identity is neither a linear track nor an easy process. This is why different authors have argued the need for a better understanding of the various strategies that are manifested in the teachers' accounts when negotiating their professional identities (Alsup, 2006; Clarke, 2008a, 2008b; Millar Marsh, 2003, Trent, 2009; Day and Gu, 2010). In this sense, focusing on teachers' conversations and stories and observing their teaching practice can expand our understanding of their professional identity evolution, especially if it includes the role of context in these processes of identity formation.

As argued by Phillips (2014: 11), human and learning experiences do not occur in a vacuum.

> Learning is a phenomenon that involves real people who live in real, complex social contexts from which they cannot be abstracted in any meaningful way. Difficult as it is for researchers to deal with [...] learners are contextualised. They do have a gender, a sexual orientation, a socioeconomic status, an ethnicity, a home culture; they have interests—and things that bore them; they have or have not consumed breakfast; and they live in neighbourhoods with or without frequent gun violence or earthquakes, they are attracted by (or clash with) the personality of their teacher, and so on. (Phillips, 2014: 11)

In our research, context is proving to be fundamental in order to explore the complexly interwoven and often contradictory elements embedded in the social, educational, cultural and professional context of teachers. In this endeavour, micro-ethnographic cases seem to be a powerful approach to make sense of the role of context in the constitution of the professional identity, in this case, of novice teachers.

From the five considered cases, we are able to highlight the following aspects with a positive or negative influence on the process of learning to become a teacher:

Teachers' school experiences constitute an early and essential mirror for deciding, explicitly or implicitly, the kind of teachers they are aiming to be (Rivas and Leite, 2013). It can be made up of positive (role models) or negative (something to be avoided) incidents. It seems a key element for deciding to become a teacher, or not, and the kind of teacher they would like to be.

The dominant or minority pedagogical discourses, but especially the teaching practice itself in the teacher-training colleges. Again, both what is said and what is done in the initial professional development can act as something to pursue or something to avoid.

The administrative dispositions that inform the way teachers get the first job and progress within the career ladder. A teacher in their first working year can be sent to up to twenty different schools for short substitutions; or another in their second year and working part-time, is doomed to act as the group tutor—responsible for the class. What kind of professional identities are fostering these working conditions: nomadic, liquid, subjugated, cynical, drifters ...? What will be the consequences for the future of education? (Sancho, 2014).

The inertial culture of schools that fosters teachers' individuality, heavily maintains compartmentalised timetables and curricula and traditional (teacher-centred) teaching practice. A situation that encourages colonised identities, adapted and maintainers of the structures, mechanisms and power relationships. Above all, however, it contributes to a type of learning to be a teacher, which displaces the personal demands to an irresponsible identity more focused on teaching than on learning.

Teaching is also a question of personality (a way of being). Initial education experiences, dominant discourses, administrative policies and school climate are certainly important circumstances in the learning process of being a teacher. Nevertheless, also of major relevance are the visions of the world held by individuals, their way of being, how each one places themselves in life ... and this is not something easy to learn at college ... or through school practices. This has much more to do with their social and cultural capital (Bourdieu, 1977; Hargreaves and Fullan, 2012).

In this context, teachers rather individually develop a set of strategies, tactics and abilities ranging from resistance (especially within their own classrooms), adaptation, confrontation, submission, looking for external support, attending in-service courses, undertaking post-graduate studies, etc. Using a war metaphor, we could say they use more guerrilla strategies than planned battles. In this process, the classroom can be both a battlefield and a haven of peace. In any case, what is remarkable is the fact that all participant teachers in this research pointed out the relationship with pupils as the most rewarding aspect of their job.

Acknowledgment

With the support of the Faculty of Education and the Department of Didactics and Educational Management, University of Barcelona.

References

Alsup, J. (2006) *Teacher identity discourses: Negotiating personal and professional spaces*. Mahwah, N.J.: Lawrence Erlbaum Associates.

Bauman, Z. (2005) *Liquid life*. Cambridge: Polity.

Bauman, Z. (2006) *Liquid fear*. Cambridge: Polity.

Boltanski, L., and Chiapello, E. (2005). *The new spirit of capitalism*. London-New York: Verso.

Bourdieu, P. (1977) *Outline of a theory of practice*. Cambridge: Cambridge University Press.

Castells, M. (2012) Networks of outrage and hope: social movements in the internet age. Cambridge, UK; Malden, MA: Polity Press, 2012.

Castells, M. (1996) The rise of the network society. The information age: Economy, society and culture Vol. I. Malden, MA; Oxford, UK: Blackwell.

Clandinin, D. J., and Connelly, F. M. (1995) *Teachers' professional knowledge landscapes*. New York: Teachers College Press.

Clarke, M. (2008a) *Language teacher identities. Co-constructing discourse and community*. Clevedon: Multilingual Matters.

Clarke, M. (2008b). The ethico-politics of teacher identity. *Educational Philosophy and Theory*, 40:1-16.

Day, C. and Gu, Q. (2010) *The New Lives of Teachers*. London: Taylor and Francis.

De Gee, J. (2001) Identity as an analytical lens for research in education. *Review of Research in Education*, 25:99-125.

De Souza, E. C. (2011) Acompañamiento, mediación biográfica y formación de formadores: dimensiones de investigación-formación. *Revista de Educación y Pedagogía*, 23(61):41-56.

Denzin, N. (1997) *En Interpretative Ethnography*. London: Sage Publications.

Elliott, J (2006) Educational Research as a Form of Democratic Rationality. *Journal of Philosophy of Education*, 40(2):169-185.

Fullan, M. (2007). *The new meaning of educational change*. New York : Teachers College Press. 4th ed.

Giddens, A. (1991) *Modernity and Self-identity: self and society in the late modern age*. Stanford, Calif.: Stanford University Press.

Hargreaves, A. and Fullan, M. (2012). *Professional capital: transforming teaching in every school*. New York, NY: Teachers College Press.

Jeffrey, R. A., and Troman, G. A. (2004) Time for ethnography. *British Educational Research Journal*, 30(4):535-548.

Johansen, B. (2007) *Get there early: Sensing the future to compete in the present*. San Francisco, CA: Berrett-Koehler Publishers, Inc.

Le Baron, C. (2006) Microethnography. In V. Jupp (ed.), *The Sage dictionary of social research methods* (177-179). London: Sage Publications.

Millar Marsh, M. (2003) *The social fashioning of teacher identities*. New York: Peter Lang.

Mlodinow, L. (2012) *Subliminal: How your unconscious mind rules your behaviour*. New York: Pantheon Books

Nind, M. (2014) *What in inclusive research?* London/New York: Bloomsbury Publishing.

Padilla-Petry, P. (2014) El papel de los colegas en la constitución de la identidad docente, in J. M. Sancho and F. Hernández (coord.), *Maestros al vaivén. Aprender a ser docentes en el mundo actual* (87-106). Barcelona: Octaedro.

Paris and M. T. Winn (ed) (2014) *Humanising research: Decolonising qualitative inquiry with youth and communities*. Los Angeles, CA: Sage.

Phillips, D. C. (2014) Research in the hard sciences, and in very hard 'softer' domains. *Educational Researcher*, 43(1):9-11.

Rivas, J. I. and Leite, A. (2013) Aprender la profesión desde el pupitre. *Cuadernos de Pedagogía*,436:34-37.

Sancho, J. M. (2014) Las identidades docentes en la perspectiva de 40 años. *Cuadernos de Pedagogía*, 451:48 -51.

Sancho, J. M. and F. Hernández (coord.) (2014) *Maestros al vaivén. Aprender a ser docentes en el mundo actual*. Barcelona: Octaedro.

Sarason, S.B. (1990) *The predictable failure of educational reform: can we change course before it's too late?* San Francisco: Jossey-Bass.

Sennett, R. (1998). *The corrosion of character: the personal consequences of work in the new capitalism*. New York: Norton.

Sennett, R. 2012) *Together: The rituals, pleasures, and politics of cooperation*. London: Penguin Books.

Sfard, A. and Prusak, A. (2005) Telling identities: In search of an analytic tool for investigating learning as a culturally shaped activity. *Educational Researcher*, 34(4):14-22.

Trent, J. (2009) From rigid dichotomy to measured contingency. *Teaching and Teacher Education*, 26(4):906-913.

Tuck, E. andYang, K. W. (2014) R-words: Refusing research, in D. Paris and M. T. Winn (ed), *Op. Cit.*

Chapter 6

Tales from the field: Student teachers' ups and downs during their first professional experiences

José Miguel Correa, Asunción Martínez-Arbelaiz, Estibaliz Aberasturi, Luispe Gutiérrez

Abstract

The very first encounter teachers have with the joys and sorrows of their career usually takes place during the teaching practicum, and we believe that this experience leaves an indelible trace. During their practicum, student teachers have to negotiate their rights and obligations with different stakeholders (practicum instructor, practicum supervisor, teaching colleagues, parents, pupils, etc.), and as a consequence, they go through a great deal of emotional turmoil. As part of their required work for their teaching degree, student teachers posted a problem or a real case that they were experiencing during the practicum in an online forum. We observed through the resulting narratives that student teachers fight to integrate what they experience with their previous ideas of the ideal teacher. The discourse generated in the forum is analysed against the *Communities of Practice theory* (Lave and Wenger, 1991). We contrast two opposing cases: a student teacher who could not integrate her identity as a caring, passionate person with her idea of what a teacher should be, and a second case where a student managed to successfully integrate her membership in another community of practice, that of sign language users, with her teaching identity.

Introduction

The main aim of our research project, *The construction of the professional identity of pre-school teachers during initial training and the first years at work*[1] is to describe, examine and interpret the ideas, reflections and experiences that go into the construction of professional identity by primary and pre-primary school teachers, especially those in the initial training period and their first few years as a teacher. Our research intends to link personal issues to cultural and social issues in order to build ways of understanding how new teachers build their sense of being

1. This chapter is part of the larger project, *The constriction of the professional identity of pre-school teachers during initial training and the first years at work* (MICINN-EDU2010-20852-C02-02).

and consequently put into practice improvements in education. As part of this project, we asked students in the teacher education programme, where several authors of this chapter work as faculty members, to post a pedagogical problem or a remarkable experience that wanted to share with the group. These postings are a mandatory task within the practicum and they were intended to minimise the feelings of isolation that student teachers usually go through in their first teaching duties and obligations. The participation in the forums acted as an electronic umbilical cord with the School of Education, i.e. with their professors and their peers who were in similar situations but in different schools.[2]

The student teachers were asked to reflect on a situation they considered to be a critical incident (Shapira-Lishchinsky, 2011). They had to narrate this critical incident in an interactive manner, as the rest of the members of the group had to react to these postings. The faculty member in charge of the group could participate in the forums but he did not have to lead the discussion. On the contrary, it was the student teacher the one who had to open, lead and close the discussion. With these simple instructions we triggered a number of narratives that vividly describe how student teachers often struggle to make sense of what they observe in their schools. This 'making sense' has be coherent not only with their previous ideas of what the ideal or imagined teacher has to do but also with their inner self or what have been called the core qualities of the teacher (Korthagen, 2004). This process is not an easy one, particularly when students are on the verge of becoming teachers, or what can be considered a liminal situation or space (Stroud and Wee, 2007).

In this chapter, we analyse two particular cases as described by student teachers and negotiated in a group through the lens of the *Communities of Practice theory* (CoP) (Lave and Wenger, 1991; Wenger, 1998)[3]. In the first case, the student teacher struggled to fully integrate her identity as a caring, passionate

---

2. A more detailed description of the impact of the forums in the practicum and its evolution through a series of academic years in can be found inMartínez-Arbelaiz, Gutierrez Cuenca, Jimenez de Aberasturi, Correa Gorospe and Ibañez Etxeberria (2008).
3. Unlike other academic experiences (Sim, 2006), we did not design the practicum with the model of *Communities of Practice* in mind. After the narratives from the student teachers had been collected, we decided to analyse them against this particular heuristic. We agree with Eckert and McConnell-Ginnet (1998:491) when they say '[t]he community of practice is where the rubber meets the road—it is where observable practice and interaction do the work of producing, reproducing, and resisting the organisation of power in society'.

person with her notion of a 'professional' teacher. In the second case, however, the student teacher successfully managed to blend her membership in another community of practice, that of sign language users, with her teaching identity.

Identity and communities of practice

Chris Weedon (1997) has often been cited as the first scholar who 'deconstructed' the concept of identity, proposing in a post-modern manner 'a subjectivity which is precarious, contradictory and in process, constantly being reconstituted in discourse each time we think or speak' (Weedon, 1997:32). While Weedon talks of 'subjectivities', her definition maps well onto the current ideas regarding identity in the social sciences, namely, the view that identity is not fixed but rather is in constant evolution and going through multiple—and sometimes painful—contradictions. Another key concept in Weedon's definition of identity or subjectivity is 'discourse', which is defined by Blommaert (2005) as follows: '[d]iscourse comprises all forms of meaningful semiotic human activity seen in connection with social, cultural, and historical patterns and developments of use'. The advantage of this definition is that it allows multimodality. In other words, discourse not only comprises language—although without doubt this form of discourse has a pre-emptive position in the research on identity—but also other forms of communication such as painting, drawing, photography, video, and other media.

In her influential work on how gender identity develops, Butler (2004) argues that gendered selves are not determined by nature or by nurture. Rather, a given gendered identity is the consequence of day-to-day 'acting' in ways normatively defined as masculine or feminine. Expanding this idea to identity in general, we can state that a given identity is the set of bodily and linguistic enactments—or performances—of discourses at particular times and particular places.

A crucial aspect to understanding these performances or enactments is the concept of communities of practice (CoP) (Lave and Wenger, 1991; Wenger, 1998), since the actual performances we observe will be in alignment or misalignment with what a given community of practice establishes as its norms. DePalma (2009) points to the fact that previous examples of this model have been relatively simplistic, closed, and reproductive systems, such as the claim processor company, Alinsu, which Wenger (1998) describes in his book. In fact this model has received some criticisms for being a social reproductive system where 'opportunities for co-constructing linguistic symbols and resisting power seem overshadowed by the so-called mutual focus on, quite literally, business as usual' (p. 354). Nevertheless, without denying the reproductive potential of this model, DePalma underscores its transformative power that can be ingrained in some CoPs by describing the No Outsiders project, whose purpose is to challenge heteronormativity and homophobia in primary schools. By applying the CoP model to a social activism project DePalma points 'the way toward the possibility of learning and practice communities that are more transformative and less reproductive' (p. 354). We, together with other researchers in education, embrace the metaphor of CoP as a powerful research lens to unveil legitimised power relations that affect the participation or non-participation of new members of a given social group. In addition we adopt a postmodern (Sumsion, 2005; Clarke, 2003) definition of identity, for our educational research purposes.

In summary, CoPs correspond to the different positions, performances or enactments individuals adopt on a moment-to-moment and day-to-day basis, and indeed throughout their lifetimes. Individuals gain entry to a CoP by means of 'legitimate peripheral participation'. The concept of peripheral participation is crucial since it entails that we learn by practice but without being subject to the demands of full membership in the initial phase of a given membership. This peripheral participation is achieved via exposure to 'mutual engagement with other members, to their actions and their negotiation of the enterprise, and to their repertoire in use' (Wenger, 1998:100). In the case of student teachers doing their practicum, they are clearly given the permission to legitimate peripheral participation. They learn by observing the practicum instructor in action, by giving little teaching tasks, but they are not given the responsibility of the group of students.

While identity is conditioned by social interaction and social structure, at the same time it also conditions social interaction and social structure. Thus, interaction is crucial since it is constitutive and constituted by the social context. This is the two-way action commonly described in the work of sociologists such as Bourdieu (1977) and Giddens (1995). A given practice, that is, one way of being or acting, becomes the norm or is constitutive of a given community when fellow members of the community accept the symbolic behaviour of an individual as appropriate and real. This process is often called 'authentication'. Teachers form their CoP like any other social group, and each group has a way of behaving that is constitutive of membership in a given CoP.

We follow authors such as Wenger (1998), Gergen (1992), Burr (1995) and Kincheloe (2001) when dealing with the study of identity by analysing it from multiple perspectives, which entails change, co-construction, contextualisation and limitation. In the same fashion, the identity of future teachers is developed through their experiences in the school, that is, in the context of learning where they are exposed to the regulatory socio-political rules, with its cultures and tasks, whether implicit or explicit. In this way, the practicum experience contributes directly to the building of the teachers' identity.

In this chapter we observe the ups and downs of student teachers on their way to becoming fully participating teachers. Some core features of the student teachers' identities are in alignment with the CoP of teachers, while other features are in clear conflict, forcing the student teachers to create third spaces or arrive at a bearable hybridity.

Communities of practice and research in education

Grounded in the notion of community of practice, a number of studies have observed the complex path, crucially including conflicts and resistances, of certain new-comers that try to access a given CoP. In the field of language education, several projects have found this model of CoP useful. Morita (2004), for example, examines how six graduate students from Japan, whose native language was not English, socialised in order to become legitimate members of the academic community of a North American university. The study demonstrated that the students struggled to negotiate their competence in the second language and their identities. Their silences in class were given new meanings, unveiling power relations that could eventually block full participation.

Warriner (2009) observes that adult learners of English adopted the practices of one CoP, the language school, but that they remained excluded from legitimate membership in other CoP, which roughly corresponded to the job market. Also in the field of second language acquisition, Norton (2001) and Kanno and Norton (2003) highlight the importance of the imagination in the Wengerian sense, to explain how individuals create a community they desire to belong to and how this can be a moving force for their learning endeavours. The relevance of imagination is also crucial in Pavlenko's (2003) work who adds that non-native speakers of English can choose between seeing oneself as either peripheral members of the 'English Teachers' community or as legitimate multicompetent members of a larger imagined community. This choice is likely to affect how they engage with learning opportunities in the classroom. Finally, the relation between identity and practice is the object of research in Kanno and Stuart (2011), who follow two novice teachers of English in their first year of teaching, unveiling the inextricable relation of identity and classroom practice.

Moving to the field of Teacher Education, Yandell and Turvey (2007) interviewed two newly qualified teachers analysing their experiences against the CoP model. They underscore the complex role of the teachers' subjectivity and larger power structures such as the schools where they start their teaching. Woodgate-Jones (2012) equates a given school where student teachers do their practicum with a CoP that resists or welcomes the newcomers to different degrees. By interviewing the old-time teachers, the students and the families involved, Woodgate-Jones finds that in principle the CoP is open to new ideas and changes that the student teachers can bring about, but that there are serious limitations for those innovations to actually take place. She further recommends that the schools should be open to the innovations that student teachers can trigger when she concludes that '[t]hose COPs (and old-timers) that recognise this [that legitimate peripheral participants can be considered skilled newcomers in some respects] and respect the knowledge/skills of the student teacher allowing them to make a contribution will benefit more than those that do not' (p. 158).

Finally, in Correa, Martínez-Arbelaiz and Gutierrez (20014) we discussed the conflicts and dilemmas that student teachers experience in reconciling the pressure they feel to conform to the teaching practices and become a full member of their corresponding CoP with their drive for innovation and transformation. Using the same narrative methodology that will be explained in the next section, we concluded that student teachers mentioned changes they could implement in their schools, but at the same time they also felt the pressure to align themselves to already established and legitimised practices (Tyack and Tobin, 1994).

Methodological perspective

The methodological perspective adopted in this research study is a narrative one. As suggested by Flick (2004), Denzin and Lincoln (2005), or more specifically by Gubrium and Holstein (2008), when talking about narrative and ethnographic research, the use of different strategies to collect multiple data is an appropriate way of solving problems raised in the study. A particular focus is also required in the places where events take place and for the conditions and the resources of the narrative process.

Following Connelly and Clandinin (1988), MacLure (1993), Alsup (2006), Clandinin et al. (2006) and Cohen (2010), we assume that research on teachers' narratives can bring to light reflexive and analytic processes that help build the teaching identity. Teachers, and people in general, assign meaning to what has happened, integrating what is going on into one or various stories. Within these stories we have identified key passages (Clandinin and Connelly, 1996) and we have interpreted these key moments as constitutive of the participants' teaching identity.

Nine student teachers took part in our research project, and from this pool two cases will be discussed as exemplary illustrations of the two extremes in the trajectory of becoming a teacher. Although the nine threads or topics that each student narrated and shared with the group were amenable to analysis and elaboration, we followed Polkinghorne´s (2005: 140) 'purposive selection' and chose two student teachers and their respective critical incident. According to Polkinghorne, '[t]he purposive selection of data sources involves choosing people or documents from which the researcher can substantially learn about the experience.' Thus, the data collected in this study came primarily from two on-line postings. The six students and the practicum supervisors participated through asking questions and commenting on the case being discussed. The relevance and meaning of the cases presented here was evaluated by the research team, who assessed their resonance (Conle, 1996) and coherence within the theoretical framework by Lave and Wenger (1991) and Wenger (1998). This phase required the research team to interpret and reconstruct the student teachers' meaningful experiences, as told in their narratives. We should not forget that to narrate is a form of investigation (Clandinin and Connelly, 2000); it is not just a form of representation, rather it is a form of searching (Conle, 2000).

In the six-week period of the practicum, students took part in several face-to-face discussions with the practicum supervisor[4] and when they were assigned to their corresponding schools, they took part in an on-line forum in groups of six student teachers. Each participant had to open the discussion by posting a critical incident they had experienced, and the rest of the students were required to respond. Thus, each participant had to lead a discussion on a critical incident and participate in the other five discussions. Students were provided with a calendar so that they knew when they were required to post their critical incident, as well as with a model of a critical incident and guidelines on how to take part in the discussion.

4. We use the labels 'student teachers' and 'future teachers' to refer to the participants in this study. We will refer to the university faculty member that is in charge of coordinating the student teaching as 'practicum supervisor' and also as 'researcher'. The person that oversees the student teaching at the school is the 'practicum instructor'.

The practicum supervisor recommended that the posting on the critical incident be six-hundred words long and that the replies to the initial posting by the rest of the group members be around two-hundred words. He also participated by commenting on the critical incidents. The forum was open for a week. The first critical incident selected, which dealt with a personal dilemma generated the five required comments (one by each students) and also a comment by the practicum supervisor. In addition, this posting generated three unsolicited comments. In the second critical incident regarding a child with hearing impairment, the five students and the practicum supervisor posted one message each. These postings were followed by two more messages from the supervisor and another student. In addition, after deadline had passed, the student in charge of leading the forum discussion summarised the conclusions in a two-hunudred and fifty word text.

This pedagogical intervention is reminiscent of case-based pedagogy, which has been advocated by some teacher educators (Harrington, Quinn-Leering and Hodson, 1996; Hsu, 2004). The main difference between this approach and the one described here is that in the two mentioned references the actual case studies came from a textbook or were presented by the professor. In contrast, in our project, the student teachers were living and narrating the experiences in the schools. This made the discussion not only relevant to the members of the group, but also realistic.

We decided to share a definition of critical incidents (Flanagan, 1954) with the student teachers. Critical incidents were defined as those events in our professional practice that cause perplexity, doubts, surprise or that have bothered or worried us because they lack coherence or they are unexpected. Critical incidents are events from daily life that impact us or surprise us and thus trigger reflection. They do not necessarily involve extreme consequences or risk of death. Denzin (1989) considers them to be interactive moments that constitute a turning point. Returning to teachers, for Kelchtermans (1994) a narrated event is a critical incident because that is how the teacher perceives it. The practicum is a foundational period for teachers, who are particularly sensitive to the situations of conflict where they are required to act and make quick decisions.

As we show in the following sections, the analysis of the two student teachers' critical incidents allows us to explore the meaning that the student teachers give to their work in the schools and how they incorporate or reject the pedagogical routines they see. The mixed emotions that these student teachers bring up have a relevant place in these narratives.

Tales from the field

Leyre's dilemma

We focus our attention on Leyre,[5] one of the student teachers in the discussion group who, like the other members, was about to obtain her teaching degree. As mentioned earlier, the data collection process involved several face-to-face meetings with one of the researchers, either one-to-one or in a group. The student was interviewed and the meaning of her critical incident was explored, shared and reviewed different times.

In this particular case, the opportunity to discuss the critical incident with Leyre face-to-face in a very detailed manner was not programmed in the research study. It came about when she paid a visit to the office of one of the researchers, who happened to be also her university practicum supervisor. In this meeting she clarified the incident to the professor and researcher. Later, in the forum, Leyre agreed to discuss the same critical incident and began by describing what had happened in playground of the school where she was doing her practicum. This school is a state school in the outskirts of Bilbao, a large city in the Basque Country, Spain, that had pupils of different ethnic groups, some of them of Gypsy or Romani ethnicity. The incident is summed up in the following lines.

What Leyre told us face to face and described later in the forum was that she witnessed a brawl between two Romani children, because one of them was swearing. The student teacher thought that she could separate the two children but was unable to do so. She ended up protecting the child she believed to be the most vulnerable, inevitably taking sides. This incident brought her into a crisis and made her question her identity as a teacher. This conflict made her feel divided between emotion and rationality, between a caring climate and a formal climate (Shapira-Lishchinsky. 2011):

> That was when I felt myself come into conflict. What should I do? I looked at the other teachers, looking for a clue as to how to act, but they didn't look at me. Meanwhile, I used my arm to protect Sara, but only half-heartedly. What was wrong with me? I don't have a problem with showing affection in front of others. I now think that I realised how

5. All the names have been changed to ensure participants' anonymity.

> many different variables where going through my head at that moment: What will the more experienced teachers think of me if I get too close? What will happen to Sara if her fellow pupils see an adult protecting her? Should we give a cold and distant impression or should we take into account the needs of the student teacher? As you can see, I was swamped with doubt.
>
> Student Teacher Leyre

In this narrative, Leyre debates between what she wants to do, that is, hug the girl, and what she thinks the ideal teacher should do. She debates whether showing her emotions is appropriate or coherent with her image of a 'professional' or an old-time teacher. Being in the school yard, she is also worried about her public image (Goffman, 1959), and whether her teaching career could be ruined for having been seen by the old-timers to show affection to the children. She is granted legitimate peripheral participation in the school, which means that she is allow to interact with the children, but she is definitely not a full member of the CoP. That is why she observes at the old-timers to see what the appropriate behaviour is in the particular situation.

Following Wenger's definition, a type of identity is the connection between or at the junction of different memberships. The student teacher sees herself as an affectionate person, but this subjectivity goes against her future teacher membership in the school community. In her image of the professional identity there is a belief that a teacher should be distant, and this belief is backed up when she looks at the other teachers on the playground. Leyre looks at the old-timers in this particular CoP and sees that they are not reacting to the situation. She tries to reconcile her two identities, that of the distant teacher as per her preconceived belief of what a teacher should be, and her affectionate self. Her emergent teacher identity requires that she add boundaries to her display of emotions.

In the middle of this reflection Leyre realises that her affection has to have a limit. At university she has learned that showing her emotions is something positive, but this clashes with what she sees on the playground. She observes that the old-timers, the more experienced teachers who she considers to be her models, do not show their emotions. Leyre thus negotiates the conflict by drawing boundaries. This critical incident involves a reflection on Leyre's code of conduct, since it has to be genuine and credible (Bucholtz, 2003) for the CoP where she is discussing and assigning meaning to the incident.

When the initial mandatory round of postings is over, Leyre, in a new posting, claims a utopian identity for herself and for her future CoP. This reminds us of the concept of imagined communities, echoing recent research in the field of language acquisition reviewed in the introduction. In this respect, Norton (2000) has shown how the way immigrants view their identity as language users can have a clear impact on their degree of participation in the host community. Similarly Pavlenko (2003), reveals how international graduate students' self-perception as either incompetent non-native speakers of English or as multicompetent, bilingual or multilingual speakers can make a difference. Through her classroom intervention, Pavlenko plays an important role in 'shaping the student's memberships in imagined communities and legitimising new identity options' (p. 266). These two studies underscore the fact that the imagination is a very powerful tool in second language pedagogies, as well as in teacher education. According to Wenger (1998: 272) if the purpose of education is to give the students 'a sense of the possible trajectories available in various communities, then education must involve imagination in a central way'. What Leyre posted in her closing message is clearly linked to future trajectories and an imagined teaching identity. In her message she reminds the group that new teachers have the potential to change the actual school, implying that emotions should be an integral part of the school.

> Without a doubt I know that I am very idealistic when it comes to what working at a school should involve, but shouldn't all teachers and future teachers be idealistic and utopian in order to make the school a better place? A place where children feel protected, safe and free to be themselves?
>
> Student Teacher Leyre

Summarising this first case, we observe how Leyre moves from describing an internal conflict to its resolution by drawing invisible limits on her display of affection. We know that one of the forms of identity construction comes from finding ourselves at the limit. As Bernstein and Solomon (1999: 273) frame it, '[t]here is always a boundary. It may vary in its explicitness, its visibility, its potential and in the manner of transmission and acquisition.' Leyre reflects on her own reactions, as well as on the old-timers' reactions, which are crucially in conflict. Her reaction is to attempt to put limits to her display of emotions and find a state of harmony with herself. After her struggle, nevertheless, with the support of the teacher supervisor and her peers, she emerges from the initial dilemma feeling empowered and cognizant of her idealistic and utopian self. Her last rhetorical question, 'Shouldn't all teachers and future teachers be idealistic and utopian in order to make the school a better place?' points to a different imagined scenario where she does not feel refrained by the old-timers, as in the incident reported.

Blanca's expert voice

Blanca narrates the second critical incident, which starts with the description of a particular child in her school. Two features are selected to describe this child, his Romani background and his hearing impairment. Although the first feature selected is not mentioned in the critical incident, it is in the background of the student teachers' discourse. What is relevant in the present forum discussion, is that the roles are reversed. In this sense, the expert, the old-timer, is no longer the practicum supervisor, nor the practicum instructor. In this particular forum the leading student is the expert of a new CoP where the practicum supervisor or the other students do not happen to belong. The new CoP that we are referring to is the community of hearing impaired people.

In the case we discuss in the following lines, the student teacher Blanca identifies herself as an expert in sign language. She feels so sure that she dares to correct the other students in the forum and even the practicum supervisor, Begoña, on the correct way of designating sign language, as can be seen in the following excerpt:

> Regarding the use or lack of sign language, which is not sign speech Begoña you ask who he will be able to communicate with during the time that he is far away from the school environment using the sign language. Well, with other deaf people he will end up sooner or later getting together with. We all need to socialise with others and from my experience; I can tell you that deaf people look for deaf people's company. Being among them or with listening people you would use the sign language and then they feel totally integrated, where they have access to information and they take part in a conversation. They feel they belong to the group.
>
> Student Teacher Blanca

She makes reference to her experience with deaf people and goes on with a long posting where she describes her previous work with families with one or several deaf members. She displays wide and precise knowledge on the topic of cochlear implants, as well as on the different functions of sign language in the lives of these students. In this sense, Blanca can build a useful bridge between the two CoPs she belongs to. She has a membership in the CoP of the hearing impaired, as well as in the CoP of the school where she is doing her practicum. Using Wenger's terms, we can characterise the link between these two CoPs as a case of brokering. For Niesz (2010), belonging to different CoPs and reconciliation are prerequisites for brokering to take place.

Through her narrative, Blanca connects the two CoPs in a very productive and instructive way for the other five student teachers in the forum. Perhaps more interestingly, these postings are also very productive for the practicum supervisor. As Kwan and Lopez-Real (2010) point out, very often the practicum supervisors are the ones who learn from the student teachers. In this particular case, it seems that the topic of hearing impairment is not a familiar one for the practicum supervisors. The following excerpt from one of the practicum supervisors and researchers publicly acknowledges this gap and the benefits of bringing up such a topic, not only for schools but also for the university community:

> I know it is a very different context (the university) from compulsory education schools, but they have been useful for reflecting on the communicative context, the exchange of expectations and the complexities of the teaching-learning process, not only for these people but also for the teachers and students who know and participate in the classrooms with deaf people. Practicum Supervisor

In this sense, the roles are subverted, since the practicum supervisor is the novice who is not familiar with the practices of the particular CoP of hearing impaired individuals that the student teaches brings up. In this particular case, the student teacher plays the role of the teacher, the one in possession of the relevant and valuable knowledge for the practices of this community. In her summarising message, Blanca gives more details on her personal involvement in this CoP:

> What a boring and long speech I gave you! But as I told you at the beginning, this topic interests me and really fills me with satisfaction, I know a lot of deaf people and I have been through extraordinary situations with them, even surrealistic ones and I could not help freeing myself, although I do not know if I have made myself clear.

> At these moments I would like to get together in person and talk about all the questions and problems that we have raised. Bye Bye
> Student Teacher Blanca

With her comment, Blanca asserts that she has gained competence through experience, underscoring the idea that learning to be a teacher cannot be separated from all the other aspects of our lives; instead, it has to be an integral part of who we are and how we live. In addition, the virtual CoP that has just been established, together with the reflexive dialogue generated among its members, acts as emotional support and a place of resistance where future teachers can build and negotiate their identities together. It is through this discourse that initial resistances and reconciliations become apparent. In Blanca's case, she is a full member of a CoP that is not shared by the other student teachers nor by the practicum supervisor. Thus, instead of feeling that she is only allowed legitimate peripheral participation in the school, by concentrating in the CoP of the hearing impaired, she positions herself as a full participant and at the same time, by correcting the other group participants, she is telling them that they are not members of that CoP.

The postings in this forum, then afford a space for emotional support, where student teachers can manage the different and, as in the case just discussed, complementary aspects of their identities more broadly and their teaching identities in particular. In addition, we have observed that through these interactions student teachers can create and build upon strategies to actively participate in the different social contexts related to the schools, such as the CoP of the sign language users.

Conclusions

The theoretical construct of CoPs and the related construct of legitimate peripheral participation have been useful in analysing the collectively constructed student teachers' narratives in the forum. The narratives, as expected, revolved around critical incidents that the student teachers experienced while doing their teaching practicums. The perspective gained through CoP theory has allowed us to unveil roles, attitudes and reactions in the students' trajectory towards full participation. Specifically, this analysis has revealed the emotional difficulties and internal contradictions that student teachers go through and have to overcome in order to become a legitimate member of a teaching community. In addition, we have shown that certain previous identities, such as Blanca's membership in the hearing impaired community, can have a positive and unexpected impact on this trajectory.

This research highlights the emotional turmoil student teachers go through primarily because of their peripherality, as well as the means and strategies they must display so that this peripheral participation does not lead to disappointment regarding their teaching roles. Practicum supervisors and instructors have to be aware of this and should not forget that student teachers have other identities and are members of other CoPs, and that novice teachers have to reconcile several memberships. As Wenger (1998:159) states, 'identity should be viewed as a nexus of multi-memberships.' In this sense, we have documented how Leyre struggles to find a nexus between her two roles: her caring, affectionate self and the 'professional' teacher she aims to be. In Blanca's case, however, the nexus is easily established, since being an expert or a full member in the CoP of the hearing impaired does not conflict with the school community. This is a case of successful brokering, since Blanca can bring concepts, information, and knowledge from one CoP to the other, the school where she is doing her teaching practicum. Blanca happens to be more expert than the practicum supervisor or the practicum instructor.

Returning to the case of Leyre, we saw how tensions were caused by uncertainties in the socially accepted teaching behaviour, when there was discrepancy in how to solve emotional problems. Her perception of the facial expressions of the more experienced teachers and their lack of affection toward the unprotected child triggered an internal dilemma regarding how to behave. The shared reflection with other students through the online forum helps to assign meaning to Leyre's experience. In this fashion, student teachers build their own teaching narrative collaboratively, analysing their peripheral participation in the schools and establishing a moral self, with their negotiated rights and duties. In this co-participation (Niesz, 2010), a new interpretative structure that must be coherent with the new CoP, the schools where each student teacher is assigned, is generated.

Another conclusion of this study is that practicum supervisors play a very delicate role in guiding student teachers' along their learning trajectory, mediating between the university and the school. In general, they are considered experts by virtue of belonging to the university CoP, and as such, they are vested with power by the institution (Bourdieu, 1985), although their discourse is not in line with that of the experienced teachers (the old-timers) or the practicum instructor. They have the difficult task of finding the middle point between utopia and reality, between innovation and the limits imposed by the school. This research unveils the difficulty and responsibility that practicum instructors have as mediators between the university CoP and particular schools.

Finally, this research emphasises the importance of narrative work. Narratives become an element that generates meaning; they facilitate reflection, and they constitute a stage for sharing and negotiating the meanings of experiences. While describing and discussing their critical incidents, the student teachers analysed their participation in the school and created spaces to portray an imagined teaching practice. This created a support system and established moral guidelines and accountability, and it also established a good reputation that needed to be maintained in subsequent interactions, whether face-to-face or through other forums.

Tabachnick (1980) has already observed that the practicum is probably the most valuable experience future teachers go through before being in full control of a class. The conflicts that were discussed and the multiple memberships that had to be reconciled—the need to limit emotions, the integration of children with special needs for instance—are issues that these student teachers will be address and negotiate in the CoPs where they will accumulate experiences in the future. The road towards full participation in the CoP is a long and bumpy one, but as Yandell and Turvey (2007) show, it is not only student teachers who have difficulty gaining full access to the community; newly qualified teachers struggle as well. Nevertheless, according to Yandell and Turvey, 'there is a world of difference between the roles occupied by student teachers (...) and what is expected of even the newest of newly qualified teachers. (p. 547). We believe that the student teachers that shared the rich critical incidents with us have become aware of the difficulties and complexities inherent to teaching. They have also reflected on their own identities and we agree with Beauchamp and Thomas (2009) when they say that '[w]hile it is clear to us that further identity development will take place in actual practice later on, a teacher education programme seems to be the ideal starting point for instilling not only an awareness of the need to develop an identity, but also a strong sense of the ongoing shifts that will occur in that identity' (p. 186). Teacher education programmes should make an effort in enhancing interactive reflection on teaching identity while student teachers are doing their practicum. The experience reported here has been an attempt to promote this type of reflection.

We cannot end without emphasising the performative power of narratives. The actual task of narrating a personal experience or a critical incident is an opportunity not only to reflect on students' practice but, more importantly, to facilitate discourse that offers a window on making the process of identity construction explicit. To narrate is to accept that we are narrating for others, and this dialogue inevitably weaves together multiple perspectives. In this chapter we have seen that joint narration of the critical incidents through the forums offers the opportunity to tap into the ups and downs that future teachers go through in a shared and negotiated manner with other student teachers, university profess ors and researchers.

Acknowledgments

We are grateful to Wendy Baldwin for her impeccable work of translating this text into English. We could not have a more careful reader who pointed to inconsistencies and areas that needed clarification.

References

Alsup, J. (2006) *Teacher identity discourse: Negotiating personal and professional spaces.* Mahwah, NJ: Lawrence Erlbaum Associates.

Beauchamp, C. and Thomas, L. (2009) Understanding teacher identity: an overview of issues in the literature and implications for teacher education. *Cambridge Journal of Education,* 39(2): 175-189.

Bernstein, B. and Solomon, J. (1999) Pedagogy, Identity and the Construction of a Theory of Symbolic Control. *British Journal of Sociology of Education,* 2(2): 265-79.

Bloommaert, J. (2005) *Discourse: a critical introduction.* New York: Cambridge University Press: New York .

Bourdieu, P. (1977) *Outline of a Theory of Practice.* Cambridge: Cambridge University Press: Cambridge. .

Bourdieu, P. (1985) *¿Qué significa hablar? Economía de los intercambios lingüísticos.* Madrid: Akal, DL.

Bucholtz, M. (2003) Sociolinguistic nostalgia and authentication of identity. *Journal of Sociolinguistics,* 7(3): 398-416.

Burr, V. (1995) *An introduction to social constructionism.* London: Routledge.

Butler, J. (2004) *Undoing gender.* New York: Routledge.

Clandinin, D. J. and Connelly, F. M. (1996) Teachers' professional knowledge landscapes: Teacher stories–stories of teachers–school stories–stories of schools. *Educational Researcher,* 25(3): 24 -30.

Clandinin, D. J. and Connelly, F. M. (2000). *Narrative inquiry: Experience and story in qualitative research.* San Francisco: Jossey-Bass.

Clandinin, D. J., Huber, J., Huber, M. and Murphy, M. S. (2006) *Composing diverse identities. Narrative inquiries into the interwoven lives of children and teachers.* New York: Routledge.

Clarke, A. (2003) Situational Analyses: Grounded Theory Mapping after the Postmodern Turn. *Symbolic Interaction,* 26(4): 553-576. .

Clarke, L. (2009) The POD model: Using communities of practice theory to conceptualise student teachers' professional learning online. *Computers and Education,* 52: 521-529.

Cohen, J. L. (2010) Getting recognised: Teachers negotiating professional identities as learners through talk. *Teaching and Teacher Education,* 26: 473-481.

Conle, C. (1996) Resonance in pre-service teacher inquiry. *American Educational Research Journal,* 33(2): 297-325.

Conle, C. (2000) Narrative Inquiry: Research tool and medium for professional development. *European Journal of Teacher Education,* 23(1): 49-63.

Connelly, F. M. and Clandinin, D. J. (1988) *Teachers as curriculum planners: Narratives of experience.* New York: Teachers College Press.

Correa, J. M., Martínez-Arbelaiz, A. and Gutierrez, L. P. (2014). Between the real school and the ideal school: another step in building a teaching identity. *Educational Review,* 66*(*4): 447-464. .

Denzin, N. K. and Lincoln, Y. S. (2005) *The Sage handbook of qualitative research. Third edition.* Thousand Oaks: Sage Publications, Inc. .

Denzin, N. K. (1989) *Interpretative biography.* Newbury Park, CA: Sage University Press. .

DePalma, R. (2009) Leaving Alinsu: Towards a transformative community of practice. *Mind, Culture, and Activity,* 16: 353-370.

Eckert, P. and McConnell-Ginnet, S. (1998) Communities of practice: Where language, gender and power all live, in J. Coates (Ed.), *Language and gender: A reader* (484-494). Oxford, UK: Blackwell.

Flanagan, J. C. (1954) The critical incident technique. *Psychological Bulletin,* 51(4): 327-358.

Flick, U. (2004) *Introducción a la investigación cualitativa,* Madrid: Ediciones Morata. .

Gergen, K. (1992) *El yo saturado. Dilemas de identidad en el mundo contemporánea.* Barcelona: Paidós.

Gergen, K. (2007) *Construccionismo social,* Bogotá: Ediciones Uniandes. .

Giddens, A. (1995) *Modernidad e identidad del yo: el yo y la sociedad en la época contemporánea.* Barcelona: Península.

Goffman, E. (1959) *The presentation of self in everyday life,* Garden City, NY: Doubleday/ Anchor Books.

Gubrium, J. and Holstein, J. (2008) *Narrative Ethnography*, in S. Hesse-Biber and P. Leavy (Eds.). *Handbook of Emergent Methods*, New York: The Guilford Press. .

Harrington, H. L., Quinn-Leering, K. and Hodson, L. (1996) Written case analysis and critical reflection. *Teaching and Teacher Education*, 12(1): 25-37.

Hsu, S. (2004) Using case discussion on the web to develop student teacher problem solving skills. *Teaching and Teacher Education,* 20: 681-692.

Kanno, Y. and Stuart, C. (2011) Learning to become a second language teacher: Identities-in-practice. *The Modern Language Journal,* 95.

Kanno, Y. and Norton, B. (2003) Imagined communities and educational possibilities: Introduction. *Journal of Language, Identity, and Education,* 2(4): 241-249.

Kelchtermans, G. (1994) Biographical methods in the study of teachers' professional development, in I. Carlgren, G. Handal, and S. Vaage (Eds.), *Teachers' minds and actions: Research on teachers' thinking and practice* (93-108). London: The Falmer Press.

Kincheloe, J. (2001) *Hacia una revisión crítica del pensamiento docente.* Barcelona: Octaedro.

Korthagen, F. A. J. (2004) In search of the essence of a good teacher: towards a more holistic approach in teacher education. *Teaching and Teacher Education,* 20(1): 77-97.

Kwan, T. and Lopez-Real, F. (2010) Identity formation of teacher-mentors: An analysis of contrasting experiences using a Wengerian matrix framework. *Teaching and Teacher Education,* 26: 722-731.

Lave, J. and Wenger, E. (1991) *Situated learning: Legitimate peripheral participation.* Cambridge: Cambridge University Press.

Martínez-Arbelaiz, A., Gutierrez Cuenca, L. P., Jimenez de Aberasturi, E., Correa Gorospe, J. M. and Ibañez Etxeberria, A. (2008) ICT in Teacher education: Designing a practicum for reflection and inquiry, in K. McFerrin, R. Weber, R. Carlsen and D. A. Willis (eds.), *Proceedings of the Society for Information Technology and Teacher Education International Conference 2008.* Chesapeake, VA: AACE, 3341-3346.

MacLure, M. (1993) Arguing for yourself: identity as an organising principle in teacher's jobs and lives. *British Educational Research Journal,* 19(4): 311-322.

Morita, N. (2004) Negotiating participation and identity in second language academic communities, TESOL Quarterly, 38(4): 573-603.

Niesz, T (2010) Chasms and bridges: Generativity in the space between educators, *Teaching and teacher education,* 26: 37-44.

Norton, B. (2000) *Identity and Language Learning*, London: Longman.

Norton, B. (2001) Non-participation, imagined communities, and the language classroom, in M. Breen (ed.), Learner contributions to language learning: New directions in research, London: Pearson Education Limited, 159-171.

Pavlenko, A. (2003) I never knew I was bilingual. Reimagining teacher identities in TESOL. *Journal of Language, Identity, and Education,* 2(4):251-268.

Polkinghorne, D. E. (2005) Language and meaning: Data collection in qualitative research, *Journal of Counseling Psychology,* 52(2): 137-145.

Sim, C. (2006) Preparing for professional experiences –incorporating pre-service teachers as 'communities of practice'. *Teaching and Teacher Education,* 22: 77-83.

Shapira-Lishchinsky, O. (2011) Teachers' critical incidents: Ethical dilemmas in teaching practice. *Teaching and Teacher Education*, 27: 648-656.

Stroud, C. and L. Wee (2007) A pedagogical application of liminalities in social positioning: Identity and literacy in Singapore, *TESOL Quarterly,* 4(1): 33-54.

Sumsion. J. (2005) Putting postmodern theories into practice in early childhood teacher education. *Advances in Early Education and Day Care,* 14: 193-216.

Tabachnick, B. R. (1980) Intern-teacher roles: Illusion, disillusion and reality. *Journal of Education,* 62(1): 122-137.

Toohey, K. (1996) Learning English as a second language in kindergarten: A community of practice perspective. *Canadian Modern Language Review,* 52: 549-576.

Tyack, D. and Tobin, W. (1994) The 'grammar' of schooling: Why has it been so hard to change? *American Educational Research Journal*, 31(3): 453-479.

Warriner, D. S. (2010) Competent performances of situated identities: Adult learners of English accessing engaged participation. *Teaching and Teacher Education,* 26: 22-30.

Weedon, C. (1997) Teaching Post-structuralist Feminist Theory in Education: Student resistances. *Gender and Education,* 9(3): 261-269.

Wenger, E. (1998) *Communities of practice: Learning, meaning and identity*. Cambridge: Cambridge University Press.

Woodgate-Jones, A. (2012) The student teacher and the school community of practice: an exploration of the contribution of the legitimate peripheral participation. *Educational Review,* 64(2): 145-160.

Yandell, J. and Turvey, A. (2007) Standards or communities of practice? Competing models of workplace learning and development. *British Educational Research Journal*, 33(4): 533-550.

Chapter 7

Raising the standard: A research-based agenda for teacher education in England

Alaster Scott Douglas

Introduction

This chapter considers the value of focusing on a research-based agenda for teacher education. The purpose of the chapter is to suggest developments in the preparation of new teachers in order to create learning opportunities in schools for both student teachers and teachers. I shall argue, with illustrations from my own empirical research, that if simply meeting government teaching standards is the focus with higher education marginalised in the preparation of teachers in England, then schools need to provide working environments which are open to challenge and debate in order for new and expansive developments in teaching and learning to occur. Such developments are necessary for enabling teachers to work successfully in an ever-changing teaching and learning environment.

The history of teacher education in England shows a gradual development of centralised requirements outlined by successive governments for how teachers are to be prepared for the profession. Circular 3/84 (Department of Education and Science, 1984) prescribed specific conditions in order to establish a national model of initial teacher education. A new organisation was established by the government to oversee initial teacher education in England and Wales (the Council for the Accreditation of Teacher Education) which regulated the duration of teacher education courses and the amount of time student teachers had to spend in schools. The introduction of new government inspection procedures supported the Council effectively enabling the Secretary of State to influence both the content and structure of initial teacher education (Furlong, 2013: 35). The circular was the first of a number of government documents changing the nature of teacher education in England with new routes into teaching introduced (some excluding higher education), new teaching competencies outlined, and the prescription of how university-school partnerships were to be formed. Three themes ran through a series of government directives: a forced reduction of higher education's contribution to teacher education, attempts to control the form of this input, and the monitoring of compliance (Wilkin, 1999). Alternative teacher education routes in recent years have shown 'a proliferation of training routes and a marked reduction in university-led provision' (Gewirtz, 2013: 10). Promotion of the craft of teaching by the UK government looks 'favourably on practice-based forms of Initial Teacher Training' (Marshall, 2014: 268). This has been further enhanced with the introduction of School Direct (McNamara and Murray, 2013) a scheme set up to promote greater time for novice teachers to 'learn on the job'. The main aim of the policy was to give schools the lead in the initial training of teachers through the new programme. Thus, the position of higher education is being potentially marginalised and the value of knowledge about education that higher education institutions provide is being called into question.

Increased school-based training emphasises the skills element in learning to teach, and thereby highlights the apparent relevance in course content to the task of teaching in schools (Blake et al., 1995). Government literature in England now refers to teacher training and trainees as opposed to teacher education and student teachers and this has come about through the continued UK government's approach to learning to teach being a craft or an apprenticeship 'best learnt as an apprentice observing a master craftsman or woman' (Department for Education (DfE) 2010b). Originally termed competencies, national teaching standards are regularly revised in order to assess student teachers during their teaching course and school practices. The Teaching Standards (DfE, 2013) are presented as the baseline standard for teaching in England and focus on thresholds for competence and conduct in setting high expectations, promoting pupils' progress and outcomes, demonstrating curriculum knowledge, planning and adapting lessons, using assessment, managing behaviour and fulfilling professional responsibilities. The managerial tone of the standards document is conveyed by the repetition of 'a teacher must' at the start of each standard description.

However, concern that some of the government imposed standards do not require students to be critically engaged in their practice, or to consider educational resources, educational values and disciplinary based knowledge has been expressed (Hordern, 2014). Proponents of higher education input argue that schools are not well placed or necessarily equipped with the expertise to enable student teachers to be critical and to reflect rationally on teaching and learning practice. Nevertheless, increasing pressures from the education inspectorate (Office for Standards in Education) with greater emphasis on quality assurance for higher education when working with student teachers and schools, means that those institutions seen to be under-performing are allotted reduced student teacher numbers and consequently financial penalties.

The current situation with teacher education playing a major part in many Faculties of Education in English universities is likely to be unsustainable (Furlong, 2013). Some English universities have stopped offering courses for student teachers altogether. This crisis, it could be argued, has partially come about from a lack of public justification for the importance of the university in professional teacher education. Arguments have started to surface in relation to what the university's unique contribution is for student teachers taking a course leading to qualified teacher status (HEA, 2013; BERA and RSA, 2013). Reports highlight the value of research in developing student teacher learning opportunities. This chapter considers why a research-based agenda could be important for teacher education by exploring the findings from three empirical research studies. These studies focus on a standards and school-based approach to teacher education in England and report on the potential conflict between prescribed teaching standards, school-based training and the learning opportunities for student teachers. The findings from the final study suggest future developments for developing learning opportunities for student teachers and teachers in schools and looks to the possibility of effective teacher education with less university input.

The research studies

In order to explore the role of the university and the standards-based approach in the process of educating student teachers, this chapter considers three research studies I have undertaken in recent years with student teachers and others involved in teacher education. The first study, based in a secondary high school, was a year-long ethnographic study which explored the learning opportunities for student teachers when on their school teaching practice. For the purpose of this chapter I shall discuss the learning opportunities of the student teachers in the Science department. The student teachers were undertaking a one year university postgraduate certificate in secondary education (for 11-18 year-old pupils) in the south of England. The second study is a follow up to the first. However, this project worked with student teachers participating in a teacher education course for primary (elementary) school teachers (for 7-11 year-old pupils). The research school is in London. The second research study develops the theoretical premise of the first by utilising an interventionist research methodology in an attempt to address some of the previous findings which highlighted a need to promote greater challenge and critique in teacher education. The third research project is designed as a pilot study. The study explores the possibilities of introducing a research-based agenda into university teacher education courses in order to help develop a 'critical pedagogy of teacher education' (McNamara and Murray, 2013: 17). This is advocated in the previous two studies. The pilot study was undertaken with twelve student teachers who were studying for a postgraduate certificate in education and training to teach Religious Studies to 11-18 year-old pupils. The discussion here is timely for teacher education policy in England in that all the research studies highlight the developing importance of schools in the student teacher learning process but the difficulties inherent in enabling learning opportunities for student teachers and teachers in the classroom. The chapter will argue that if the university is being marginalised in teacher education then in order for developments in teaching and learning to occur in schools, the schools will need to provide a setting which is more open to challenge and change.

Study 1

The study was a year-long ethnographic doctoral study (2006-2007) exploring teacher education work in four subject departments in one secondary school in the south of England (Douglas, 2014). The research focused on a one-year teacher education programme at an established university. The course had consistently been rated as highly successful in the Office for Standards in Education inspection grades and course evaluation outcomes. The school in which the student teachers were placed was well regarded for the way its staff worked with the university and had many connections with the work of the university's course, with which it had been involved for over fifteen years. The data were generated by asking two research questions:

(1) What are the opportunities for student teacher learning in different departments in one school?

(2) To what extent and why are these learning opportunities constructed differently?

These questions were addressed through participant observation of sixty-two meetings between student teachers and their mentors; twenty-seven meetings between university tutors, mentors and student teachers; fifty-two lesson observations with feedback sessions from mentors; sixty-one interviews with participants involved in teacher education (mentors, teachers, student teachers, university tutors and senior school managers); and numerous occasions observing social interaction in subject department 'team rooms'. The data-set comprises extensive field notes written in situ, transcripts of recordings of formal meetings such as interviews and numerous documents.

Secondary school student teachers' school practices are centred on teaching in specialist subject areas with subject teachers and the support of a subject specialist mentor and university tutor. The structure of the school experience requires a specifically designated school-supervising teacher (the mentor) who arranges and co-ordinates the teaching practice with the teacher educator (the university tutor) and liaises with the class teachers who are working with the student teachers (being observed by them and then observing their lessons as they gradually take on teaching the classes themselves). The movement to school-based teacher education has meant that school practices not only take up a larger amount of time in the teacher education course, but the onus and responsibilities of the school staff in the student teachers' learning have increased considerably. Greater importance has been given to the mentor's role with arrangements necessary for creating student teacher timetables and mentor meetings (usually timetabled for an hour a week). They also have responsibility for assessing the student teachers against the national standards for teaching. The university tutors visit the schools approximately three times in the teaching practice to observe the student teachers and support the mentor in discussing progress and assessing the student teachers against the teaching standards.

A Cultural Historical Activity Theory (CHAT) methodology was adopted to focus on questioning why the school learning environment was like it was and how practices had evolved over time and in relation to other practices. It, therefore, analysed the social situation of student teacher development (here seen in the major influence of the subject department). A central concept in this CHAT analysis is the idea of an activity's object. This is often described as the true motive of an activity (Leont'ev 1981). This is evident because it is true to the specific practices in which it is located. Nevertheless, an object is always open to negotiation in an activity like teacher education where participants have different opinions and intentions with regards to the activity. Motives are revealed in how subjects (participants) interpret and respond to the object. For a researcher, understanding how participants see the object is possible by analysing how they work and use tools within the departments' teacher education activity system. Tools are understood as anything that mediates subjects' actions upon objects (Russell, 2004). Physical tools (for example, course handbooks, lesson plans, student teacher reports, lesson observation feedback forms) and non-physical tools (such as discussions with mentors and tutors during meetings and visits, debates on teaching and learning) were evident in the subject departments' teacher education work. By using tools, participants act on the object in order to produce an outcome. So a teacher mentor might use a planning framework as a tool in a conversation with a student teacher.

The initial aim of the research was to produce case studies of the separate departments by using the data to inform coherent descriptions that succinctly established the contexts of the departments in relation to their teacher education work, their uniqueness and the complex nature of their settings. Because of limited space in this chapter, the data analysis here focuses on data from just one of the four subject departments (the Science department) as this case study particularly highlights the impact of working with teaching standards in the teacher education process. Because the school Science department concentrated on helping the student teachers meet the teaching standards for gaining accreditation, the standards were constantly referred to as needing to be evidenced in the student teachers' lessons and planning. The extensive use of the standards terminology in lesson plans and observation summaries encouraged a focus on these in post lesson discussions. Meeting these descriptors therefore became the priority in lesson feedback. The practice of meeting the standards sometimes appeared to be prioritised before an understanding of why the standards needed to be met:

> *School Science mentor*: You are not just teaching from the front now. So select this week what you want staff to look for ... so how about PV2 (planning), P1 pitch and assessment opportunities and teaching ones, time limits and clear transitions?. (Field notes. 16 January)

Monitoring of the student teachers' files took place at the university with a tick sheet designed to do this, and thus this was seen as a university task to do with checking the requirements of the course.

The mentor used the curriculum handbook produced by the university as a mechanism for setting out the respective roles of those in the teacher education activity. In this respect, it often served to close down discussions with its emphasis on standards and codified learning points: "I found at times that I had to be quite forceful and say 'no this is the case, you can't do that; you have to do this'" (interview with school Science mentor, 27 June). This went against the idea of opening out differences of opinion, as the handbook appeared to provide all the answers, and the student teachers' practices were viewed in terms of the requirements set out. Tensions in ideas on teaching and learning were rarely brought to the surface, but instead there were tensions in the student teachers not meeting the expectations of the school department staff.

Opportunities for enhancing student teacher learning in the science department were governed by demands for completing the student teacher education paperwork. This became the main focus of discussions and was time consuming, and allowed little room for student teacher agency when participating in learning opportunities. General conversations personalising the required codified teaching standards to the viewpoint of the student teachers rarely occurred. Instead, completing the paperwork from the university became the main activity in mentor and tutor meetings. There was an emphasis on written recording in the handbook:

> You should maintain good records of your observations and discussions with your mentor, experienced teachers and your [university] tutor, using the questions and suggestions that **we** [emphasis in the original] provide as guidelines. These records can be kept on the reverse side of the school-based activity sheet in the notes section. (Science Handbook p. 51)

There was also a weekly profile with open spaces for comments and these were 'formally checked' three times during the year. The design of the handbook suggested that it was seen as part of a monitoring process. The emphasis on following the recommendations of the university department by emboldening the 'we' in the quotation above appeared to come from a wish to heighten the student teachers' awareness of the status of the document, and therefore the expected manner in which it should be used. By constantly trying to evidence that they were meeting the teaching standards required to gain accreditation in both the mentor and tutor meetings, the student teachers were always giving input from an 'unqualified' position, and as such they may have perceived their ideas as being unequal in comparison to the other participants in the activity system. Hence, their feelings of agency were challenged, and the freedom of movement possible in using the handbook as a tool and a way of mediating learning was restricted.

There was also an acceptance by the university Science tutors that the handbook was not necessarily mediating student teacher learning. Both university Science tutors questioned the value of some of the paperwork and wondered how much of an evidence gathering exercise it was purely to satisfy their, and the government's, need for accountability. The standard of the portfolios was often felt to be 'shockingly poor':

> It's just formulaic writing; it's not very good. I would say it's the weakest part of our course. (Interview with Science tutor, 24 May)

> As a useful document, it's useful for what? I think the portfolio was done as an assessment activity for us to monitor different aspects of the meeting of the standards. But is it a document that helps them learn? I couldn't hand on heart say that. We have never had a proper conversation about why we have got this and what should be in it.
> (Interview with Science tutor, 3 July)

Therefore, the school Science department appropriated the tools at a functional level within the work ensuring that forms were completed and progress recorded. Like the handbook, the way many tools were used in Science, with the school mentor seeing the observation feedback summaries as evidence for progress, for example, frequently appeared to replace possible discourse on specific contexts of teaching and the student teachers' interpretations of these. This carried over into the university tutor visits, where in preparation for the second school practice, the university tutor noted down development points for the next school mentor:

> *University tutor*: Let's carry on through your profile then—I'll write that—use information technology more for help. How are we for time [mentor]?
> *School mentor:* fifteen minutes
> *University tutor*: Come on then.
> (There are more quick fire questions about the scheme of work and how [student teacher] plans activities.)
> *Student teacher:* Lesson plans
> *School mentor:* Much better, only one teacher has given 'attention needed' for pitch. No one has said 'consistent' but you have improved a lot considering the initial concerns.
> *University tutor*: Ok, I'll make a note of that—pitch improved but still needs working on. (Field notes, 17 April)

As an opportunity to open out the issues of the practice of teaching and learning, it was noticeable that checking forms dominated the visits: University tutor: 'share that now so we can tick more boxes off' (Field notes, 21 November).

For the student teachers, this meant that some tools occasionally appeared threatening, as they were being used explicitly as monitoring devices. This impersonal approach was also evident when the student teachers produced lesson plans that did not match the required format. Rather than questioning why they had veered from the expected style, and what this said about how the student teachers were approaching issues of teaching and learning, the rules for how the lesson plans should be completed were stressed. The activity system's rules were emphasised and the tools used as a means to enforce them.

On the few occasions where considerations of the importance of professional values when conversing on matters of pedagogy were apparent (for example, when considering wider perspectives on how work in classrooms was viewed) this initiated discussions about the point of being there, and the value of education for both pupils and teachers. Nevertheless, the majority of the specific student teacher learning opportunities were couched in a rule-bound notion of complying with the course requirements and using tools to evidence the meeting of codified standards. When opinions were challenged by the student teachers in mentor meetings this was in contrast to the established way of working:

> *School science mentor*: I had a couple of staff come and say that they were concerned about how you [student teacher] were taking advice. I had that in mind when you didn't agree with my problem. I thought I was wasting my time as you didn't want to know, and I thought that other people were also feeling you were not taking advice. That is why I wanted to end the conversation on Friday.
>
> (Field notes, 30 January)

General debates on pedagogy were overridden by discussions on the schemes of work, and meeting the standards required for gaining qualified teacher status.

The movement to school-based teacher education has meant that school teaching practices not only take up a larger amount of time in university teacher education courses, but the onus and responsibilities of the school staff in the student teachers' learning have increased considerably. Greater importance has been given to the school mentor's role with responsibilities for assessing the student teachers against the national standards. But 'overly concentrating on prescribed teaching standards limits the opportunities for student teachers to learn, as a standards-based technicised approach is unlikely to be responsive either to social contexts or to individual needs' (Menter, 2009: 226). The recently revised standards (DfE, 2013) approach the initial professional development of teachers in managerial terms, in so far as the standards mostly offer a list of pre-defined tasks and responsibilities (Marshall, 2014). By focusing so much on what new teachers are expected to do, it might be argued that the standards fail to adequately address what new teachers are thinking. It may therefore be sufficient for a new teacher to simply perform well with 'little encouragement to take risks or to be experimental in one's approach to teaching' (Menter et al., 2006: 281). The standards do not indicate how an understanding of for example, pupils' learning and needs is created or that this might be developed through an engagement with educational theory. The second research study illustrates how engagement with theory encouraged by the university tutor and a researcher may enhance the richness of teacher education work in schools.

Study 2

The second research study (2010) considers how one may negotiate the teacher education activity system's object in a primary school with a researcher central to the negotiation process. The shift from academic emphases to concentration on craft knowledge and professional relevance has meant that higher education institutions may feel that they need to create courses which both meet the government's guidelines and the national standards for fulfilling a school-based design, while at the same time ensure that student teachers are critically evaluating their practice and engaging in debates on educational values, which may or may not be taking place in the school setting. The student teachers in this study are working within a postgraduate partnership scheme. The study aimed to open up new possibilities for learning by creating the opportunity to negotiate the object of teacher education activity in order to encourage greater discussion of the learning process noted as missing in the first study. The fieldwork (observations and interviews) took place over two weeks and was followed by a workshop with school staff and the university tutor. The research draws on the Developmental Work Research (DWR) methodology of Engeström (2007) using the change laboratory method. DWR is a mode of research intervention where researchers and practitioners jointly interrogate the structural tensions in and between different dimensions of activity (in this case teacher education) as defined by CHAT, such as the rules, tools and divisions of labour that have emerged in teacher education practices over time and which constrain the development of future teacher education activity. The desired outcome of the DWR meetings is expansive learning at a systemic level; promoting the possibility of new learning through developing increased abilities to interpret situations.

Possibilities are negotiated of how tools could change in order to prevent the tensions noted from the research data. For the purpose of this chapter, one tension noted in the data will be discussed. Facilitated by the researcher, the change laboratory uses research data as evidence of current teacher education practices in the school (known as 'mirror' data — for example, 'everyday understandings of practices collected from individual interviews with staff') (Edwards, 2010: 162). These data are pre-selected by the researcher for their capacity to highlight tensions in the teacher education practices. Owing to the research in the study being small-scale with only two weeks of fieldwork undertaken, the mirror data were also supplemented by, and compared to, data from the earlier ethnographic research in the first study (termed 'window' data). Accepting that the secondary school research data are different, they can help to illuminate points of comparison when considered alongside the primary school data.

An aim was to highlight possible tensions in learning opportunities for student teachers and this was inherent in the research question: What are the opportunities for student teacher learning in a primary school? The research school had three school-based teacher education tutors who took responsibility for teacher education at the school and liaised with the university tutor who visited the school during the year. The school tutors, after having undergone training at the university, were responsible for supporting and assessing the three student teachers. Each of the student teachers was paired with a class teacher (their mentor) and taught their classes. Situated in London, the school is a comprehensive mixed primary school (4-11 year-olds) with over four-hundred pupils. It is an oversubscribed school and serves a generally advantaged area. The overall effectiveness of the school was classed as 'outstanding' in the most recent Office for Standards in Education inspection.

The contradiction identified in the primary school teacher education activity system relates to how critiquing and debating ideas on pedagogy can be seen as negatively impinging on personal support in working relations. The university encouraged and wanted a 'kind of critical enquiry':

> I see it as our responsibility in uni to say 'look there are other ways of doing it' so that they can bring that critical lens to bear on what they see in the classroom. (University tutor, 18 June)

In interview, the student teachers and the school mentors emphasised the supportive nature of the work: 'there's this sort of policy of everyone's helping everyone else and everyone's learning from everyone else's experience' (mentor, 14 June). But the notion of challenging one another's viewpoints was seen as possibly problematic:

> I haven't been challenged about that (teaching ethos); I think that would be hard to be challenged by a student, but interesting.
> (School mentor, 11 June)

Although not dismissing that there could be interest in having to defend one's approach to teaching and learning, it was not an expected way of working that was integral to teacher education. Similarly, student teachers did not see such challenge as particularly necessary when asked if they would openly challenge teaching strategies:

> I would definitely say 'interesting why did you do that because I never would have thought to do that' or something like that … But I've seen it more as I'm here to learn, to expand my horizons rather than to shrink someone else's, so if I needed to, I would definitely have that chat, but I've never had that opportunity, or that need.(Student teacher, 16 June)

Commenting in terms of 'shrinking someone's horizons' if questioning their choice of teaching practices, suggests a view of criticism and challenge that is negative and not expansive; in fact quite the opposite. This student teacher feels that communication is important and suggests that commenting on teaching and learning choices is something she would do. However, she focuses on her own learning rather than adopting an expansive learning approach, where the class teacher could learn too.

In the change laboratory workshop school staff readily recognised this contradiction and acknowledged that it was desirable to accept the importance of critical enquiry. When negotiating the tension of questioning accepted practices, one school mentor commented: 'I am not particularly thinking about their role [as a student teacher] carefully enough' (16 December). She felt that her concern for personally supporting the student teacher sometimes discouraged her from challenging the ideas behind the teaching practice. Another school mentor also felt that careful consideration was needed in order to develop genuine debate, and suggested ways forward for encouraging collaboration:

> You have to make an agreement between you if you are observing one another for example, what the purpose of the observation is and what is going to happen after the observation. (Mentor, 16 December)

Receiving feedback from student teachers 'felt strange' for one of the school mentors when she was observed in her classroom. In the change laboratory she accepted that 'maybe it shouldn't' (school mentor, 16 December) as it was crucial that everyone was open to learning. This illustrated the value of discussing teacher education activity for all participants, which was emphasised in the workshop where new ways of appropriating teacher education tools (such as the example of observation above) were suggested. The university tutor also acknowledged the thought provoking nature of negotiating tensions observed during the fieldwork. She commented in the change laboratory workshop: 'I've only just thought about this because you [researcher] are making me think about it' (16 December). Such comments suggest that seeking out tensions in teacher education practices was not a natural way of working in the school setting.

When asked how one school mentor felt about the opportunities student teachers get to try out different ways of teaching, she acknowledged the tension:

> It's a very good point. In many respects they don't [get the opportunities]. If they have an excellent role model as a class teacher then they're in a very good position. Even if you have a very good role model, that doesn't address the issue of different approaches. I see trainees attempt to model themselves on an outstanding teacher but they don't actually see what underpins the excellence of the teaching. They purely mimic what they're doing without realising what underpins it. (School mentor, 14 June)

The temptation to emulate teachers when working in such a close-knit community and to replicate the social practices evident in the school is understandable: 'watching [teacher] teach has just been amazing and then me trying to do something similar myself' (student teacher, 16 June). However, this way of working does not allow for the possibility of two way learning, but appears like an apprenticeship model, often critically evaluated in teacher education literature for 'privileging mastery of techniques of management of the classroom and behaviour of pupils [rather than developing] inquiring minds and reflective approaches' (Spendlove et al., 2010: 65).

Criticism of teacher education has suggested that there is too much 'emphasis on curriculum delivery at the expense of the experience of responsive pedagogical decision making' (Edwards and Protheroe, 2003: 240). Practices may be seen to be responsive if they are developed through questioning and challenging pedagogical decisions with regards to specific contexts. Teacher education tools can help this by initiating debate about established pedagogical meanings. This was evident in the fieldwork when the university tutor observed one of the student teachers, and noted in the feedback session how she, as a tutor, needed to think carefully through the topic that had been taught (getting pupils to write explanations rather than instructions) and work out how she would have approached this lesson. She proceeded to discuss this openly with the student teacher and they shared their opinions:

University tutor: We try and simplify it for them but actually in this case you know the overlap, this is not a criticism, because it took me most of the lesson to kind of sort this out for myself. I kept thinking hang on what, why do they keep doing this [mixing the two writing genres]. You've got some lovely bits of writing and this is much more about untangling a little bit the difficulty of trying to teach genres discretely. So just think about that one.

Student teacher: What's in the national strategy is to recommend these volcanoes [for writing explanations] but they also talk about using a video and that's what [mentor] and I discussed, and it was like actually we've got this opportunity, let's ... but then once we watched the video yesterday we suddenly realised actually there's a really strong crossover there and we have to be careful. (Field notes: 18 June)

Resulting discussions from feedback sessions like the above may feed into student teachers' thinking, which along with the ideas of other participants should be open to critique. If discussions arising from the tools are meaningful to student teachers' pedagogical experiences, these can affect their practices, which may in turn feed back into how future discussions arising from the tools are shaped. Thus, opportunities for mutual and expansive learning can arise when tools are appropriated in this way, with the relationships of the participants using them being open to learning ('you made me think a lot about that', university tutor, 18 June). If the tools (in this case the feedback session) had been appropriated in a regulatory way with the tutor giving an 'assessed' response to the lesson on how well the writing genres had been taught, the tool would have simply worked as a rule in the activity system and learning would have been restricted, as new interpretations would not have been enabled. If information is imparted as a one-way process focusing on how student teachers are meeting teaching standards, contestation is repressed and compliance encouraged. This suggests that the teacher education activity system's object is seen as less complex with its principal motive being to develop student teachers as able practitioners managing their classrooms.

An interventionist research model such as a Developmental Work Research enables a researcher to work directly with participants in the school teacher education activity system in order to start to test hypotheses about the conditions for expansive learning and see how expansive learning may be encouraged in practice. Opening out participants' thinking by presenting possible tensions and contradictions observed in the activity system encourages negotiations on the object of the teacher education activity, and develops a shared understanding of this. This then enables participants to look closely at the way they use tools in order to mediate work on the systems' objects. A better understanding of practice by analysing the discussion in the change laboratory workshop in relation to the mirror and window data was characterised by an awareness of the multi-voiced nature of teacher education. Opening this up for discussion sought to 'stimulate a system of possible alternatives' (Engeström, 1993: 68) in order to negotiate the object of teacher education activity and to develop teacher education practices and consequently student teacher learning opportunities.

Such work would necessitate a paradigmatic shift for participants in the teacher education process with a deconstruction of established norms in order to set the context for future practice. This finding sits alongside other research findings which have noted how demands on teacher educators have changed as a result of initial teacher training shifting from earlier notions of promoting teacher autonomy for student teachers to be educated to supporting trainee teachers in being trained to comply with externally imposed teaching and assessment regimes (Brown et al., 2014). With the teacher educator's role moving into schools (White, 2014) and university-based teacher educators being marginalised by new school-based training routes, ways for encouraging expansive learning opportunities are needed in schools if learning to teach is to involve forms of critical enquiry. The final study in this chapter reports on a pilot study aimed to develop critical enquiry in schools by incorporating a research project into student teachers' first school teaching practice

Study 3

The research was undertaken with a group of twelve Religious Studies student teachers on a one year teacher training course (2013). The group of students made up the full cohort of a Religious Studies one year postgraduate certificate of education course at a university in England. As part of their first term's work for their Professional Studies assignment the student teachers attended four research training workshops taught by a researcher at the university and then undertook classroom research, each observing and interviewing three different experienced teachers who taught the same class of students. The research questions asked:

1. Did student teachers view their development as researchers during the research process as significant to their learning?
2. Did the study enable student teachers to integrate their empirical findings into a theoretical background?

The research presented draws upon the analysis of data generated from a student teacher focus group interview (audio recorded), and the student teachers' course assignments as well as field notes taken during the four research methods workshops based at the university. These different research methods were used in order to generate data on the student teachers' experience of taking part in a research project and their perceived learning as a consequence. The strength of the evidence supporting the interpretation of the learning opportunities in the research is recognised in terms of the limitations of doing a small scale pilot study for one group of student teachers in one teacher education course. The participants are not representative and the data are not viewed as being open to generalisation. However, multiple perspectives within one course provided rich data that were central to understanding the complexity of introducing a research-based assignment into student teachers' school teaching practices.

All the student teachers undertook their fieldwork individually in their first teaching practice schools. Analysing the student teachers' research data was supported at the university. Their research work was written up as part of their Professional Studies assignment and assessed for their course by tutors not undertaking the research. The student teachers linked their data analysis to their reading of the literature which focused on an aspect of classroom differentiation of their own choice, for example, the use of teachers' questioning, working with pupils with special educational needs. The task for the assignment was a compulsory part of the course. However, participating in the research pilot study with the university researcher was voluntary as was taking part in the focus group interviews, and giving consent for course assignments to be analysed.

Findings from the study suggest that conducting research was a significant learning event for the student teachers in that their analysis of their development as researchers was seen to enhance their developing appreciation of the importance of differentiation strategies when observing teaching in diverse classrooms. The student teachers felt that the knowledge gained from undertaking their research changed their understanding and thinking about classroom practice and helped them be more reflective in their own teaching:

> From not knowing what I was really looking for, when I had the research workshops you think 'so this is how I can observe' and then you start to analyse a bit more specifically and I think it was really helpful to have that focus as you can start to really look at what is going on and when you reflect critically on that, it does have a lot more meaning.
>
> (Focus Group, 2 June, 2014)

The research activity appeared to facilitate early and meaningful links between research and practice with the student teachers specifically differentiating between the social situation of development for the pupils and the more generic ideas often forwarded in the literature:

> I picked two students to observe and I chose EAL [English as an additional language] as my focus and how strategies for teaching these students work. Do the strategies work across the board or are they effective in this particular classroom with this student? So I am trying

> to identify the best strategy for an individual student in a particular situation as opposed to finding a strategy like an umbrella strategy for everyone, which doesn't always work. (Focus Group, 4 June, 2014)

The data from the focus group interview with the student teachers highlighted a positive response to undertaking research in schools. Regarding the research methods workshops in the university as 'useful' they particularly valued the opportunity to consider ethical issues with regard to working in classrooms as a 'researcher' rather than as a student teacher. When asked what the difference was they pointed out how for some, they felt nervous undertaking a new role where research was for them associated with academic pursuits and 'with professors in their offices' (4 June, 2014) rather than seeing research as relevant to all practitioners who as potential researchers of their own practice can benefit from participating in the research process.

The research work was seen as contributing to the teaching practice in the school with the idea that outcomes of observations and interviews may help to increase the perceived value of the research process for school teachers as well as student teachers. An aim was also to develop student teacher confidence to be critical and to see differently with research data generated for specific research questions. Ideally, this could create a 'powerful pathway for exploring challenging issues' (Merino and Holmes, 2006: 95) and provide a non-judgemental basis for considering teaching strategies. The outcome could pave the way for ongoing critical reflection as a means for understanding classroom practice and appreciating the value of this way of working in future practice.

In their Professional Studies assignments the student teachers noted how teachers' thinking was often spontaneous:

> After observing RE lessons I became aware that teachers were hesitant to use group work within their lessons. Quite often teachers would have a group work activity planned but steer away (skip the *PowerPoint* slide) from the task due to the class behaviour or engagement.

The student teacher goes on to cite literature in terms of practical theories, which recommend structuring group work so that it builds upon smaller interactions in order to counter the behaviour of challenging pupils which may dominate the classroom environment. This student teacher then explained in her assignment that 'through her research [she had] highlighted conditions for successful group work: pupils must feel safe, secure and confident in sharing ideas with their group' (Baines et al., 2004: 20). This could be seen as beginning to think in terms of meta-theories of education in order to inform future practice: 'I have chosen to try and implement group work in my classroom that will engage the whole class.' Identifying through observations and interviews how teachers' thinking was believed to work on a number of different levels enabled student teachers to articulate more carefully how the literature could inform analyses from their empirical data.

The relative richness of the data generated from the student teacher-as-researcher in comparison to the opportunities the student teacher may have had when considering the situation when not operating as a researcher (but when working with the class as a novice teacher) may be seen to encourage a view of the educational setting from a number of different perspectives. These perspectives may encompass examples of teachers' thinking in the classroom as well as thinking in terms of practical theories and potentially meta-theories of education. Many of the student teachers were aware that teaching is a complex activity and they did acknowledge both in their assignments and in the focus group interview that they, as student teachers, were on a learning trajectory. They also felt that an appreciation of the complexity of teaching effectively was not something that was easily explained or observed:

> I am self-aware enough to consider that the poor levels of speaking and listening that I have experienced in the classroom are perhaps due to the shortcomings of my own practice. While I see the value and sense in the strategies discussed, it is important to remember that they can only be effective when used in conjunction with the many other skills and experiences that make an effective teacher. Furthermore, teaching is such a complex activity which makes it difficult to underpin one or even several strategies that will indefinitely meet the needs of disengaged learners.

In order for student teachers to fully consider their empirical findings with a theoretical background, the study indicated that they would need to further develop their conceptualisation of the teacher learning process which could be enhanced by their own developing and ongoing experience of teaching in the classroom. Ideas for building on the student teachers' research analyses throughout their teacher education course and into their second teaching practice (where they experience more classroom teaching as teachers themselves) are being considered in the course. This could potentially further help develop understanding of teacher learning and be advantageous for embedding a research-based agenda within the teacher education programme.

The research literature highlights the value of research work playing an integral part of teacher education courses with student teacher research having the potential to create important influences on the ways in which classroom teachers come to view links between practice and research and to foster communities of inquiry and critical alignment (Kotsopoulos et al., 2012: 35). This and other research studies have shown how reflective skills of student teachers are enhanced by participation in classroom-based qualitative research (Lambe, 2011).

Concluding comments

The three studies outlined in this chapter emphasise the importance of what Furlong (2013) has described as the 'contestability of knowledge' which he advocates as the primary purpose of the university: to challenge underlying assumptions and to teach students to think critically about knowledge and values so as to gain the skills needed to form their own judgements. Student teachers strongly advocate embedding coursework assessment in their school teaching practice (Allen and Wright, 2014: 149) and research has been seen to provide opportunities for teacher candidates to transform their orientation towards teaching through personal, systematic and intentional exploration of practice (Price, 2001: 71).

The changes to impact on teacher education in England have been the continuing political drive for school-based teacher education. It has been predicted that within a year the university will no longer be the leading provider of teacher education in England (Furlong, 2013). There are also growing numbers of student teachers in England in work-based learning that are not taking part in teacher education courses. Ways of analysing alternative experiences recognising the influence of schools in affecting the kinds of learning available to these student teachers are also needed in order to increase understanding of the benefits of new and different approaches to teacher education. With less university input in these work-based schemes, and with changes in school governance and centralised requirements for teachers entering the profession (for example, English state schools , Academies, which are funded directly by central government are no longer required to employ teachers in possession of qualified teacher status) school leaders are crucially placed to facilitate new alternative experiences in learning how to teach.

> The use of the Teaching Standards (DfE, 2011) as a benchmark for the 'good teacher' enables government to wield considerable power over identifying the 'products' of teacher formation processes in England, but this may be increasingly complicated by systemic fragmentation resulting from recent reform. (Hordern, 2014)

In the current climate of educational reform, considerations about standards draw attention away from the role of the educational community and forms of participation within the community (Moate and Ruohotie-Lyhty 2014). However, with the nature of the teaching communities also diversifying, instead of building teacher education practices on competence standards or considerations of important content in an attempt to predetermine what kind of teachers students should become, it is even more important to focus on the 'why' questions of education. Extending the notion of novice teachers researching with more experienced practitioners in the classroom as a process could also be developed by using a version of the Developmental Work Research change laboratory workshops (Engeström, 2007; Douglas, 2012). These are designed to promote a shared purpose to research work by involving classroom practitioners in exploring the data with the aim of developing shared values on the principles of teaching. Student teachers who are more predominantly based in schools on the School Direct scheme (DfE, 2010a) where the involvement of universities is being reduced through government pressures (Medwell and Wray, 2014: 75) could also benefit from working in this way. Exploring the potential of the teacher, school mentor and student teacher partnership as a way of embedding research-based agendas into both school-based as well as university-based teacher education courses could further support an enquiry based approach to learning to teach. The findings from the three research studies discussed above suggest this is important for the development of learning opportunities in teacher education.

References

Allen, J.M., and Wright, S. (2014) Integrating Theory and Practice in the Pre-Service Teacher Education Practicum, *Teachers and Teaching: theory and practice,* 20(2): 136-151.

Blake, D., Hanley, V., Jennings, M. and Lloyd, M. (1995) *Researching School-Based Teacher Education.* Aldershot: Avebury.

British Educational Research Association (BERA) and Royal Society of the Arts (RSA) (2013) The Role of Research in Teacher Education: Reviewing the Evidence. http://content.yudu.com/Library/A2mkmg/BERAoneoffJanuary201/resources/index.htm?referrerUrl

Brown, T., Rowley, H. and Smith, K. (2014) Rethinking Research in Teacher Education, *British Journal of Educational Studies*, 62(3): 281-296.

Department for Education (DfE) (2010a) The Importance of Teaching: The Schools White Paper, 2010 [online]. Available at: https://www.gov.uk/government/uploads/system/uploads/attachment_data/file/175429/CM-7980.pdf [10 October, 2012].

Department for Education (DfE) (2010b) Michael Gove Speech to the National College Annual Conference, Birmingham. Available at: www.gov.uk (accessed 1 June, 2014).

Department for Education (DfE) (2013) Teachers' Standards (rev. Jun), London.

Department of Education and Science (DES) (1984) *Initial Teacher Training: Approval of Courses (Circular 3/84)*. London: DES.

Douglas, A.S. (2012) Creating Expansive Learning Opportunities in Schools: The role of school leaders in initial teacher education partnerships, *European Journal of Teacher Education*, 35(1): 3-15.

Douglas, A.S. (2014) *Student Teachers in School Practice: An analysis of learning opportunities*. London: Palgrave Macmillan.

Edwards, A. (2010) *Being an Expert Professional Practitioner: The relational turn in expertise*. London: Springer.

Edwards, A. and Protheroe, L. (2003) Learning to See in Classrooms: What are student teachers learning about teaching and learning while learning to teach in schools? *British Educational Research Journal*, 29(2): 227-242.

Engeström, Y. (1993) Developmental Studies of Work as a Test Bench of Activity Theory: The case of the primary medical care practice. In: S. Chaiklin and J. Lave (eds.) *Understanding Practice: Perspectives on Activity and Context*. Cambridge: Cambridge University Press, 64-103.

Engeström, Y. (2007) Putting Activity Theory to Work: The change laboratory as an application of double stimulation, In: H. Daniels, M. Cole, and J. Wertsch (eds.) *The Cambridge Companion to Vygotsky*. Cambridge: Cambridge University Press.

Furlong, J. (2013) *Education—An anatomy of the discipline: Rescuing the university project?* Abingdon: Routledge.

Gewirtz, S. (2013) Developing Teachers as Scholar-Citizens: Reasserting the value of university involvement in teacher education, HEA Learning to Teach Part 1, http://www.heacademy.ac.uk/assets/documents/disciplines/socialsciences/Strategic_2014/LearningToTeach_Part1_Final.pdf

Higher Education Academy (HEA) (2013) Learning to Teach Parts 1 and 2 http://www.heacademy.ac.uk/assets/documents/disciplines/socialsciences/Strategic_2014/LearningToTeach_Part1_Final.pdf

http://www.heacademy.ac.uk/assets/documents/disciplines/socialsciences/Strategic_2014/LearningToTeach_Part2_final.pdf.

Hordern, J. (2014) The Logic and Implications of School-based Teacher Formation, *British Journal of Educational Studies*, 62(3): 231-248.

Kotsopoulos, D., Mueller, J., and Buzza, D. (2012) Pre-service Teacher Research: An early acculturation into a research disposition. *Journal of Education for Teaching*, 38(1): 21-36.

Lambe, J. (2011) Developing Pre-Service Teachers' Reflective Capacity through Engagement with Classroom-Based Research, *Reflective Practice*, 12(1): 87-100.

Leont'ev, A. N. (1981) The Problem of Activity in Psychology, In: J. V. Wertsch (ed.) *The Concept of Activity in Soviet Psychology*. New York: Armonk NY.

Marshall, T. (2014) New Teachers Need Access to Powerful Educational Knowledge, *British Journal of Educational Studies*, 62(3): 265-279.

McNamara, O., and Murray, J. (2013) The School Direct Programme and its Implications for Research-Informed Teacher Education, In *Learning to Teach Part 1*. http://www.heacademy.ac.uk/assets/documents/disciplines/socialsciences/Strategic_2014/LearningToTeach_Part1_Final.pdf

Medwell J., and Wray, D. (2014) Pre-Service Teachers Undertaking Classroom Research: Developing reflection and enquiry skills, *Journal of Education for Teaching*, 40(1): 65-77.

Menter, I. (2009) Teachers for the Future: What have we got and what do we need? In: S. Gewirtz, P. Mahony, I. Hextall and A. Cribb (eds.) *Changing Teacher Professionalism, International Trends, Challenges and Ways Forward*. London: Routledge, 217-228.

Menter, I., Brisard, E. and Smith, I. (2006) Making Teachers in Britain: Professional knowledge for initial teacher education in England and Scotland, *Educational Philosophy and Theory*, 38(3): 269-286.

Merino, B., and Holmes, P. (2006) Student Teacher Inquiry as an 'Entry Point' for Advocacy, *Teacher Education Quarterly*, 33(3): 79-96.

Moate, J. and Ruohotie-Lyhty, M. (2014) Identity, Agency and Community: Reconsidering the pedagogic responsibilities of teacher education, *British Journal of Educational Studies*, 62(3): 249-264.

Price, J. (2001) Action Research, Pedagogy and Change: The transformative potential of action research in pre-service teacher education, *Curriculum Studies*, 33(1): 43-74.

Russell, D. R. (2004) Looking Beyond the Interface, Activity Theory and Distributed Learning, In: H. Daniels and A. Edwards (eds.) *The Routledge Falmer Reader in Psychology of Education*. London: Routledge Falmer, 307-326.

Spendlove, D., Howes, A. and Wake, G. (2010) Partnerships in Pedagogy: Refocusing of classroom lenses, *European Journal of Teacher Education*, 33(1): 65-77.

White, E. (2014) Being a Teacher and a Teacher Educator—Developing a New Identity? *Professional Development in Education*, 40(3): 436-449.

Wilkin, M. (1999) The Role of Higher Education in Initial Teacher Education, Universities Council for the Education of Teachers (UCET) London, Occasional Paper No 12.

Chapter 8

Discourses of performativity and educational effectiveness: Contesting and shaping teacher identity in a neoliberal world

Lawrence Angus

Abstract

The starting point for this chapter is a general acceptance of certain key elements of the postmodern condition; namely, the provisional nature of, culture, identity and discursive construction, and the importance of signifiers. These elements render any single definition of teacher identity or teacher professionalism extremely problematic, and put the focus squarely on both the assertion of, and the subjective construction of, norms, values and commitments about curriculum and pedagogy among teachers. The broad argument of this chapter is that powerful global movements in education policy and teaching practice have generated widely-accepted discourses of performativity and educational effectiveness that have had pedagogical effects on constructions of teacher identity. The chapter attempts a deconstruction of prevailing discourses and the development of partial understanding of the complexity and multi-directionality of the social relations of educational politics. Gaining insight into such complexity, in this case into notions of teacher identity within a globalised neoliberal world, is an important step in the process of challenging and subverting the perverse effects of prevalent discourses and neoliberal education policies.

During the past thirty years, there have been major changes in government and public thinking about education. This has occurred in Australia and in most Western countries, particularly the English-speaking ones (Alexander, 2009; Lingard, 2010), and also in many developing nations (Nordtveit, 2010); and while it is obviously important to recognise that education systems in Europe vary markedly across and even within national borders, there is nonetheless a strongly emerging literature which associates the 'Europeanisation' of education and the 'construction of the European Education Space' (e.g. Grek et al., 2009) with neoliberal policy themes of strong accountability, competition, high-stakes testing and a strong connection between education and the economy. There has been what Ball (2006: 10) and many others regard as 'a major transformation in the organising principles of social provision right across the public sector' (emphasis in original). Although Ball's main concern is with educational provision, his point is that the nature of western society, economy and politics as a whole, including its underlying values and organising norms, has substantially changed within a generation. In this chapter, I describe changes in values and policy directions that have occurred within education discourses throughout most of the western world and, increasingly, beyond, and attempt to explain the impact of such changes on the construction of teacher identity. I argue that the changes, by and large, have had a deleterious or perverse effect on teaching and have, in fact, contributed to a substantial de-professionalisation of teachers to the point that serious debate is needed on what kind of education is desirable for the twenty-first century and what kind of teachers are needed for the task.

The contested professional capital of the teaching profession

When it comes to education as a social institution, Anderson (2009) maintains that, compared with the humanistic and educative goals that had largely characterised education a generation ago, 'economic goals have undeniably become front and centre in the wake of the ascendancy of neoliberalism with its emphasis on the individual's human capital and its promotion of a competition state that has intensified competition among individuals' (p. 51). The discourse of neoliberalism has had a profound effect on the nature of education and the education profession. In particular, there has been an emphasis on so-called 'failing' schools and teachers, and on regulating schools and teaching in order to ensure that 'standards' are raised. This type of thinking has resulted in policies of narrow accountability and market competition among schools, and the use of 'league tables' to rank 'successful' and 'failing' schools against each other. The logic assumes that individual teachers and students are to blame for 'poor performance'. This way of framing education and student 'achievement' is extremely dangerous and damaging to educational values as it decreases the professional autonomy of educators (Ball, 2006: 2003; Anderson, 2009). Of course, teacher professionalism and teacher identities are continually being constructed and reconstructed. The point is, that a significant and powerful shift has occurred over the past three decades in the professional capital and personal identities of many teachers. This is important because part of being a member of a profession is being able to assert what Bourdieu might call its 'professional culture' or, more precisely in his terms, being able to define the 'professional field of teaching' in terms of its cultural and symbolic capital. That is to say, members of the teaching professional field have long attempted to define, assert, and defend the body of norms and knowledge that that they believe are the ones that give the teaching profession its internal and external legitimacy. Therefore, although professional knowledge and norms are always being contested from different positions within the teaching professional field, the profession's legitimacy rests largely on its shared sense of its own distinctiveness and purpose. Thus, although contested, members are likely to try to keep asserting, through somewhat competing and somewhat overlapping discourses, what they believe are the professional norms and commitments that should characterise their profession. If they are unable to do this, then the nature and status of the profession becomes more uncertain as 'the cultural capital of the [professional] field is lost' (Oakes et al., 1998: 263) or becomes highly problematic. The argument I am making is that previously asserted professional capital of teachers, in Bourdieusian terms, has been contested and largely reconstructed in recent decades. As Oakes et al., (1998: 273) explain:

> ... redefining the [professional] field's dominant capital may not directly affect actors' intrinsic properties [e.g. a teacher's knowledge about and commitment to inclusive curriculum], but it does affect their relational properties (their position), because it affects their overall capital, and, therefore, their standing in the field. This, in turn, will have implications for an individual's sense of positional identity.

The professional field of teachers has certainly been challenged during the era of neoliberalism. The pressures on schools and teachers that has been brought about by the increased public visibility given to teachers' work because of policies such as the publication of student and school results, often in the form of league tables, has been less than subtle. The almost universal government and public acceptance of such policies of narrow accountability, and of managerialism and market competition in schooling, has been steadily reshaping conceptions of the teaching profession during the past three decades. As a result, the cultural capital of the professional field, it could be argued, has been deeply problematised. That is, the constituents of what had been regarded in the 1970s and 1980s as comprising 'a good teacher' (e.g. curriculum relevance and innovation, student-centred pedagogy, a social justice orientation; see discussion in Brown and Angus, 1995) would seem to have been revalued and challenged by greater esteem being given to the importance of testing, market competition among schools and the need for schools to attract 'good' students, which have been promoted by governments and education authorities, and which have been generally accepted as a pragmatic imperative by most teachers and school principals. Schools and education authorities, particularly throughout the English-speaking world, but also in Europe, Scandinavia and elsewhere, have increasingly adopted the language of competitive educational markets, standards, managerialism, and other neoliberal themes. As Saltman (2014: 251) explains, 'Neoliberal ideology sees education not as a public good ideally serving a democratic society but as a private good primarily useful for preparing workers and consumers for the economy'. Schooling, in this view, should therefore 'be oriented toward educational competition in preparation for economic competition, initially against others in the nation and then for competition against other nations' (Saltman, 2014: 251). Such an orientation has, over time, reframed the public discourse about education.

The neoliberal policy emphasis on accountability, particularly the accountability of teachers and schools for the achievement of performance targets set for students and the comparative scores they achieve in national standardised tests and public examinations, has made schools directly answerable to an external audience of education hierarchies, governments, and local communities. Many concerned citizens have responded positively to the government rhetoric of schools needing to reverse allegedly declining educational standards, and many aspirational citizens seek reassurance that their school's academic performance is sound as judged by the various standardised tests. This is a strong illustration of the actualisation of the performance orientation that increasingly frames the pedagogy of teachers within the competitive market relationship among schools. Such a performance orientation is also manifest in the pressure applied to schools and teachers by governments wanting to claim that their nation is among those deemed to be educationally successful due to the nation's children performing well on international standardised test, particularly the Programme for International Student Assessment (PISA). The ever-present awareness among teachers of the importance of their students' success on such tests amounts to what Ball and colleagues (2012: 518) refer to as 'calculated technologies of performance' and, for individual teachers at the classroom level, the 'terrors of performativity' (Ball, 1993). Commenting on national testing of students' basic skills in Australia, Hardy (2014: 16) explains that such test results, when published, 'constitute a form of objectified, and also institutionalised capital, [which seems] to shift the curricula focus from an emphasis upon learning for its own sake, to a focus upon securing the best possible test scores as markers of esteem'.

The educational effectiveness movement and standardised testing

It is important to emphasise that the enormous significance attributed to standardised testing in the current era predates the strong emergence of the neoliberal emphasis on educational accountability, setting and measuring standards, and comparing schools within a market environment. Considerable educational legitimacy had already been conferred upon the mass usage of standardised testing by the so-called 'Educational Effectiveness Movement' (EER), whose pervasive influence on international education policies is celebrated in a special issue of the journal, *School Improvement and School Effectiveness*, published in 2014, which is sub-titled: 'A state-of-the-art review—educational effectiveness, teacher effectiveness and professional learning, and school and system improvement'. In this special issue, Reynolds and colleagues (2014) celebrate the successes of the early years of EER, when 'school effectiveness' studies emerged in reaction to the massive, ground-breaking, quantitative studies conducted in the USA by Coleman et al. (1966) and Jencks et al. (1972). These research projects concluded that students' school achievement is heavily influenced by their family backgrounds. But Educational Effectiveness (EE) authors continue to maintain that this seminal research was misguided and led to the 'commonplace' belief that 'schools make no difference' (Reynolds et al., 2014: 198) to the educational outcomes of young people. The Coleman and Jencks findings were regarded as 'counter-intuitive' and 'disquieting' (Reynolds et al., 2014: 198) by effectiveness researchers who, initially, simply refused to accept the possibility that schools had a relatively minor influence on student outcomes. Their response was to shoot the messenger and ignore the message. They vowed to demonstrate that individual schools could make huge differences to educational achievement regardless of the 'outside-school' influences that bore down on students and their families, such as poverty, fractured families, unfamiliarity with the language and culture of schooling, racial discrimination, unsuitable housing or deprived neighbourhoods.

The method proposed by EE researchers for lifting the standards of students and making their schools more 'effective' involved a huge emphasis on standardised testing. Indeed, it was only on the basis of the standardised tests of basic skills that schools were to be compared with each other in terms of their levels of relative 'educational effectiveness'. One might argue that there was another way of responding to the somewhat pessimistic findings of Coleman and Jenks, which would have required schools and teachers trying to adjust to, and engage with, the different cultures and needs of the kinds of children (working class, low SES, minority, disadvantaged, and poor) who generally did not succeed in school. But rather than reaching out to diverse young people and attempting to reform education by making schooling more directly relevant to their needs and interests, the better way to go, it was claimed within EER, was to stick with what schools had traditionally done and try to do it more tightly and effectively. This emphasis is, of course, similar to that which applies under neoliberal logic.

The main task of educational effectiveness research (EER), then and now, according to Reynolds and a large number of contributing authors to his lead paper in the special issue of *School Effectiveness and School Improvement* mentioned above (Reynolds et al., 2014: 197), is 'distinguishing the effects of schools from other effects such as those of student intake and educational background' on the educational 'achievement' or 'performance' of students; that is, to concentrate on 'inside-school factors' and not the social and economic factors that Coleman and his colleagues (1966) calculated had the greatest effect on students' education prospects. Nothing much seems to have changed in this respect. The 'educational effectiveness' (EE) idea is still to identify specific inside-school factors that are apparently statistically associated with student learning outcomes, as measured by ubiquitous standardised tests, which exceed 'statistical expectations' given a student's family background. I am not suggesting that educational effectiveness researchers do not recognise that factors such as social class or race, for example, have a strong effect on educational outcomes; the point is that, in EER, such factors are said to be statistically controlled in order to determine which schools are the most effective in that they appear to contribute a 'value added' increment to a child's 'expected' level of success in basic, standardised tests of literacy and numeracy. That is, within EER, the very purpose of effectiveness research is typically defined as identifying factors that are associated with student learning outcomes which exceed statistical expectations given a student's family background. Yet family background, social class, and any notion of context, are typically regarded merely as 'noise' as is EE research as 'outside' background factors which must be statistically controlled for and then stripped away so that the researcher can concentrate on the important domain of inside-school factors. The process of schooling, the culture of pupils, the nature of the community, the society, the economy—all of which bear down heavily on teachers' work are not seen in relation to each other or to student 'achievement'.

It is the presumed direct connection between results on standardised tests and particular student outcomes which is important. All else is 'simply' regarded as background context, which is presumed to be beyond the capacity of educators to influence.

I do not wish to be disparaging of EE work because any attempt to identify ways in which schools can engage with students, especially less-advantaged students, and generate good educational outcomes is to be commended, and was an understandable response to the empirical findings of Coleman and Jencks. There is certainly a strong positive moment in this kind of educational effectiveness work in its well-meaning commitment to equality of outcomes. But the EER approach is disconnected from social and cultural constructions, and from considerations of political and economic interests. In other words, educational effectiveness researchers, even when they accept that family and social circumstances do strongly influence the ways in which young people experience schooling, do not take such factors into account when comparing student results or comparing schools. Moreover, the key point to be made here is that the educational effectiveness movement has gained tremendous momentum since the 1980s because of its congruence with neo-conservative and neoliberal policy agendas. The notion of educational effectiveness, in which centrality is given to standardised testing and basic skills, was music to the ears of neo-conservative, 'New Right' governments in the UK under Prime Minister Margaret Thatcher and in the USA under President Ronald Reagan. EE was soon influential throughout New Zealand and Australia by the late 1980s, and in parts of Europe and Scandinavia. It was taken up with particular gusto by New Labour governments in the UK in the 1990s and beyond (Reynolds et al., 2014), and was similarly influential in the United States, particularly at state level and within the deliberations of the self-styled 'education governors', many of whom legislated for state-wide testing (Reynolds et al., 2014).

The quantitative, pseudo-positivistic paradigm of EER, and its functionalist, decontextualised and ahistorical view of schooling, helped to give spurious legitimacy to political pressures from governments seeking greater control over education through the introduction of increased 'accountability' of teachers and schools and insisting upon supposedly objective measures of young people's educational achievement. In the 2005 edition of a major work on school effectiveness, Harris and Bennett (2005: 1) could claim with apparent pride that 'the school effectiveness and school improvement research fields are likely to remain influential with policy makers and practitioners alike'. This claim has proven to be a significant understatement. In the event, the international reach of both the educational effectiveness movement and neoliberal education policies has led to what Lingard and Sellar (2013) refer to as 'perverse effects' in that the integration of narrow measures of educational performance into the day to day work of teaching and learning has had anti-educational results, such as a severe narrowing of both curriculum and pedagogy as well as assessment. Such narrowing would seem to have had a deleterious effect on previously asserted notions of teacher identity.

Neoliberalism, educational effectiveness, and restricted teacher professionalism

The term 'educational effectiveness', as used currently, embraces the fields of school effectiveness (SE), teacher effectiveness (TE) and 'system-level effectiveness'(Reynolds, 2014). The broad effectiveness movement has had powerful effects in contributing to an educational climate that promotes a severely restricted sense of teacher professionalism (Hoyle, 1975). The underlying features of EE largely paved the way for key aspects of the current, neoliberal education policy assemblage in the UK, Europe and most nations globally. Such policies have done particular damage to notions of equity and social justice in education. The easy absorption of educational effectiveness discourse and priorities into the prevailing neoliberal educational policy regime has had the effect of bestowing legitimacy on educationally damaging policies that embrace and promote undue competition, marketisation, performativity and managerialism. Education policy imperatives, such as the neoliberal insistence on market comparability of schools, rely on general public acceptance of the mechanisms of standardised testing and strict accountability, and the public dissemination and display of test results, often in the form of 'league tables'. The logical endpoint, as Ball (1995: 261) predicted quite some time ago, has been the establishment an unsubtle 'technology of control which enables the monitoring and *steering* of schools by applying apparently *neutral* indicators'. Within the top-down, technicist perspective that characterises both EER and neoliberal education policy, teachers, students and communities are positioned as objects to whom educational effectiveness is 'done' rather than as a social agents within socio-political contexts. Most importantly, the general professional identities of teachers have been manipulated and shaped by policy requirements for improved outcomes of students on standardised tests.

So far in this chapter I have tried to demonstrate that, although it is only one element of the neoliberal policy complex, and although terms like 'school effectiveness,' 'teacher effectiveness' and 'educational effectiveness' sound extremely innocuous, these are very significant and extremely powerful concepts. They act as relay devices or policy vehicles for the implementation in schools of other key neoliberal policy elements that tend to restrict the ways in which teachers and school principals think about their work and their identities. By relay devices, I mean that the discourse of 'educational effectiveness' has played a substantial role in securing the commitment of many educators, at all levels of national educational hierarchies, to the broad modalities of linear control, management-driven policy and practice, and a misguided belief in the common-sense necessity of testing and accountability measures which feed into the marketisation of schooling. Lewis and Hardy (2014: 1) describe how 'national policies are enacted and mediated (i.e. practised) at the level of the school, and how these same policies discursively constitute the teacher as a performative subject—not merely changing what teachers *do*, but also ultimately who teachers *are*' (emphasis in original). Therefore, although the concept of educational effectiveness, on the face of it, may seem reasonable and sensible—which in many respects it is the effectiveness movement allows only a particular type of definition of what an effective school or an effective teacher can be.

A narrow emphasis on standardised testing in order to 'measure' educational effectiveness has been promoted by this movement, which distracts the attention of teachers and educational leaders, and the general public, away from many of the most important educational aims and purposes of schooling. These latter have become severely neglected, and changing notions of teacher identity are being played out in the critical educational message systems of curriculum, pedagogy and evaluation identified by Bernstein (1971a) as the pillars of educational approaches and identities. Indeed, the 'effectiveness' agenda displaces equally important, previous asserted educational agendas that were related to values of democracy and social justice in education. In fact, the importance of these latter purposes dates back to the founding days of public education in countries like the USA, Australia and elsewhere.

It is impossible to over-emphasise the extent to which the EER perspective, however well-intentioned, continually reinforces neoliberal education policy and conservative assumptions, while it minimises and displaces alternative educational ideals and values, which in previous eras had been, to some extent at least, asserted as legitimate elements in teacher professional culture (Brown and Angus, 1995). In the special issue of the journal, *School Effectiveness and School Improvement* mentioned above, the editor assures readers that the articles 'continue to expand knowledge about both what makes *good* teachers and schools, and about how to make schools and educational systems *good* ones' (Reynolds, 2014: 196). Harris (2014: 194) maintains that the articles in the special issue 'take stock of *what is known* ... [and that the special issue] defines a field that continues to influence policy, research, and practice'. I am particularly concerned about the easy merging, casually suggested here by Harris, of educational effectiveness discourses and practices into the prevailing neoliberal educational policy regime. I would certainly agree with Harris that the educational effectiveness movement has had a strong and enduring influence on educational policy and practice, but such influence has not been educationally positive. Indeed, the educational effectiveness movement has been the result of the flawed logic that, because schools have been found by various studies to contribute in only a minor way to the educational success or otherwise of young people compared with the massive effects of their own and family circumstances, then schools should ignore these external effects and concentrate on basic skills and standardised testing. The teacher identity implied in this narrow approach is that of a technically-competent instructor, not a student-centred educator capable of making informed professional judgements and exercising a repertoire of educational approaches.

Teacher professional identity and the purposes of education

The emphasis on standardised testing of lower-order, basic skills in the areas of literacy and numeracy is a major limitation of EER, as some educational effectiveness practitioners concede (Muis et al., 2014: 231). Yet, through its linear educational rhetoric and comforting qualitative, pseudo-positivist approach, educational effectiveness paved the way for, and continually reinforces, neoliberal policies in education. Most educators accept that the concept of 'education' is an inherently contestable one and that, therefore, it is difficult to obtain agreement on its specific nature and purposes. Nonetheless, compared with the multiple aims and purposes that have commonly been ascribed to schooling such as contributing to democracy and social justice, assisting the full flowering of young people's creativity and inquisitiveness, preparing young people for full and active participation in civic affairs, and generally enhancing their full range of potentials that may help them to lead happy and fulfilling lives—limiting one's sense of 'educational attainment' to performance on narrow, standardised tests of basic skills seems an extraordinarily restricted way of measuring the richness of learning that one normally associates with a 'good' education. Consistent with the education policy objectives of neoliberalism, effectiveness scholars have little if anything to say about equally important educational outcomes such as the development of motivation, social skills, self-esteem, broad general knowledge, the capacity to form opinions and defend them, creativity, international understanding, multicultural awareness, understanding the social and ecological issues of our time, human social interaction and empathy, health and well-being. The almost-exclusive emphasis on improving performance on standardised tests reinforces an outdated notion of teaching as merely transmission. As Cochran-Smith and Lytle (2006) emphasise, 'the distorted and highly reductionist conceptions of teaching practice and the work of teachers, and the explicit narrowing of the purposes of teaching and schooling, … results in an impoverished view of the curriculum and the broader social and democratic goals, processes, and consequences of education.'

In contrast to the view expressed by Cochran-Smith and Lytle, Muijs et al. (2014) summarise the restrictive kind of teacher behaviour that effectiveness scholars believe contributes to educational effectiveness in a 'state-of-the-art' essay on teacher effectiveness that contains the following:

> Teacher effectiveness research has consistently found that the way that the classroom is managed is important to avoiding misbehaviour and therefore to maximising time-on-task. Student misbehaviour is most likely to occur during the start of the lesson, at the end of the lesson, during downtime (which should be limited as much as possible), and during transitions. In all four cases, it is important to establish clear procedures for student behaviour … [R]ules must be rigorously enforced, otherwise they will soon be ignored by students … Having a quick pace will stop students becoming disengaged and bored, and will thus further help avoid student misbehaviour. (Muijs et al., 2014: 233)

These proclamations about effective teaching are reminiscent of the kind of advice given to novice teachers in the nineteenth-century. There is 'an emphasis on procedural efficiency' (Muijs et al., 2014: 248). Teacher-centred, whole class instruction is clearly assumed. Knowledge is seen as objective and, in the style of 'banking' education, is merely to be transmitted. Low test scores are presumed to be the fault of the students or of underperforming teachers rather than attributable to structural issues in society that contribute to unequal educational outcomes (Angus, 2012). There is a dour concern with issues of time-on-task and ensuring that the curriculum is covered or, more specifically in this case, that whatever material will be included in 'whatever test is being used to measure student progress' is covered (Muijs et al., 2014: 232). There is no mention of the joy of learning. Tests define what is officially important and also shape the processes that are regarded as effective pedagogy. Advice that Muijs and colleagues provide on the topic of 'effective questioning' further illustrates the point:

> Effective questioning is one of the most widely studied aspects of teaching, and therefore a solid body of knowledge exists on which strategies are most effective. Questions need to be asked at the beginning of the lesson when the topic of the last lesson in that subject is being reviewed, after every short presentation, and during the summary at the end of the lesson ... Correct answers need to be acknowledged in a positive but businesslike fashion ... When a student answers a question incorrectly, the teacher needs to point out swiftly that the answer was wrong. If the student has answered incorrectly due to inattention or carelessness, the teacher must swiftly move on to the next student.
>
> (Muijs et al., 2014: 234)

In these extracts, students are represented as disembodied objects to whom the teaching, or, better, in the discourse of educational effectiveness and neoliberal policies, 'instruction', is done. The state-of-the-art advice is about behavioural strategies, instructional techniques and didactic methods that are to be applied to generic, disempowered, anonymous students. The importance of teaching to the test is reinforced, and there would seem little opportunity for seizing teaching moments or pursuing student interest, curiosity or creativity. To the extent that teachers do act in this way, however, they entrench a top-down, positivistic, reductionist approach to pedagogy and surrender control of education to an impersonal bureaucracy. There is no consideration of the professional autonomy and professional judgment of teachers, which has been seriously undermined. Nor is there any sense that the legitimate work of teachers involves understanding, provoking and responding to students' imagination and fantasy. It all seems so backward-looking, heartless and soulless, devoid of any attempt to do as Gannon (2013: 26) encourages us 'to know more about the micropolitics of pedagogies in context and about the productive little swerves that teachers and students make as they work together to co-construct knowledge from the resources that all of them bring to that pedagogical space'. That kind of spontaneity and creativity, and professional awareness and judgements about the needs and interests of students, is lacking in the educational effectiveness approach and in neoliberal education policy. Instead, the 'reforms' associated with neoliberalism, and legitimised by educational effectiveness rhetoric, are, as Saltman (2014: 257) points out, 'utterly antithetical to teachers acting as intellectuals or performing the public role of fostering that dialogue, debates, and critical thought that is the lifeblood of public democratic lives outside of schools'. The current political framing of education, Salman (2014: 257) concludes, is antithetical to an educative view in which 'youth, the very embodiment of hope for the future, can be invested with the tools and skills for creative and critical thought to comprehend and ruthlessly criticise the present so as to imagine a future that is not just free and equal, prosperous and peaceful, but survivable'.

The current hero among TE commentators is John Hattie, whose book *Visible Learning* (Hattie, 2009) is said to provide the 'most influential set of recent meta-analyses relevant to teacher effectiveness research' (Muijs et al., 2014: 237). Hattie's book provides a synthesis of over 800 meta-analyses of research on a range of influences on students' school 'achievement'. Typically, however, the studies examined are quantitative comparisons of the performance of students on standardised tests. Hattie's research, according to Muijs and colleagues (2014: 237), 'generally concur[s] with the main body of educational effectiveness research in finding that classroom practice is the strongest determinant of student outcomes'. Hattie, himself, is a little more cautious and makes it clear that his book is only about 'within-school factors' and that he has expressly excluded discussion of other factors that 'may be more important'. Specifically, in introducing the book, Hattie cautions:

> It is *not* a book about what cannot be influenced in schools—thus critical discussions about class, poverty, resources in families, health in families, and nutrition are not included—but this is NOT because they are unimportant, indeed they may be more important than many of the influences discussed in this book. It is just that I have not included these topics in my orbit. (2009: viii-ix, emphasis in original)

Muijs et al. (2014: 238) do concede that meta-analyses are always problematic and that there is 'inherent difficulty of combining studies in a field [like EE] where clarity and agreement over concepts and the application and measurement thereof is very often missing'. Moreover, one could argue, as Coe and Fitz-Gibbon (1998: 430) do, that the 'repeated confirmation of [educational effectiveness] factors depends in part on the vagueness of their formulation' and their compatibility with the neoliberal education policy requirement of narrow, teacher-centred instruction in basic skills that are to be measured by standardised tests, the results of which are believed by proponents to indicate whether a teacher is sufficiently 'good' at his or her profession. As well as being vague, the factors that are said to contribute to educational effectiveness also tend to be entirely predictable. All are conventional school-level modalities that have long been associated with narrow, conservative forms of schooling. Their continual 'validation', therefore, continually legitimates what has become the policy status quo in the neoliberal era. For example, a review conducted by Sammons and her colleagues (1995) specifies the following eleven categories of effective schooling: professional leadership, shared vision and goals, a learning environment, concentration on teaching and learning, purposeful teaching, high expectations, positive reinforcement, monitoring progress, people's rights and responsibilities, home/school partnerships, and a learning organisation. Such factors are obviously imprecise and lend themselves to a wide range of interpretations. For instance, judging that 'a learning environment' exists, however such a thing might be defined, can surely be only impressionistic at best. Likewise, what exactly would be required for leadership to be judged as 'purposeful'? Moreover, the process of measuring each school variable separately and calculating its relationship with each of the other variables and with the single control variable of 'student achievement' in order to get some sense of the overall 'effectiveness' of the school and its teachers, as Luyten et al. (2005) put it, 'does no justice to the complexity of the realities experienced by these schools'. Yet, in the many highly influential reviews of the EE field (e.g. Scheerens and Bosker, 1997, Teddlie and Reynolds, 2000), 'effectiveness factors' are presented with such a sense of clarity, confidence and numerical precision that one feels almost obliged to agree with them.

The strong impression is conveyed in EER discourse that almost everything that needs to be known about effective learning and teaching is now known; the answers have been provided by EER and have been the basis for neoliberal 'reforms'. The superficial conclusion is that we just need teachers, principals and school communities to implement the appropriate, 'best practice', effectiveness measures. Yet the critical point is that the educational achievement of teachers and schools is measured only by the performance of students on standardised tests—which provides an extremely narrow sense of the nature of the work of teachers and schools. This means that the concentration of EER on so-called 'effectiveness factors' ignores the enormous complexities of student-teacher relationships and the incredible diversity of students' lives and the ways these play out in schools and classrooms. Bourdieu (1977, Bourdieu and Passeron, 1977) in France, and Bernstein (1971b, 1977) in England, for example, have made it abundantly clear that students of less-advantaged cultural backgrounds tend to struggle at school in comparison with students from middle class cultures. They and others have illustrated that subtle and largely unrecognised processes of advantaging and disadvantaging occur in schools because of the general preference in schooling for language, practices, norms and values that are, in the main, consistent with the habits and dispositions of middle class families.

The major outcome of such critical sociological work since the 1970s is that it has opened up sophisticated analyses and theorising about the nature of schools as organisations, the complexity of their cultures, the problematic relationship between schooling and society, and, in particular, the highly problematic nature of teacher identity and culture. Although some insights from these critiques may have been expressed in a somewhat reductionist manner at times, this important work has enabled educators and researchers to understand that teaching is a complex social, political and cultural process that is far from neutral. It is precisely this fundamental lesson that is still ignored in EER and which, largely because of the broad acceptance of educational effectiveness thinking among governments and policy makers, is being engrained in current neoliberal education policy and in general public understandings of 'good' teaching. Moreover, even despite its almost total concentration on standardised test scores as indicators of effective teaching and effective schooling, the size of the 'school effect' identified by EE researchers has turned out to be about the same as that identified in the 1960s by Coleman and his team, who put it as contributing about fifteen per cent of the explanation of a pupil's school achievement compared with about eighty-five per cent being due to the pupil's family and social circumstances (Teddlie, Reynolds and Sammons, 2000). This point is emphasised by Luyten et al. (2005: 269), who state that 'the school effects reported in [effectiveness] studies hardly ever exceed fifteen per cent for studies based on achievement scores'. In other words, and this critical point needs to be emphasised, almost all SER [i.e.

school effectiveness research] findings reinforce the point that school success is overwhelmingly associated with social and economic advantage. As Luyten et al. (2005: 269) conclude:

> Even though almost every SER study confirms the limited influence of school factors and the substantial impact of family backgrounds on learning, the latter relation is hardly ever investigated thoroughly … SER studies usually treat family background, peer groups, and similar factors as control variables in data analysis, in an attempt to estimate the effects of the particular factors on which the studies focus (e.g. teaching time, amount of content covered, educational leadership) more accurately. The notion that factors outside the school and classroom may cancel out the efforts of schools and teachers, however, is not within the scope of SER.

Instead of considering social and cultural factors, the pervasiveness of policies of 'effectiveness', measurement, choice, markets and accountability bears down upon, and shapes, the ways in which teachers, students, parents and communities engage with their local or 'chosen' schools, which are likely to be quite different places than they would have been if such priority had not been given to such concepts that are related to high-stakes testing. These key elements of the neoliberal world-view have been, to a large extent, normalised in the day-to-day practices of teaching and learning. The upshot is that a neoliberal social imaginary has been asserted rather fluidly over time and now seems so intransigent that alternative imaginaries are displaced by the broad acceptance of what is presented as the neoliberal 'reality'. Such policies have imposed a very powerful disciplinary template over schools and teachers. Within this performative and regulatory policy regime, the edicts of 'the neoliberal global consensus' (Rizvi and Lingard, 2010) have been incorporated into national education legislation, which has effectively brought education into the service of the economy. The cold and distal form of teacher engagement that characterises the currently prevailing 'measuring and reporting' approach to education, with its limited aspiration of improving test scores, is very different from the 'much richer notion of teaching and learning advocated by Cochran-Smith and Lytle (2004):

> Teaching goes far beyond what teachers do when they stand in front of students, just as student learning is not limited to the classroom … It is about how teachers and their students construct the curriculum,

> commingling their experiences, their cultural and linguistic resources, and their interpretive frameworks. Teaching also entails how teachers' actions are infused with complex and multilayered understandings of learners, culture, class, gender, literacies, social issues, institutions, 'herstories' and histories, communities, materials, texts, and curricula.

Cochran-Smith and Lytle (2004) present an argument for asserting social and educational values within education, and for teachers to work with families and communities to provide better opportunities for young people. An important element of teacher identity, in this view, is to keep chipping away at the greater goal of achieving democratic schooling for social justice.

Alternative, more authentic ways in which 'schools make a difference'

Effectiveness rationality has had a profound effect upon school practitioners and, particularly through the legitimacy it gives to neoliberal policy themes, on educational politics and governance throughout OECD countries and, increasingly, everywhere else. This is not surprising as the effectiveness movement purports to offer direct, evidence-based solutions to educational problems. The effectiveness literature, therefore, should never be taken lightly. The trouble is that its putative solutions turn out to do little to solve, and much to exacerbate, existing problems of educational inequality. Concern with measurement and comparison in schools, when linked with policies of high-stakes testing, competition and marketisation, has steadily displaced what had been emerging, to some extent at least, in the 1960s and 1970s as a professional ethos of concern for equity and social responsibility, which required teachers to try to get to know their pupils, understand where they were coming from, and to move to meet them by moderating or negotiating the curriculum and their pedagogy to make learning more relevant to their everyday lives and experiences. Such ideas have now well and truly been replaced by the more impersonal ethos of narrowly-defined effectiveness, teacher instruction, competition, accountability, market and performativity, which allows little place for attempts to understand and be inclusive of the everyday lived experiences and cultures of young people. Pedagogy and curriculum have increasingly narrowed. The hardening of the education policy regime has meant that schools, particularly those in areas characterised by poverty and disadvantage, are less likely to deliberately seek to change their ways of operating in order to accommodate the diversity of students.

Instead, they are pushed towards compliance with a policy overlay defined by testing and competition.

To cope with competitive market arrangements, 'effectiveness' mentality, and the heavy accountability regime, students and teachers are expected to turn themselves into the kind of people demanded by ostensibly effective, high performing schools that excel in high-stakes testing. The 'high stakes' bring teachers to 'the point where power reaches into the very grain of individuals, touches their bodies and inserts itself into their actions and attitudes, their discourses, learning processes and everyday lives' (Foucault, 1980: 39). This is an example of disciplinary power that affects the professional autonomy and professional repertoires of teachers, and imposes upon their self-concept and professional identity. As Foucault (1977: 187) puts it: 'It is the fact of constantly being seen, of being able always to be seen, that maintains the disciplined individual in his (sic) subjection'. Such a form of visibility—in this case data surveillance—'compels educators to comply with [government] standards through threats of sanctions and promises of rewards' (Webb, 2005: 194). Teachers' sense of themselves as teachers is continually being constructed in these ways and through discourses of accountability and performativity.

Some students are able to fare very well in the competitive environment prescribed by neoliberalism despite the bland curriculum, unimaginative pedagogy, and relentless measurement that characterise 'effective' schools. These are the kind of students who have always done well at school. They are typically highly motivated, well-resourced, and culturally equipped for educational and future life success. For them, the 'decision' to be successful at school is, as Ball and colleagues (2002: 54) put it, 'a non-decision' because it is part of a 'normal', unthinking and expected social trajectory. But such is not the case for less-advantaged children. For them, the decision to make a real effort to be successful at school has to be an active one. But it is a problematic decision because they and their families lack the social and cultural resources and supports that are generally available to more advantaged families. This makes the reproduction of disadvantage, for them, much more likely, which is why it is critically important for schools to reach out to engage such students—to understand them and their neighbourhoods, to ensure that they can have a personal connection with teachers and a stake in what the school is perceived to offer. Instead of being expected to simply adjust to, and comply with, the entrenched school and teacher paradigms that are characteristic of EE modalities and neoliberal education policy, students should be engaged in relevant and interesting school experiences in which they can recognise themselves, their neighbours, and their communities.

This kind of injustice within schooling practices is unrecognised within neoliberal policy framing or effectiveness rationality, which tend to eschew the socio-political, cultural, and economic factors that bear down on families and communities and infuse education with complexity and uncertainty. The entrenchment of narrow, reductionist thinking about such an infinitely complex and contestable conception as education is an example of what Bourdieu means by symbolic domination:

> The effect of symbolic domination (whether ethnic, gender, cultural or linguistic, etc.) is exerted not in the logic of knowing consciousnesses but through the schemes of perception, appreciation and action that are constitutive of habitus and which, below the level of the decisions of consciousness and the controls of the will, set up a cognitive relationship that is profoundly obscure to itself. (Bourdieu, 2004: 340)

There is now a generation of students and teachers in the English-speaking countries in particular, and increasingly in Europe, Scandinavia and the rest of the world, whose perceptions of teaching and learning have been framed by the competitive, test-oriented norms and values of neoliberal education policy, for which EE rationality paved the way. Such is now the educational status quo. The danger is that, as Bourdieu and Wacquant (2004) explain, our propensity to take existing arrangements for granted is a result of our 'being born in a social world, [and so] we accept a whole range of postulates, axioms, which go without saying and require no inculcating' (p. 272). The milieu of EE has gradually become more and more entrenched and taken for granted. And, although acceptance of the status quo can be seen an act of 'misrecognition' on the part of educators in general, it is precisely the kind of misrecognition that constitutes 'symbolic violence' (Bourdieu, 2004; Bourdieu and Wacquant, 2004), an illustration of which is schools trying to demonstrate to governments, education authorities and the school marketplace that they are 'successful' and 'effective' because they perform well on high-stakes tests while, at the same time, they are failing to engage with the most vulnerable of students for whom they are responsible. This limited educational perspective does symbolic violence to all students and to alternative educational ideas and imagined educational futures that might be built along inherently 'educational' rather than economic and competitive lines.

That is, the pervasive discourse of 'school effectiveness', 'teacher effectiveness' and 'system effectiveness', and the competition among schools to be successful in the market, reduces education to a mind-numbing uniformity which displaces richer, more humane conceptions of learning and teaching.

Conclusion: activist and socially critical teacher identity

Research conducted at Federation University Australia (e.g. Smyth et al., 2008: 2009; Smyth and McInerney, 2012, Angus, 2012, 2013), some of which I have participated in, and the research of many others (e.g. Wrigley et al., 2012, Hattam et al., 2009), suggests we need to critically examine the effects of EE thinking and neoliberal policies on the everyday life-worlds of students, teachers and schools, who, within neoliberal discourses, are decontextualised and pathologised, and represented in negative and inappropriate ways. The heavy policy overlay of accountability and competitiveness weighs heavily on teachers, students, and parents and tends to leads us, even if unwillingly, to accept dominant meanings that shape our identities as educators. Under such conditions we are more likely to overlook the moral purpose of education to promote in schools the core values of social justice, democracy, and equity. Shields (2004: 122) explains this point in relation to US schooling:

> When children feel they belong and find their realities reflected in the curriculum and conversations of schooling, research has demonstrated repeatedly that they are more engaged in learning and that they experience greater school success. ... Unless all children experience a sense of belonging in schools, they are being educated in institutions that exclude and marginalise them, that perpetuate inequity and inequality rather than democracy and social justice.

The research cited above indicates multiple direct and indirect ways in which teachers are able to exercise professional judgments in order to make a difference to students' learning, and, more importantly, their lives and their sense of themselves. The ethnographic data reported in the research indicates that teachers and school principals have the capacity to influence organisational norms, practices, and structure, while also simultaneously both adapting to and influencing professional expectations within organisations and, more broadly, within educational policy and governance. Ethnographic analysis of such processes and discourses, through which social relations and identities are constituted, sheds a little light on how management and organisational change gets 'accomplished' in schools. Typically, teachers in such situations engage in relational pedagogy that acknowledges students' life-worlds and recognises them as authentic and agentic beings who are co-constructors of knowledge and not just passive recipients. Such teachers, and their students, reject the passive identity that is typically constructed for them within so-called effective classrooms in which direct, whole-class instruction and standardised testing is typically preferred. Instead, as Hattam and others (2009: 305) conclude:

> [A]ny project that hopes to address the problem of cultural capital must focus on the pedagogies that start to connect school-based learning with students' own life-worlds in their communities. Only when schooling is organised to make this link can the experience of intrinsic value in education become established, and enable scaffolding to success in the mainstream curriculum, leading to extrinsic rewards from schooling.

It is important to foster the belief that students have voices and opinions and wisdom that are to be taken seriously by their teachers so that their values, cultures, and actual life circumstances can be respected, engaged with, and incorporated into the life of the school in curriculum and teaching practice (Angus, 2006). The currently skewed orientation does violence to professional and relational notions of teacher identity. It reinforces concerns with efficiency and effectiveness at the expense of the broader, richer aims of education. Structural inequalities in society are ignored within neoliberal policy frames while the erroneous belief that people, regardless of inequality and disadvantage, should be held responsible for their own failures is implicitly accepted. Schooling is a major social institution that contributes to the production of, as well as the reproduction of, as well as resistance to, power relations of society (Willis, 1981). In arguing for a relational approach to learning and teaching, I am also arguing that teacher identity should embrace a relational, democratic perspective in which students are regarded as contributors to a dialogical process that has some chance of re-shaping the way schooling is 'done'.

References

Alexander, R. (Ed) (2009). *Children, their world, their education: Final report and recommendations of the Cambridge Primary review*. London: Routledge.

Anderson, G. (2009) *Advocacy Leadership: Towards a Post-reform Agenda in Education*, Routledge: New York.

Angus, L. (2013) School choice: neoliberal education policy and imagined futures, *British Journal of Sociology of Education*, DOI: 10.1080/01425692.2013.823835

Angus, L. (2012) Teaching within and against the circle of privilege: reforming teachers, reforming schools, *Journal of Education Policy*, 27(2):231-251

Angus, L. (2006) Educational leadership and the imperative of including student voices, student interests, and students' lives in the mainstream, *International Journal of Leadership in Education*, 9(4):369-379.

Ball, S. (2006). *Education policy and social class*, London: Routledge.

Ball, S. (2003) The teacher's soul and the terrors of performativity, *Journal of Education Policy*, 18(2):215-228.

Ball, S. (1995) Intellectuals or technicians? The urgent role of theory in educational studies, *British Journal of Educational Studies*, 43(3):255-271.

Ball, S., Maguire, M., Braun, A., Perryman, J. and Hoskins, K. 2012) Assessment Technologies in Schools: 'Deliverology' and the 'Play of Dominations'. *Research Papers in Education*, 27(5): 513-533.

Ball, S., Davies, J., David, M. and Reay, D. (2002) 'Classification' and 'judgement': social class and the 'cognitive structures' of choice of higher education, *British Journal of Sociology of Education*, 23(1):51-72.

Bernstein, B. (1971a) On the classification and framing of educational knowledge, in M. F. D Young (ed). *Knowledge and Control: New directions for the sociology of education.* London: Collier MacMillan.

Bernstein, B. (1971b) *Class, codes and control, Volume I*, London: Routledge and Kegan Paul.

Bernstein, B. (1977) *Class, codes and control, Volume 3*, London: Routledge and Kegan Paul.

Bourdieu, P. (1977) *Cultural reproduction and social reproduction*, in J. Karabel and A. Halsey (eds) *Power and ideology in education,* New York: Oxford University Press).

Bourdieu, P. (2004) Gender and symbolic violence, in N. Scheper-Hughes and P. Bourgois (Eds.) *Violence in war and peace: An anthology* (Oxford, Blackwell):339-42.

Bourdieu, P. and Passeron, J. (1977) *Reproduction in education, society and culture*, London: Sage.

Bourdieu, P. and Wacquant, L. (2004) Symbolic violence, in N. Scheper-Hughes and P. Bourgois (Eds) *Violence in war and peace: An anthology* (Oxford, Blackwell).

Brown, L. and Angus, L. (1995) Reconstructing teacher professionalism: Curriculum in Victoria's Schools of the Future, paper presented to te annual conference of the Australian Curriculum Studies Association, Adelaide.

Cochran-Smith, M. and Lytle, S. (2006) Troubling images of teaching in No Child Left Behind, *Harvard educational review*, 76(4):668-697.

Coe, R. and Fitz-Gibbon, C.T. (1998) School Effectiveness Research: criticisms and recommendations, *Oxford Review of Education*, 24(4):421-438.

Coleman, J. S., Campbell, E., Hobson, C., McPartland, J., Mood, A., Weinfeld, F. and York, R. (1966) *Equality of educational opportunity,* Washington, DC: US Government Printing Office.

Foucault, M. (1980) *Power/knowledge: selected interviews and other writings*, New York: Pantheon Books.

Foucault, M. (1977) *Discipline and punish: The birth of the prison*, New York: Pantheon Books.

Gannon, S. (2013) My School redux: re-storying schooling with the My School website, *Discourse: Studies in the Cultural Politics of Education*, 35(1):17-30.

Grek, S., Lawn, M., Lingard, B., Ozga, J., Rinne, R., Segerholm, C. and Simola, H. (2009) National policy brokering and the construction of the European Education Space in England, Sweden, Finland and Scotland, *Journal of Education Policy*, 45(1):5-21.

Hardy, I. (2014): A logic of enumeration: the nature and effects of national literacy and numeracy testing in Australia, *Journal of Education Policy*, DOI: 10.1080/02680939.2014.945964

Harris, A. (2014) Still making a difference: reflections on the field, *School Effectiveness and School Improvement*, 25(2):193-194.

Harris, A. and Bennett, N. (Eds) (2005) *School effectiveness and school improvement: Alternative perspectives*, London: Continuum.

Hattam, R., Brennan, R., Zipin, L. and Comber, B. (2009) Researching for social justice: contextual, conceptual and methodological challenges, *Discourse: Studies in the Cultural Politics of Education*, 30(3):303-316.

Hattie, J. (2009) *Visible learning: A synthesis of over 800 meta-analyses relating to achievement*, London: Routledge.

Hoyle, E. (1975) Changing conceptions of a profession, in H. Burher and R. Saran (Eds.) *Managing teachers as professionals in schools*, London: Kogan Page.

Jencks, C., Smith, M. S., Ackland, H., Bane, M. J., Cohen, D., Grintlis, H., Heynes, B. and Michelson, S. (1972) *Inequality*, New York: Basic Books.

Lingard, B. (2010). Policy borrowing, policy learning: testing times in Australian schooling, *Critical Studies in Education*, 51(2):129-147.

Lewis, S. and Hardy, I. (2014): Funding, reputation and targets: the discursive logics of high-stakes testing, *Cambridge Journal of Education*, DOI: 10.1080/0305764X.2014.936826

Luyten, H., Visscher, A., and Witziers, B. (2005). School effectiveness research: From a review of the criticism to recommendations for further development, *School Effectiveness and School Improvement*, 16: 249-279.

Muijs, D., Kyriakides, L., van der Werf, G., Creemers, B., Timperley, H. and Earl, L. (2014) State of the art - teacher effectiveness and professional learning, *School Effectiveness and School Improvement*, 25(2):231-256.

Nordtveit, B. (2010). Towards post-globalisation? On the hegemony of western education and development discourses. *Globalisation, Societies and Education*, 8(3):321-337.

Oakes, L., Townley, B. and Cooper, D.J. (1998). Business planning as pedagogy: language and control in a changing educational field. *Administrative Science Quarterly*, 48(2):257-292.

Reynolds, D. (2014) Editorial, *School Effectiveness and School Improvement*, 25(2):195-196).

Reynolds, D., Sammons, P., De Fraine, B., Van Damme, J., Townsend, T., Teddlie, C. and Stringfield, S. (2014) Educational effectiveness research (EER): a state-of-the-art review, *School Effectiveness and School Improvement*, 25(2):197-230.

Saltman, K. (2014) Neoliberalism and corporate school reform: 'failure' and 'creative destruction', *Review of Education, Pedagogy, and Cultural Studies*, 36(4):249-259

Sammons, P., Hillman, J. and Mortimore, P. (1995) *Key characteristics of effective schools: a review of school effectiveness research*, London: Office for Standards in Education.

Scheerens, J. (2014) School, teaching, and system effectiveness: some comments on three state-of-the-art reviews, *School Effectiveness and School Improvement*, 25(2):282-290.

Scheerens, J., and Bosker, R. (1997) *The foundations of school effectiveness*, Oxford: Pergamon Press.

Shields, C. (2004) Dialogic leadership for social justice: Overcoming pathologies of silence. *Educational Administration Quarterly*, 40(1):109-132.

Smyth, J., Angus, L., Down, B. and McInerney, P. (2009) *Activist and socially critical school and community renewal: Social justice in exploitative times*, Rotterdam: Sense Publishers.

Smyth, J., Angus, L., Down, B. and McInerney, P. (2008) *Critically engaged learning: connecting to young lives*, New York: Peter Lang.

Smyth, J., and McInerney, P. (2012) *From silent witnesses to active agents: Student voice in re-engaging with learning*, New York: Peter Lang.

Teddlie, C. and Reynolds, D. (Eds.) (2000). *The international handbook of school effectiveness research*, London: Falmer Press.

Teddlie, C., Reynolds, D. and Sammons, P. (2000) the methodology and scientific properties of school effectiveness research, in C. Teddlie and D. Reynolds (Eds) *International handbook of school effectiveness research* (pp. 55-133):London: Falmer Press.

Webb, P. (2005) The anatomy of accountability, *Journal of Education Policy*, 20(2):189-208.

Wrigley, T., Lingard, B. and Thomson, P. (2012) Pedagogies of transformation: Keeping hope alive in troubled times, *Critical Studies in Education*, 53(1):95-108.

Willis, P. (1981) Cultural production is different from cultural reproduction is different to social production is different from reproduction, *Interchange*, 12(2/3):48-67

Chapter 9

Changeability and technacy: The new professional *raison d'etre*

Karen Borgnakke

Abstract

The political discourse and educational reforms show increasing demands for professionalisation highlighted as changeability and strategies for organisational development. These approaches throughout the 2000s have stressed innovation, and IT-based strategies referring to important shifts in focus on the professionals in the educational sector. Based on case studies this chapter will analyse the shift from classical concepts centering on a single professional to current concepts having a professional mix and an inter-professional team at the centre.

The chapter identifies the demands of changeability and innovation as a political credo going across the educational sector. Following the credo the analyses show how changeability and technacy have become the current professional *raison d'être*. Educational cases provide examples for analysis and critical reflection of practical consequences and challenges for educational organisations, as well as for teachers and students.

Background: The classic concepts of professionalisation

The concepts of professionalisation examined here are related to analyses of reform trends in the Nordic welfare state (Petersen1997; Petersen 2011) and the consequences for the (Danish) educational system (Moos, Hermansen, Krejsler 2002, Hjort 2004, 2008, Krogh-Jespersen 2005, Råe 2005, Nordisk Pedagogik 2006). During the 2000s the description of teachers, nurses and pedagogues regarded as the semi-professionals of the modern welfare system or just *the welfare professions* was sharpened as a result of a post-modern critical approach to the new liberal political discourse. However, the logic behind the analyses was still the classic logic originating from the Weberian inspired concept of professions. This logic implies that compared with professions like doctors, lawyers, and engineers—regarded as full-scale professionals—the nurse, teacher, pedagogue and social worker *only* obtain semi-professional status. The semi-professions conceptualised as *welfare professions* and incorporated in the Bourdieu inspired analyses of power-relations and intersections of social, symbolic and legal closure (Harrits 2014) seem to confirm the *semi-* status in terms of reproductions of power relations in the social field.

Further, semi-professions conceptualised as *second generation professionals* (Selander 1993) or incorporated into analyses of the four ages in professionalism (Hargreaves 2000) add important contemporary historical dimensions to the concepts.

From the above, it could be concluded that despite different concepts, the current statement is that the semi-professionals and welfare professions still lack the privileges of full professional autonomy, authority and sovereignty. To understand the consequences in relation to the profession intensive systems like *health care* and *education*, the classic analysis of the *semi-status* and *lack of authority and sovereignty* serve a clarifying function. However, at the same time tendencies at the political macro-level seem to be in conflict with the classic concepts and a shift in foci on professional functions is noticed during the 1990s and 2000s.

If the main point is that we still need the classic approach regarding contemporary background and basic definitions, I will continue the argument agreeing with the approach of Thomas Brante (2011) elaborated in the article *Professions as Science-Based Occupations*. This article provides *the very simple, basic definition of professions*, by stressing as follows:

> Professions are: Occupations conducting interventions derived from scientific knowledge of mechanisms, structures, and contexts. It should perhaps be added that, of course, professions do not *only* employ science-based interventions in their practice. It is a necessary but not sufficient criterion. (Brante 2011:14)

However, if the concepts provide a basic platform and a theoretical position, empirically, a missing link is revealed. Empirical analyses and case studies point towards trends and strategies in opposition to the classic concepts of a profession. The empirical analyses represent a shift in focus moving from the professional as an authorised expert in one single person, towards a focus on the organisation and on the professional team.

Bearing in mind the strategies for reforms and organisational development, the empirical analyses of the interplay between the political macro- and the institutional meso-level are needed. Furthermore, analyses of the situation for educational institutions are needed where the demands of professionalisation have an impact across the sector as well as an impact on the transition for secondary, upper secondary and higher education.

The decades of reform across the educational sector

With reference to the ethnographic research and analyses performed during the 2000s I refer to what can be characterised as the decades of reforms across the sector ranging from kindergarten to university. Further, I draw from empirical analyses exposing the consequences for higher education and the different scholastic, academic and profession oriented learning contexts. Overviews and details are given in former case analyses (Borgnakke 2005, 2011, 2012, 2014). In this chapter, going across these cases, my focus is on the common tendencies and consequences for the institutional and organisational level referring to policy documents, case-study multi-level materials and interviews with leadership teams and teacher teams (Borgnakke 2010).

Against this backdrop both the reforms, processes of implementation and school cases serve as the empirical background for analysing professionalisation as a main political theme and an issue in the field of practice.

The examples in the following sections start at the political macro-level concentrating on the discursive shift *from a single expert to the professional team*. Next, the analysis concentrates on professionalisation at the organisational level. The IT-based strategies and *The IT-upper secondary school* are the *pioneer* examples of the 2000 decade (Borgnakke 2012). These are followed by examples from the academic context (*The innovative university campus*). At this stage, the analyses include different voices and professional role models. The trend-analyses end with examples from the profession-oriented context concentrating the institutional development and formation project on online learning: *NETeducation, online-learning nursing program*.

The macro-level and the political project: From the single expert to the professional organisation and the professional team

The political discourse and official agenda in educational contexts represented up till the 1990s is characterised by dynamic signs of modernisation and societal development. In view of the obligations to pursue *equality through education* and life-long learning, educational organisations were additionally required to have strategies to change the former selective educational patterns. This implied the introduction of strategies to neutralise power relations, gender and class patterns by changing the traditional education system and elite institutions from the inside.

During the 1990s a shift could be recognised and the political point seemed to be that the strategy should concentrate on quality assurance, enhancing the concrete process of modernisation and professionalisation by focusing on the professional key tasks related to the sector. With this background there are issues with both the concepts of welfare professions and power relations as well as the battles between the professions, as it is shown in the Danish analyses given by Weber (2001), Jørgensen and Eriksen (2005), and Hjort (2008).

These analyses show how semi-professions are placed in a specific vulnerable situation expressed as the dilemma between professionalisation and its contradiction, de-professionalisation. To understand the consequences, we need to conceptualise the political demands of reform and professionalisation within the public sphere as a late modern consequence related to what in policy analyses is summarised as postmodern *marketising* and demands of *the operational focus* (Ball 2000, Gumport 2001, Lynch 2006). At this stage, the political discourse shows a breakaway from the classic concept of professionalism and concentrates demands on an operational focus directed by the organisation and the professional leadership as the professional team. With this background we can stress that the team in a concrete manner is supposed to represent a new model and an answer to how to cope professionally with the system, the sector and the organisational key tasks.

At the macro level the process of professionalisation can be described through concepts from Anthony Giddens as a part of the societal process of structuration and disembedding (1990, 1991). Further, the professionalisation of the key tasks in the health care and educational sectors, which were marked by conflicts at the institutional meso-level, can be conceptualised through Jürgen Habermas (1981), as conflicts between the system and the lifeworld and as social pathologies being provoked (Borgnakke 1996, 2003). In decades with political reforms, such as the Danish waves of reforms during 1990-2010, the political discourse mirrors these conflicts between system and lifeworld and is followed by demands expressed as in a triad of *Modernising, Qualitative Assurance and Professionalisation.*

In an empirical sense the triad points towards development of the professional organisation and a new cross professional teamwork as a breakaway from the classic concepts of the expert. At the same time a tendency referring to demands of quality assurance as crisis management can be recognised. When something is going wrong and cases are turning out as *bad cases*, these bad cases are supposed to be handled professionally. And if the welfare states' institutions are placed in areas having social conflicts, organisations and working teams are expected to tackle both such conflicts and institutional challenges in a professional manner.

Against this basic background, moving beyond Brante's description (Brante, 2011), the point is that the current political discourse disturbs the classic orientation towards the professional expert and faculty member as a single person. Instead of the traditional focus on the classic professional person, the political agenda now is recognised as being oriented towards the professionalised organisation, the professional team and towards this team as a cross disciplinary team, including a mix of professionals and semi-professionals. In the Danish cases there will be consequences of the point of view outlined above at all levels highlighted in terms of quality assurance and evaluation (Hansen 2005, Hansen and Rieper 2010, Dahler-Larsen 2003), or in terms of modernising both key tasks and institutional frameworks in a sectoral manner. *The sectoral manner* is revealed by case-analyses showing how both upper secondary schools and the classic elite institutions, The Gymnasium and The Faculty, are seen as new organisations demonstrating the breakaway from the classic basis (Borgnakke 2011). The professional contexts as well as professional functions are changing. Firstly, the professional teacher is no longer recognised as an individual teacher or just a member of faculty but rather as a member of a professional team working across expert areas and academic subjects. Secondly, the consequences for practice are visible with the professional teacher team in charge of the process of planning, teaching and evaluation.The teacher teams create new routines for organisational development by combining innovative strategies for performativity and assessments. Thirdly, the issue of professionalism spans the full spectrum ranging from the professional organisation dealing with questions about the organisational profile to the professional team dealing with questions about the professional identity.

Focusing on professional identity, the shift in orientation and values challenging the relation between the professional culture and organisational development is apparent. The professional team turns out to be a mix of classic professionals and new semi-professionals directed by the professional leadership team, already institutionalised by the short name 'LT'.

Summing up the process of professionalisation in rough historical lines:

> Instead of the ideal typical focus on the classic professional person we now observe a political agenda oriented towards the professionalised organisation and the professional team
>
> The professional team includes a mix of professionals and semi-professionals and refers to both mono- and inter-professional areas of knowledge and functions.

The new challenge for the organisation and the professional team seems to be to reconstruct the platform for the shifting mono- and inter-professional basis and competences (Borgnakke and Sand Nielsen, 2015).

With the macro-level tendencies as a common background, the important shift can be illustrated further by current Nordic cases from the field of compulsory school and upper secondary schools. Demands of professionalisation are up front and they are emphasised together with demands for change management. The political credo seems to be based on the appeal to the system, the organisation and the actors to be open for changes.

The political credo: 'We are open to change'

In the political discourse, *Schools in transition* as a political programme demonstrates how the school system is becoming involved in the process of reform and innovation. The contemporary point is that now if *reform* and *innovation* must be an integrated part of the process of professionalisation all involved parties involved will be confronted with a new magnitude for change referring to the educational system in total—from kindergarten to university. All schools and institutions will be confronted with strategies for change. Consequently this means that the professional organisation and the professional team will be regarded as the agency for change (2011a).

If the above refers to the ideal typical late modern case highlighted as *Schools in transition*, a current example is provided by The New Nordic School called *an on-going development project* and initiated in 2012 by the Danish Minister for Children and Education, Christine Antorini.

The purpose of this project is to embed changes in the Danish system and the political rhetoric recalls the New Nordic as exemplified with the famous

Dogme film tradition, famous chefs and the Danish Kitchen. Launching the New Nordic School (NNS) therefore included a manifesto and dogmas.

The Manifesto called for school development driven by a new interpretation of the Nordic tradition as a holistic approach acknowledging that:

> Professional competence is a combination of mastery in subject knowledge and the ability to combine knowledge across disciplines together with social, personal competences and motor skills. (Manifesto §5)

Further, the manifesto states that the NNS must:

> Be developed by professionals that constantly strive towards excellence in their own performance, take responsibility for their choice of methods and join in a systematically explorative co-operation with other professionals.

Regarding the dogmas, the concepts are further stressed as:

> We are systematically exploring our professional domain and we are open to change. We are curious, outreaching, innovative and risk taking in our ambition to exploit the potentials of every individual. To change the world, we must realise that matters can differ from our initial perception and we must be willing to change the way we work.

As quoted there is no doubt that the school in change is a matter of new strategies ruled by professionals from 2012. At the same time however, we recall traditions where the theme *Schools in transition* has a history. In the former decades the theme was even connected to one of the biggest programmes of development in the Danish school modern history, launched in 1987.

One of the 1987 programme's themes, namely *The School of the Future—The Universal School* concerned fourteen *school projects*, which together represented city and rural schools, large and small schools and private and public schools. One of the fourteen projects even involved an entire school community. The innovation programme was evaluated (see further Nørgaard 1992; Borgnakke 1991, 2005, Krogh Jespersen 2005) and the development tendencies could be highlighted as:

> Greater independence in the teachers' area of responsibility by increased teacher collaboration on matters of planning, execution and evaluation of teaching, supported by a school administration which emphasises the development of the school and of pedagogic methods'.
>
> (Nørgaard 1992: 217).

In the evaluative report we can also recognise statements about the characteristic movement *from ... towards* like the following:

> From predominantly subject-divided teaching based on a one-teacher principle towards a predominantly theme and project oriented teaching effected by a teacher team.

As highlighted, this is structurally and organisationally conceptualised as a movement:

> From a predominantly administrative school towards a predominantly pedagogic school management (Nørgaard 1992:2)

For the analysis of the tendencies it is of importance that *the School in transition* is related to changes in structure and pedagogy as the center for the process of professionalisation. At the same time, we realise the dilemma: if the school in change is a movement which had already started in the former decade stressing the basic structural and pedagogical issues as changeable why should the *same* strategies then be (re-) launched as new in 2012?

Launching New Nordic School in 2012 with the political text stating that the purpose is to 'create real and concrete changes in the Danish system', it seems like insisting that ideas and strategies are turned into realities.

The political level demands the impact of the concrete changes related to *strategies for change and innovation* as well as related to the new voices and actors in the process of implementation. The profession-oriented university colleges under reconstruction (in Danish: *Professionshøjskolerne*) related to reforms of the professions oriented Bachelor degrees and reforms in Higher Education and in Upper Secondary schools provides an example of these new voices.

In the process of implementation

The implementation of reforms in youth education and higher education are closely related to a political programme in 1999 followed by reforms in 2005 and 2008 in the Danish Upper Secondary School. The process of implementation directed by the political and the institutional levels can therefore be regarded as lasting at least a decade. In this period of time the interesting point is that new voices can be heard as both professional and scientific voices. As an example, a new department to support the process in upper secondary school was established at the Southern University in Denmark. The department published a series of evaluative reports in a book series called *Gymnasiepædagogik* (Upper-secondary Education), which literally mirror the whole process of implementation and depicts the full range of diversity in the interpretations of key tasks related to reforms between 2000 and 2010.

In this context the new voices and the actors have had an impact on what I call *the professional sounding board*. This sounding board affects the discourse and the concepts of being professional both in terms of scientific reflection and in terms of strategies in the organisational and professional profile in the field of practice. Recalling Brantes (2011) definition that 'interventions derived from scientific knowledge of mechanisms, structures, and contexts', you may say that the professional sounding board mirrors a relation to educational and pedagogical sciences. However, following the process a double agenda and a contradiction is revealed. This implies that interventions are derived from the political credo rather than from scientific knowledge. Further, it means that development of organisations, management and leadership is expected to demonstrate changeability and to perform professional handling of cross-disciplinary mono- and inter-professional issues. Additionally, the expected leadership includes handling of crises and handling of an organisational culture in conflict with the shifting reforms and references to learning paradigms, learning styles, tests and PISA-results.

In terms of theoretical concepts, it means that even though the case analysis still benefits from both the classic Max Weber inspired concepts of ideal typical paradigms and situations, the analysis must benefit from social cultural concepts of organisational learning as well.

Like Lave and Wenger (1991, 2003) it is important to refer to embedded and situated professional learning and to the community of practice. And Like Edgar Schein (2004) it is important for the case analyses to refer to the level of

Artifacts, espoused values and *basic underlying assumptions* (Senger 2003, Raae 2005, Borgnakke 2011a). In terms of empirical analysis of school cases, at the very center of the process of professionalisation, we also need to recognise how schools and teachers themselves reflect the official change in ability and strategies. Further, the organisation and the professional team go through the process of implementation by addressing knowledge production and exchange of experiences such as *communication among professionals*. Further, analyses show how the professional team is reflected as a part of the living interpretation of the professional functions and teacher roles connected with reflections among teacher generations, the old and the young generation (Zeuner 2012, Beck and Hansen, 2009).

At this point, case studies add a new dimension, namely that the ongoing discussions among professionals create a strategy for integrated *self-evaluation* and for a reflection of challenges and conflicts related to a contradiction in the process. On one hand the process of professionalisation means enhanced professional autonomy creating new strategies for teaching, learning and evaluation. In my case studies, IT-schools (upper sec level) and Online education in the health care sector confirm that the innovative framework was created and directed by the teacher team. On the other hand, the political and organisational framework means that the process is directed by the leadership team managing details in the process of implementation and controlling the learning outcome as never before.

The dilemma concerning professional autonomy is a part of the dilemma related to the three goals of the political demands: Modernising, Quality Assurance and Professionalisation. As a result the dilemma relates to crisis management and innovative problem solving in the shifting national political and local context. As shown in the case analysis, the IT-schools refer to a local professional voice related to educational political challenges in low-income areas. In this case, the innovative IT-strategy was initiated to provide a quality-offer in areas not familiar with upper secondary schools as elite-institutions (Borgnakke 2007, 2012).

When local conditions are reflected as in the above case, we recognise that the local political agenda is now oriented towards the professional team instead of focusing on the classic expert.

In broader perspectives the local political discourse of professionalisation represents the dynamic signs of practical development. Firstly, the historical elite institutions are aimed to challenge the former hierarchy, gender, class and ethnicity patterns by concrete strategies. Secondly, the elite institutions are aimed towards practical changes of the educational culture and learning contexts. Hereby the practical changes mirror the political demands for innovation on the local agenda. At the same time the local struggles mirror the international agenda, marketisation, performativity and implementation of *the operational focus*.

For the critical analysis it is important to recognise both new voices and the interplay between the local, national and international agenda. However, the point is that the local profiled IT-based schools must be adapted to internal strategies challenging the organisational development.

Challenging the organisational development

The process of professionalisation can be described (Borgnakke 2011a) as a process of challenges and dilemmas in which:

> The leader level being challenged to regard innovation and *how to perform with IT-strategies* as a matter of school culture and pedagogy rather than just a matter of administration or management. Implementation of The Learning Managements System (LMS) represents technical dimensions, but the important issues are connected to the professional leadership team, LT, and to the management of the whole process of implementation.
>
> The faculty and teachers (as colleagues) regard the same question as a matter of professional pedagogical acting. IT-strategies, and the new mix of internet and web-based resources are a professional challenge partly because of shifting online and offline activities partly because of the dilemma between mono- and inter-professional knowledge basis.
>
> Both teachers and groups of students at the learning practice level and in the classroom regard the process of learning related to scholastic culture as well as related to youth culture and non-formal learning. At this level, the whole mix of media and technology including the students own experiences with social media are challenging their learning process.

On this background the tendencies and the impact on the professional culture are conceptualised. Expressed by the IT-schools the professional culture further highlights a performative culture where *doing well* and *being educated* both refer to the classic and the new forms of literacy conceptualised as digital literacy, media literacy or technacy (Buckingham 2008, Elf 2009, Borgnakke 2012). The point is that technacy is the new professional addition gained by school leaders, faculty, teachers and students. An addition gained in situations of both formal and informal learning.

IT skills as the new professional addition

For the innovative IT schools technacy is a matter of developing a performative school culture where doing well not only refers to the classic concepts of education like in Danish *dannelse* or in German *bildung* but further refers to late modern questions concerning life skills and lifelong learning. From an organisational perspective this means sharpening the professional profile and identity in a process of renewing within the scholastic learning context on the one hand and continuous collaboration with non-formal learning activities on the other hand. Hereby, professionalisation and performativity are connected to both IT and to student-oriented strategies.

In the Danish context the strategies refer to both national programmes and reforms where innovation and creativity as personal qualifications are expressed by law. As stated in a paragraph:

> The education must further develop the student's creative and innovative skills and critical sense. (The Law of Upper Secondary School STX 2005).

If we go straight to the practical school level, the IT-schools as *pioneers* are up front implementing the IT-profile as the professional profile forms a new background. Organisational Technacy is a professional matter according to interviews with the leadership team (LT). And as highlighted by the LT, Technacy is also a matter of just stating the fact:

> (...) earlier you needed *to think* a lot. You do not need this as much now. Now you just need to state the fact: Is there wireless covering all the cabin? There is. And are the required network facilities present? When you have a knowledge platform like ours—namely Fronter—then you are almost good driving. You can do what you need to do.
>
> (Int. LT, IT-School)

On this basis the LT further more stresses how all aspects of communication become clearer both as demands and as a part of the IT profile of the school.

As stated by the member of LT:

> in terms of strategy, 'communication' is a basic element in our profile. Therefore, I'm certain that we will start to have much more focus on performing and we will coach and teach the student in performance. In this sense we will start to look more focused on how students perform.
>
> (Int. LT, IT-school)

These statements represent the school identity and make the profile for both the professional team of teachers and students look like a performativity brand: A high degree of IT, Communication and Performance!

In 1999 The Danish Ministry started the process focusing on IT and Learning as political headline and strategy. Eight years after the IT-schools confirm the strategy in a practical sense. However, when the school and all actors are surrounded by IT—IT in itself is no longer in focus. Rather, the focus is the new-shared background for further development. The case analysis shows the impact, but it also reveals a risk zone, namely that Technacy is performed with a lack of literacy and democracy. In the same manner, the analysis indicates the risk of transforming educational culture to technical culture: There can be a lack of reflective pedagogical culture. Further, this risk means lack of basic conditions needed for meeting the challenges from what Ball discusses as 'a move towards forms of democratic professionalism' (Ball 2013:39). In this context the turning point for meeting the challenges seems to be questions about handling the professional key task in relation to the next generation of students and learning models.

The IT-based innovative project represents the next generation of strategies, models and professionals at IT-schools. The most important point is therefore neither ICT as information and communication technology nor the IT-tools in itself. The point is IT-in-use in the professional process of teaching and learning.

For the upper secondary-teachers it is important to refer to the academic and profession oriented learning context at college and university and to refer to new forms of project and problem-based learning. Against this background the question about the next generation of learning models also implies questions about role models oriented towards professional life skills.

In symbolic terms it seems that the scholastic discourse and goal setting is renewed by technacy as one of modern societies' life skills. From the students' perspective we can add that it is also a matter of using life skills in a learning practice seen in the light of both the formal educational culture and the non-formal youth culture. In this light the analysis can be sharpened by adding the voices of next generation.

Voices of next generation

Analysis of organisational development focuses on how the teacher team create new forms of IT-management as an integrated part of curriculum planning and teaching practice. The operational focus is adopted to use the formulation from Lynch (2006) but so is the dilemma: The next generation of teaching and learning models are created in the light of both the scholastic culture and of a business organisation. Further, the case studies show activities created in the light of the new media and performed in a context of youth culture (Stald 2009, Borgnakke 2012). There will be activities and moments of musicals, films, shows, stage activities and sports activities being a vital part of the process of learning not only influenced by the scholastic culture but also by the professional culture from the world of sports, arts and media. Beside this, the new every day culture of social media is permanently present in the mediatised social cultural context (Ito 2008, Drotner 2008, Hjarvard 2008).

The voice of next generation that needs to be added then is not only youth and youth culture but the mediatised learning context and the basic relation between formal and non-formal learning as well. Let me elaborate further on this statement.

During the case study, the range and diversity in IT-competences in the professional teams was up for open discussion at the collegial level. Expressed in the Bourdieu-inspired concepts the IT-habitus of the actors represents the diversity and the spectra of types by Kolbæk (2013) called The Advocat, The Skeptic, The Opponent and The Critic. In the analysis Kolbæk also presents vertical patterns of developments stressing for example the tendency that the process is developed *from/to* like focus on

PC from an administrative to a pedagogical tool

From teaching about ICT to teach with ICT

The open discussion about the diversity in IT-habitus and the shift in the use of technology is a kind of platform for the next generation of actors and learning models. However, at the same time the open discussions reflect what is regarded as negative and positive voices respectively in the process. Technacy gained in a non-formal leisure context but being useful in the scholastic context is regarded as a positive voice in the process. At the same time to the same extent, negative transformation of behaviour from the leisure context, was remarkable. Private chats, computer games, Facebook activities would be regarded as negative youth cultural noise in the school context—noise disturbing the process of professionalisation and considered a waste of time and creativity.

Against this background, the case analysis points at the basic criteria about professional didactical relevance. Any competence or type of activity can be of didactical use in the learning context. It does not matter if the activity originates from school life, business life, leisure life, home or street life. The demand is that it demonstrates its relevance for the professional teamwork and for the process of teaching and learning in the scholastic context (Borgnakke 2012:133-136).

At this point, the process of professionalisation informs as to what gets included (or excluded) in the scholastic context as a perspective for next generation. It is a matter of ideal typical situations and of role models.

Role models related to technacy are already included in the school cases. Some of the (male) IT-school students possessed almost professional IT–skills. These skills were also indicated by the nickname given to members of this particular group of students: The Nerds. The Nerds gave the important keywords to understand the process of learning *doing technacy* in a boyish and professional manner. In addition, the competences represented by The Nerds were acknowledged with respect and gave social prestige among both teachers and students. As stressed such technacy gained in a leisure context is recognised as being useful in the scholastic context (Borgnakke 2012: 135).

The next generation of ideal type and role model: The professional mix

IT skills and the *nerd* in the scholastic context are to be regarded as a part of the next generation, both in terms of social cultural integration and in terms of the ideal type of professionals. Bearing this in mind, I will now point to a case focusing on the scientific profession-oriented context and the professional *nerd*. The professions-oriented context mirror how Academia and The University and in this case especially The Faculty of Science need to exclude the conventional academic *nerd* and needs to include the students (both male and female) in the professional team. However, mostly the context mirrors how the university need to include next generation in the light of youth culture.

In concrete descriptive terms, the case refers to a competition called *Moving Science* 2009, which was initiated at the University of Copenhagen, in response to the perception of the faculty of science as catering too specifically for the conventional nerd.

The key concept for *Moving Science* was to create an alternative picture. On this background *Moving Science* had their own website for the presentation of ideas, background and winners. As a campaign *Moving Science* was stressed with a twist of humour and as the leader said 'It is supposed to be weird, different and funny' and it is of importance for the film *not to be too intellectual*'.

The films produced in order confirm the role played within Academia and the gender roles represent the move from male to female highlighting modern Academia and the professional team, with females and multi-ethnicity included. The winning movie *Gør noget* (Do something) gave a precise and political correct illustration. Whereas the second awarded film *The power to create* humorously playing with an old-school academic, sex and gender myth: *The Nerd, The Scientist and The Blonde* illustratjng the impact of the connection to youth culture and virtual life on the internet. *The power to create* was only awarded second place in the competition and it did not have the educational nor the political correct messages. Nevertheless it became the most widespread of the movies to have links to youth culture with over one million viewers on *YouTube*.

For the reflection about next generation, the example in it-self is of importance. The students themselves use new technologies and social media when reconstructing next generation of professionals and in the process of professionalisation it is a matter of transition to a new organisational and mediatised context. But it is also a matter of *the link*, namely the link between the different generations and learning models—both those which are already available and those which they envisage. Situated in the current process of professionalisation we recognise the newest shift and the link where online learning and life-long learning combined is highlighted as the essential element of professionalism and profession-oriented education.

Life-long learning is an essential element of professionalism

The above statement is a quotation. It is the start of a description of a course to be held in the on-line bachelor programme at the School of Dentistry, University of Michigan, which provides another context and example for the exploration of tendencies described above. As an example of the newest on-line education the programme is in the forefront, like the exemplified IT-upper secondary school. However, indeed at the same time the statement refers to a classic approach in concepts of profession. Going back for example to Brante's (2011) definition we can conceptualise how the identity and the definition of being a professional are combined with profession-oriented life-long learning renewing scientific knowledge. If life-long learning is an essential element of professionalism it means that profession oriented education and professional working life as such have a link to life-long learning. The discourses and terms will vary of course but there is a link. Two important links can be mentioned as present in the Danish debate about New Nordic School and the political reforms and both can be heard as voices of professionals. The teachers and the teacher trade unions reacted to the policy presented in January 2013 initially with a massive demand of further education of teachers already working and secondly with demands of better basic education of the next generation of teachers. The professional logic seems to be: If the school must be innovative and open for changes, life-long learning must be a recognised part of the funded support to strengthen professionalism. At the same time the university colleges hosting the teacher education underlines this perception, for example by presenting the overall profile for professional bachelor degree in appealing words like:

> Your education starts at UCC, but continues the rest of your life. That is why we offer a strong further education giving you the opportunity to renew competences. University College Copenhagen website

If life-long learning is a classic and essential element of professionalism, the profession-oriented education as such will be regarded as contribution to the advancement of the profession. Further, we recognise how the IT-based strategies for educational development and schools being in front stress this contribution. Combined with the new conditions like the new welfare technologies the mentioned online programme from University of Michigan stressed that the course called *Leadership and Professional Development* was based on the fact that:

> Life-long learning is an essential element of professionalism. This course will focus on current issues in dental hygiene, and how individuals can contribute to the advancement of the profession and promotion of oral health for the public. (Cit. UM website)

In autumn 2012 I had the opportunity to converse with the teaching- and leadership teams of the above mentioned programme. This conversation made it clear that professional self-evaluation and programme evaluation were high on the agenda. The teacher teams further referred to articles in *Journal of Dental Education* (Gwozdek 2011, Springfield 2012). Their descriptions echoed the steps undertaken in the article *Using Online Program Development to Foster Curricular Change and Innovation.* As stressed in this article 'Programme evaluation is a necessary component of curricular change and innovation.' In the teachers point of view self-evaluation went hand in hand with the progressive development of the new online learning model. And, as shown in my field notes:

> (...) when I asked the teachers to highlight the four most important experiences from the process with the Online programme, they gave me the following list:
> 1) developing the curriculum
> 2) acting like a team
> 3)making it happen
> 4) contribution to lifelong learning
>
> (Field notes University of Michigan, Borgnakke 2012)

In this case *acting like a team' and 'contributing to lifelong learning* were closely related to challenges for educational development among professionals. At the same time the challenge is also related to development of Online settings and strategies aimed at student activity.

As stressed in the following section, the important experiences must be seen in light of the professional practice and in the light of the need of renewed strategies for profession-oriented learning.

Renewed strategies for profession-oriented learning?

The definition from Brante stressing that professions are 'Occupations conducting interventions derived from scientific knowledge of mechanisms, structures, and contexts'(Brante 2011) can be reflected in relation to the consequences in the education of the next generation of professionals. Currently, the Danish reform shows how the Professional Bachelor-degree education tries to sharpen *interventions* and *scientific* knowledge of mechanisms, structures, and contexts'. However, in most cases this is done as a matter concerning the scholastic curricula. This is confirmed by case-studies in the profession-oriented learning context, where schoolification and limitations in the current development of professional education are regarded as important empirical findings. At the same time evaluation of development projects in Nursing programmes point at the necessity of renewing the practical profession-oriented core question (Borgnakke 2014). According to teachers and clinical supervisors it is not only a matter of sharpening the scientific knowledge, but also a matter of sharpening the strategies for how to learn *to act and reflect professionally*. Moving further, it is not only a matter of sharpening the professional training for the individual professionals, but as much a matter of participation in cross-disciplinary processes training *professional acting* in inter-professional teams (Borgnakke and Nielsen, 2015). The demanded professional changeability and the relation to sectors in change leaves both educators and students in a dilemma in terms of shifting strategies regarded as either work-based strategies or scholastic strategies.

Rooted in John Dewey's concepts of *Learning by doing* and combined with project learning or understood as practice learning and situated learning (Kvale and Nielsen 1998, 2003, Lave and Wenger 1991, 2003), models of profession-oriented learning already are conceptualised as workplace based strategies—at least for the practical part of the educational courses. The different cases confirm this even though the cases represent different nuances in the constructions of learning models and strategies. Nevertheless, the cases point to a new common challenge referring to the professional standard as having consequences in relation to both students' profession-oriented study work and the professional teamwork of the teachers.

In the case at University of Michigan mentioned above. The Online Dental programme and the it-based strategies were aimed to enhance students' profession-oriented action and reflection. As one of the leadership teams stressed: 'Acting/reflection close to the professional standard is implicit in the reference for the development'. Further, the leader refers to the professional team as a background for the group and as the basic unit. As the leader puts it: 'The professional team is certainly a group and one learns and reflects better in groups, therefore we consider the group to be the unit.' At the same time, the leader exemplified the stages for the learning process, described as:

> The Triple Jump
> 1. Students start with ideas and a description of a patient situation;
> 2. Students realise the pressure from the professional practice, and are capable of raising the question of 'what to do';
> 3. Students are forced to reflect (diagnosis/treatment, suggestions) and to decide 'what I can do'.

(Leader conversation UM, Borgnakke 2012, field notes).

In this context the important question to the profession-oriented learning context can be stressed as a matter of to which degree:

professional tools and standards are integrated into the daily routine of teaching and in the learning practice

learning models are related to the scholastic and to the clinical practical learning context

learning situations are related to classic lecturing, classroom teaching, skills lab, project work or work related professional teams and task forces

Summarising experiences from the practical process, it is a matter of strengthening the profession-oriented strategies for blended learning, flipped classroom and student-directed group work calling for professional tools and standards to be implemented in the process.

With reference to current ethnographic studies these tendencies are confirmed at the institutional level by experiments in full-scale health care education. A NET-education Nursing Programme exhibits new models for Online education (Lyngsø 2015) and development of game based learning in courses for veterinarian student displays new strategies for profession-oriented learning (Nielsen 2015). Further, the project InBetween demonstrates the need to strengthen both the inter-professional competences and the integration of *Inter-professional Elements* in the curriculum of educational programmes (Borgnakke and Nielsen 2015). However, as these models and development projects are clearly oriented towards the professional practice they are also as *situated* in the educational practice clearly oriented towards the conventional and scholastic learning outcomes paradigm.

In the official description, terms indicating a profession-oriented didactical manifold are generously used. The overall aim is that students must obtain *knowledge, skills and competences* necessary to meet the requirements to function as professionals. In the course descriptions, needed knowledge is described using the verbs: Describe and understand. Skills are described using: Access and evaluate and finally, the competences that students are required to obtain are described as being capable to handle complex professional situations. Clearly, such course descriptions reflect the use of the so-called SOLO taxonomy.

The paradox underlined is neither the reference to the scholastic component nor the reference to a professional function. The paradox is the silence and the almost non-existent reference to professional learning as a learning process where students *learn to become* professionals. Further, another paradox is revealed; a paradox related to the development of curricula, which to a high extent are exclusively focused on the scholastic and formal description.

The fieldwork in the NET-education Online Nursing programme was of course not initiated so as to reveal or confirm OBL paradigmatic conditions. However, the influence of the OBL paradigm became visible through both documents and participant's voices as the fieldwork progressed. In this sense both the OBL-paradigmatic dominance in the scholastic settings and the re-contextualising aspect that the online learning situation reconstructed the classroom and the teacher-student interaction are to be regarded as significant empirical findings.

Covering these innovations and inter-professional practices the point for the ethnographic approach is that the fieldwork needs to cope with the whole process of professionalisation from vision and mission to practical reality in the clinical training setting. Hereby, the ethnographic studies move between the political macro-, the institutional meso- and the practical micro-levels covering the spectrum of issues and voices from organisational leadership teams to the professional teams involved in the practical process. For the ethnographic studies this spectrum is a challenge to be met by exploring the late modern conditions for blended learning and mixed professions. However, the process of professionalisation and the challenges from former decades will also be rediscovered. In a critical and analytical sense, this means to rediscover the lived dilemma between scholastic and profession-oriented learning strategies and the dilemma between the mono- and inter-professional knowledge basis and acting repertoire.

References

Ball, S. J. (2000) Performativities and Fabrications in the Education Economy: Towards the Performative Society?, *Australian Educational Researcher*, 27(2): 1-23.

Ball, S. (2013) Policy Paper Education, justice and democracy: The struggle over ignorance and opportunity, Class, Centre for labour and social studies. London: http://classonline.org.uk/docs/2013_Policy_Paper_-_Education,_justice_and_democracy_(Stephen_Ball).pdf

Beck, S. and Hansen, D. R. (2009) Teacher generations in an area of reform, *US-China Education Review*, 6(8): 1-16.

Borgnakke, K. (1992) The Universal School-The School of the 1990's? In Nørgaard, E. (ed.) *School improvement, Development and Innovation*, Copenhagen: The Royal School of Educational Studies.

Borgnakke, K. and Raae P. H. (2004) Professionaliseringsgevinsten—lærerprofessionalisering gennem forsøgs—og udviklingsarbejde [The gain of professionalism—teacher professionalism through experiments- and development]. In K. Hjort (ed.) *Professionsforskning i Danmark* [Professional research in Denmark], Roskilde: Universitetsforlag.

Borgnakke, K. (2005) *Læringsdiskurser og praktikker* [*Discourses on learning and practices*], Copenhagen: Akademisk Forlag.

Borgnakke, K. (2006) Professionaliseringens kønsdiskurs. Tema: Dominerende diskurser i talen om professioner [The gender discourse of professionalization. Special issue/ Theme: Dominant discourses in the speech on Professions], *Nordisk Pedagogik*, 4 (6): Oslo: Universitetsforlaget, 346-357.

Borgnakke, K. (2008) Professionsorienteret forskning: Hvad er opgaven, krumtappen og den videnskabelige basis? [Profession-oriented research: What is the task, the crank and the scientific basis?]. In Petersen, K. A. , Hoyen, M. (ed.) *At sætte spor på en vandring fra Aquinas til Bourdieu—æresbog til Staf Callewaert,* Forlaget HEXIS: www.hexis.dk

Borgnakke, K. (2010) Project ITAKA (IT and Learning in Academia) project portal http:// pur.mef.ku.dk

Borgnakke, K. (2011) Blandt professionelle idealister og pragmatikere—en caseanalyse om professionalisering i gymnasiefeltet [Among professional idealists and pragmatists—a case analysis on professionalization in secondary schools]. In Christensen and Bertelsen (ed.) *Pædagogiske perspektiver på arbejdsliv* [Pedagogical approach to work]. Copenhagen: Frydenlund.

Borgnakke, K. (2011b) *Et universitet er et sted, der forsker i alt—undtagen i sig selv og sin egen virksomhed, Rapport om den forskningsfaglige baggrund for udvikling af universitetspædagogisk forskning* [A university is a place that researches everything—except academia. Report on the research professional background for the development of university educational research], Copenhagen: Københavns Universitet.

Borgnakke, K. (2012) Challenges for the Next Generation in Upper Secondary School—Between Literacy, Numeracy, and Technacy, In Pink, W. T. (ed.) *Schools for Marginalized Youth: An International Perspective*. Cresskill, New Jersey: Hampton Press.

Borgnakke K. (2013) *Etnografiske metoder i uddannelsesforskningen—mellem klassiske traditioner og senmoderne udfordringer* [Ethnographic methods in educational research—between classical traditions and late-modern challenges]. Copenhagen: Institut for Medier, Erkendelse og Formidling. Det Humanistiske fakultet, Københavns Universitet.

Borgnakke K. (ed) (2014) *Vekselvirkning og samspil—mellem teoretiske og kliniske studier i Sygeplejerskeuddannelsen* [Interplay and Interaction—between theoretical and clinical studies in nursing education], Aarhus: VIA Systime.

Borgnakke, K. and Nielsen, C.S., 2015. Etnografiske studier i interprofessionalitet og forandringer af klassiske koncepter. (Ethnographic studies of inter-professionalism and changes of classic concepts) *Tidsskrift for professionsstudier*, Gjallerhorn, (20): 48-60.

Brante, T. (2005) Staten og professionerne [State and professions], In Eriksen and Jørgensen (eds.) *Professionsidentitet i forandring* [Professional identity in transision], Copenhagen: Akademisk Forlag.

Brante, T. (2011) *Professions as Science-Based Occupations, Profession and professionalism*, 1(1) 4-20. www.professionsandprofessionalism.com

Buckingham, D. (ed.) (2008) *Youth, Identity and Digital Media*, Cambridge, MA: MIT Press

Bøje, J. D, Hjort, K. , Larsen, L. and Raae, P. H. (2007) Gymnasiereform 2005. Professionalisering af ledelse, lærere og elever? [Professionalising leaders, teachers and students?], Book series *Gymnasiepædagogik* nr. 66. Odense: Syddansk Universitet.

Dahler-Larsen, P. (2002) *Evalueringen kartlagt* [Evaluation mapped], Aarhus, Systime.

Dahler-Larsen, P. (2003) *Selvevalueringens hvide sejl* [The white sails of self-evaluation] Odense, Syddansk Universitetsforlag.

Dale, E. L. (1987) *Opdragelse fri fra 'Mor'og 'Far'* [Education free of 'mom' and 'dad'], Oslo: Gyldendal.

Dale, E. L. (1998) *Pædagogik og professionalitet* [Pedagogy and professionalism], Aarhus: Forlaget Klim

Dovemark, M. (2004) *Responsibility, flexibility, freedom of choice: An ethnographic Study of a School in Transition.* Ph. D. thesis, Göteborg: Acta Universitatis Gothoburgensis.

Drotner, K. (2009) *Digitale læringsressourcer i folkeskolen og i de gymnasiale ungdomsuddannelser* [Digital learning resources in primary and secondary schools], Dream projektet, Syddansk Universitet http://www.dream.dk

Elf, N. (2009) *Towards Semiocy? Exploring a New Rationale for Teaching Modes and Media of Hans Christian Andersens Fairytales in Four Commercial Upper-Secondary 'Danish'. Classis.* Ph. D. thesis, Odense: University of Southern Denmark.

Eriksen, T. and Jørgensen, A. M. (2005) *Professionsidentitet i forandring* [Changes in Professional Identity], Copenhagen: Akademisk Forlag.

Gwozdek, Springfield, Peet and Kerschbaum (2011) Using Online Program Development to Foster Curricular Change and Innovation, *Educational Methodologies Journal of Dental Education*, 76(4): 414-426.

Gjallerhorn (2005) *Tidsskrift for professionsuddannelser* [Journal for professional education], nr. 1, Århus: CVU-MidtVest.

Giddens, A. (1990) The consequences of Modernity, Cambridge: Polity Press; Stanford University Press.

Giddens, A. (1991) *Modernity and Self-Identity*, Cambridge: Polity Press

Gumport, P. J. (2000) Academic restructuring: Organizational change and institutional imperatives, *Higher Education* 39: 2000. Kluwer Academic Publishers, 67-91

Gymnasiepædagogik (2000-2010) *Upper-secondary Education, Institut for filosofi, pædagogik og religionsstudier*, Odense: Syddansk Universitet, 1-80.

Habermas, J. (1981) *Theorie des Kommunikativen Handelns* [Theory of communicative action], 1 and 2, Frankfurt: Suhrkamp.

Hansen, H. F. (2005) *Evaluation Practice in the Nordic Countries. Different National Traditions or a Common Approach?* Keynote speech, NERA Congress Mars 2005.

Hansen, H. F. And Rieper, O. (2010) The Politics of Evidence-Based Policy-Making: The Case of Denmark, *German policy Studies*, 6(2): 87-112.

Hargreaves, A. (2000) Four Ages of Professionalism and Professional Learning, *Teachers and Teaching: History and Practice,* 6(2): 151-182.

Harrits, G. S. (2014) Professional Closure Beyond State Authorization Professions and Professionalism. In K. Hjort (ed.) *De professionelle, forskning i professioner og professionsuddannelser* [The professional, research on professions and professional education], Roskilde: Universitetsforlag.

Hjort, K. (2008) *Demokratisering af den offentlige sektor* [The democratization of the public sector], Roskilde: Universitetsforlag.

Ito, M. (2008) *Living and Learning with new media: Summery of findings from the Digital Youth Project, MacArthur Foundation Report,* http://digitalyouth. ischool. berkeley. edu/report. html

Jensen, A. A. and Rasmussen, P. (eds.) (2009) *Læring og forandring. Tværfaglige perspektiver* [Learning and Change: Interdisciplinary Perspectives], Aalborg: Universitetsforlag.

Krogh-Jespersen, K. (2005) *Lærerprofessionalitet—illusion og vision* [Teacher professionalism—Illusion and vision], Århus: Forlaget Klim.

Lading, Å. (2006) Vi er jo kolleger ikke konkurrenter—en analyse af moderniserede samarbejdsstrategier i grupper [We're colleagues not competitors—an analysis of modernized strategies for cooperation in groups], Ph. D. thesis, Odense: Syddansk Universitet.

Laursen, E. (2009) Helskoleforsøg som rammer om organisatorisk læring [Experiments on entire schoolas frameworks for organizational learning], In A. Jensen and P. Rasmussen (ed.) *Læring og forandring: Tværfaglige perspektiver* [Learning and Change: Interdisciplinary Perspectives], Aalborg: Universitetsforlag.

Lave, J. and Wenger, E. (1991) *Situated learning. Legitimate peripheral participation.* New York: Cambridge University Press.

Lave, J. (1997) Learning, apprenticeship, social practice, *Nordisk Pedagogik* 3/97, 197-212.

Lynch, K. (2006) Neo-liberalism and Marketisation: the implications for higher education, European, *Educational Research Journal*, 5(1): 11-17.

Lyngsø, A. 2015. At home with students–Observing online and offline contexts, *International Journal of Media, Technology and Lifelong Learning*, seminar.net. 11(1).

Mendillo, H. (2012) *Social Media Advancing at the School of Dentistry, Dental UM, Spring and Summer 2012*, University of Michigan.

Moos, L. , Hermansen, m. and Krejsler, J. (eds.) (2002) *Professionalisering og ledelse* [Professionalism and leadership], Fredrikshavn: Dafolo Forlag.

Nielsen, C.K. 2015. Ethnography in the Danish veterinary learning environment, *International Journal of Media, Technology and Lifelong Learning*, 11(1).

Nordisk pedagogik (2006) Tema: Dominerende diskurser i talen om

professioner [Theme: Dominant discourses in the speech on professions], Nordisk pedagogik 4/2006.

Olesen, H. S. (2006) Diskurs og erfaring: Eksempler fra lægeprofessionen [Discourse and experience: Examples from medical professionals], *Nordisk Pedagogik*, 4, 358-371.

Petersen, K. (1997) Fra ekspansion til krise—Udforskning af velfærdstatens udvikling efter 1945 [From expansion to crisis—Exploring the development of the welfare state after 1945], *Historisk Tidsskrift*, Bind16, 6(2): 357-375.

Petersen, O. K. (2011): *Konkurrencestaten* [The Competition State], Copenhagen: Hans Reitzels Forlag.

Raae, P. H. (2005) *Træghedens rationalitet* [Rationality of the slow]. Ph. D. thesis, DIG. Odense: Syddansk Universitet.

Saks, M. (2012) Defining a Profession: The Role of Knowledge and Expertise, *Professions and professionalism*, 2(1): 1-10

Selander, S. (1993) Professioner och professionalisering [Professions and professionalisation], In J. Cederstrøm (ed.) Lærerprofessionalisme [Teacher professionalism], Købehavn: Unge Pædagoger.

Senger, U. (2003) *Organisatorisk læring og lærerprofessionalisme i gymnasiet* [Organisational learning and teacher professionalism in secondary schools], Ph. D. theises, Odense: Syddansk Universitet. Springfield, Gwozdek, Peet,

Springfield, E. , Gwozdek, A. E. , Peet, M. , Kerschbaum, W. E. (2012) Using Multiple Methods to Assess Learning and Outcomes in an Online Degree- Granting Dental Hygiene Program, *Journal of Dental Education,* 76(4): 414-26

Søndergaard, K. D. and Hasse, C. (eds.) (2012) *Teknologi forståelse—på skoler og hospitaler* [Understanding technology—in schools and hospitals], Århus: Universitetsforlag

Sørensen, B. H. and Olesen, B. R. (eds.) (2000) Børn i en digital kultur [Children in a digital culture], Copenhagen: Gads forlag.

Ve, H. (1987) Rasjonalitetsbegreper [Concepts of rationality], *Nordisk Pedagogik* 1.

Weber, M. (1994) *Magt og bureaukrati* [Power and bureaucrazy], Oslo: Norsk Gyldendal

Weber, K. (ed.)2001 *Experience and Discourse—Theorizing professions and Subjectivity,* Roskilde: University Press

Zeuner, L. (2012) Fagsamspil og erkendelse i de gymnasiale uddannelser [Discipline interaction and cognition in secondary schools], Copenhagen: *Nyt fra samfundsvidenskaberne.*

Chapter 10

Professionalisation in educational practice: Summary

Karen Borgnakke, Marianne Dovemark, Sofia Marques da Silva

This book discusses processes of professionalisation based on research projects on educational reforms and the related consequences for teaching practices, teacher education and educational organisation. Through empirical analyses related to the political macro level as well as to the institutional meso level and practical micro level the book chapters identify trends, dilemmas and perspectives in different national and international contexts. The aim is to come closer to an understanding of the different educational systems and teachers' training traditions in order to sharpen the critical reflection about political discourses and demands of professionalisation in educational practices.

In the book, the period from 1990-2010 is characterised by a loss of autonomy and by an organisational and educational culture overruled by political top-down processes and values of the market place. The ages of professionalism, like the ages of the pre-professional, the age of autonomy, the collegial and the post-professional age, refer, at the same time, to different phases and traditions in the process of professionalisation. As shown in the book both the Anglo-American curriculum tradition and the central European 'didactic-tradition' have impacted on the processes. Against this backdrop, the book provides an international overview as well as deeper insight into national and local practices. Based on ethnographic case studies each chapter makes its own and unique contribution by exploring empirical data and discussing theoretical possibilities related to the common current question, namely what it means to be a professional teacher in the post-modern era of professionalism.

Despite varieties the international discourse points at the post-modern professional teacher and the educational institution as the professional team who play a major role in the development of the embracing institution. The commitment of the professionals has been gained through the development of team work, distributed leadership and the nurturing of institutional careers.

The starting points for the empirical analyses are key elements of the postmodern culture and discursive construction, related to international trends and national cases. The broad argument is that global movements in education policy have generated widely accepted discourses of performativity and educational effectiveness that have had pedagogical effects. The book attempts to deconstruct prevailing discourses and to develop an understanding of the complexity of educational politics and pedagogical and social relations.

At the international and political macro levels the discourse refers to changes in government and public thinking about educational systems in Europe. At the same time there is emerging a literature which associates the 'Europeanisation' with neoliberal policy themes regarded as 'a transformation in the organising principles of social provision right across the public sector' (Ball 2006). The point is that the nature of western society, economy and politics as a whole, including its underlying values and organising norms, has substantially changed within a generation.

The book and the chapters mirror the different approaches and the shifting focus. In chapters two to four, Dovemark and Holm, Kakos, Rivas and Leite, and in chapter seven and nine Douglas and Borgnakke focus on how changes in values and policy directions have had consequences on both the institutional meso level, on both the school context and organisational context. In chapters one and fiveJeffrey and Troman, Sanch et al. and Correa et al. focus on the construction of teacher identity.

Focusing on the practical context and the involved teachers, students and families the analyses show the conditions for building a democratic model of school community. The teachers are related to their different personal and professional histories and the different experiences of teachers bring out the various views about educational practice. The questions about gender, power relationships, the sense of knowledge, the social and cultural values and different perspectives on childhood and youth, are issues that generate controversy in the relationship between schoolteachers. The different views provide a way to build the school community regarding diversity, respect and conflicts.

Examining the broader context, an example at the national level, is given of school reforms in Sweden. The analysis shows a shift from a centralised based management to decentralised management by objectives that implies 'soft governance'. Teachers' work is heavily prescribed by central government even though Sweden is said to have one of the most decentralised school systems in the world. Despite differences in working duties and assignments, the Swedish case expresses perceptions of a pervasive and strengthened performative culture in schools. In this sense the professional teacher is not only represented in situations characterised by increased workloads and stress connected to assessment and administrative work; it also implies that teachers were expected to marketise their schools.

Focusing on the consequences for teacher-student interaction the books' case analyses show the changes in the professional roles and practices. In the case of 'Citizenship education' (CE) incorporated in the English Secondary curriculum, it is notable that some of the most significant challenges that obstruct the implementation of democratic and participatory pedagogies do not relate to teachers' conscious choices and professional judgment but to embodied unquestioned social practices and everyday interactions. These practices relate equally to institutionalisation or professional roles and to the ways that performativity shapes modern educational discourse about 'being professional'.

The relation between professionalisation and what it means to 'be educated' and to 'become a professional teacher' brings next generation of teacher training and higher educational contexts in focus. However, at the same time the piratical context of school and the argument of school based training is placed in the centre of the professional teaching practicum. As emphasised in the book, the very first encounter teachers have with the joys and sorrows of their career usually takes place during the teaching practicum. During this practicum, student teachers have to negotiate their rights and obligations with different stakeholders (practicum instructors, practicum supervisors, teaching colleagues, parents and pupils), and as a consequence, they go through a great deal of emotional turmoil. In the analyses opposing cases are contrasted and related to issues concerning how student teachers manage and gain teaching identity.

Where the student teacher is central to professional identity then teacher training as a part of higher education becomes central to the whole identity of the profession. In a national case from England the value of focusing on a research-based agenda for teacher education is reflected and it is shown that schools need to provide working environments that are open to challenges and debate to enable new and expansive developments in teaching and learning.

The starting point and the end point of the book represent key elements of the postmodern conditions; namely, the provisional nature of culture, identity and discursive construction of professionalisation. These elements are a challenge and put the focus on both the assertion of, and the subjective construction of curriculum and pedagogy among teachers. Further, the key elements include underlying values and organising norms that the political and educational contexts have substantially changed within a generation. The changes in values and policy directions that have occurred within educational discourses throughout most of the western world have had an impact on both the construction of teacher identity and on the process of professionalisation.

Analyses demonstrate the double logic between the former decades' concepts of professionalisation and the contradiction de-professionalisation.

At the same time analyses of the political discourse and educational reforms show that the demands of professionalisation have been emphasised as changeability and strategies for both organisational and pedagogical development. In the book these strategies are illustrated by the Nordic cases and examples referring to both the political discourses, reform programs and innovative school projects. As a result, the demands of professional changeability are identified as a political credo going across the educational sector. Further, the analysis identifies a shift from the classic concept having the single professional at the centre to the concept of having the inter-professional team at the centre.

In the book changes in values and policy directions that have occurred within education discourses throughout the western world are analysed to understand the impact of such changes on organisational and pedagogical development and to draw a picture of postmodern teacher identity. It is argued that the consequences can be regarded as both a contribution to professionalisation and a contribution to a substantial de-professionalisation of teachers. Against this backdrop the book provides a critical wake-up call and is considered a reminder of the need for a serious debate concerning the questions of what kind of education that is desirable for the twenty-first century and of what kind of professional organisations and teachers are needed for the task.

Ethnography and Education publications

Titles in the series include›

Creative learning: European experiences, edited by Bob Jeffrey;

Researching education policy: Ethnographic experiences, Geoff Troman, Bob Jeffrey and Dennis Beach;

The commodification of teaching and learning, Dennis Beach and Marianne Dovemark;

Performing English with a postcolonial accent: Ethnographic narratives from Mexico, Angeles Clemente and Michael J. Higgins.

How to do Educational Ethnography edited by Geoffrey Walford

Ritual and Identity; The staging and performing of rituals in the lives of young people, Christoph Wulf et al.

Young people's influence and democratic education: Ethnographic studies in upper secondary schools, edited by Elisabet Öhrn, Lisbeth Lundahl and Dennis Beach

Learner biographies and learning cultures: Identity and apprenticeship in England and Germany, Michaela Brockmann

Learning care lessons: Literacy, love, care and solidarity, by Maggie Feeley

Identity and social interaction in a multi-ethnic classroom, by Ruth Barley

Further information available at

www.tufnellpress.co.uk

or

www.ethnographyandeducation.org

www.ingramcontent.com/pod-product-compliance
Ingram Content Group UK Ltd.
Pitfield, Milton Keynes, MK11 3LW, UK
UKHW020143250726
13967UKWH00002B/836

9 781872 767444